A Popular Survey
of
Bible Doctrine

A Popular Survey
of
Bible Doctrine

Norman L. Geisler
Douglas E. Potter

Indian Trail, North Carolina

Contents

Figures & Tables

Introduction

Thus says the LORD, "Heaven is My throne and the earth is My footstool. Where then is a house you could build for Me? And where is a place that I may rest? For My hand made all these things, Thus all these things came into being," declares the LORD. "But to this one I will look, To him who is humble and contrite of spirit, and who trembles at My word."
Isaiah 66:1–2

LONG technical treaties on theology or doctrine, while important, can be intimidating to the Christian that wants to dig into the study of Bible doctrine for the first time. Even some less technical approaches might not state biblical truth in as systematic or comprehensive manner as it should. As a result those new to the study of Bible doctrine may never be exposed to important concepts and issues.

Christians, more than ever, need a basic introduction to Bible doctrine that is systematic and true to Scripture. Many in and outside the evangelical church do not understand how Bible doctrine is formulated, how it intersects and informs many areas of Christian thought and life which serves as a foundation to a Christian worldview.

This book is a popular introduction to the study of Bible doctrine firmly in the evangelical tradition. Each chapter covers a biblical doctrine, stresses its doctrinal importance and interconnectedness to formulating a Christian worldview. The study questions provided help reinforce the material and make it usable even for a formal study of Bible doctrine. It is ideal for personal study and in groups for the home, church, school or ministry environment.

The approach is faithful to the historical evangelical position that integrates all truth as God's truth and upholds the classical and biblical view of God's nature and the full inspiration and inerrancy of the Bible.

Dr. Norman L. Geisler, Ph.D. has taught theology and Bible doctrine in the church, colleges and seminaries for over 60 years. Having authored many technical works in Christian apologetics and theology (*Systematic Theology In One Volume*), this work on Bible doctrine, while maintaining the precision and comprehensiveness the study needs, uniquely makes it accessible to everyone.

Dr. Douglas E. Potter, D.Min., is an assistant professor and Director of the Doctor of Ministry program at Southern Evangelical Seminary. He has been teaching Christian theology and apologetics for over a decade and is an author or co–author of several books.

| 1 |

Before we Study

For what can be known about God is plain to them, because
God has shown it to them. For his invisible attributes, namely,
his eternal power and divine nature, have been clearly
perceived, ever since the creation of the world in the things
that have been made. So they are without excuse.
Romans 1:19–20

UNDERSTANDING Bible doctrine hinges on the meaning and use of words. So to begin our study we must start with terms. The word "evangelical" comes from the Greek word for "gospel" or "good news" and historically upholds the approach to Bible doctrine that says there are certain non–negotiable doctrinal truths that must be held by Christians to support the truth of the gospel. These would include such doctrines as the Inspiration and Inerrancy of the Bible, the Trinity, the Incarnation of Jesus Christ, His virgin birth, ascension, bodily resurrection and Second Coming.

The word "theology" itself comes from the Greek word *theos* which means "God" and *logos* that means "word." Hence, *Theology* is a discourse or study of God. Because God created the world and inspired His word (the Bible); God reveals truth in both realms. The first is called general revelation. Truth in this realm can be arrived at through human reasoning. By using our reason, for example, we can show that God exists and must exist in a certain way. The second realm is special revelation, which is everything in the Bible or Scripture. Some truth revealed in the Bible is beyond human reason to obtain by itself apart from Scripture. Such truths as the Trinity and salvation through Jesus Christ are known only because God has revealed them to us in the Bible.

Our study of Bible doctrine focuses on the Bible and is divided into subjects. Each subject comes from a Greek word. Issues that need to be studied before we study the Bible are covered in the subject called prolegomena (*pro*–before, *lego* meaning "I say"). Bibliology (*biblios* meaning "Bible") is the study of the inspiration and formation of the Bible; Theology Proper (*Theos* meaning "God") is the study of God's nature and includes Creation (*cosmos*–meaning "creation"). Christology (*Christos* meaning "Christ") is the study of Jesus Christ and His work. Pneumatology (*pneumos*–meaning "spirit") is the study of the Holy Spirit. Angelology (*angelos*–meaning "angel") is the study of angels that also includes both good and bad angels. The bad angels are studied under Satanology & Demonology (*daimonion*–meaning "demon") of which the chief demon is Satan and his cohort demons. Anthropology (*Anthropos*–meaning "man") is the study of humans and Hamartiology (*harmartia*–meaning "sin") is the study of their sin and its effects. Soteriology (*soterios*–meaning "salvation") is the study of salvation. Ecclesiology (*ecclesia*–meaning "church") is the study of the church. And finally Eschatology (*eschatos*–meaning "end") is the study of last things.

IMPORTANCE OF BIBLICAL STUDY

Everything in the study of Bible doctrine flows out of prolegomena. A failure here will have serious consequences later in Bible doctrine. For example, if we want to assert that something in Bible doctrine is true, it relies on the nature of truth being absolute. But if truth is relative, as many in our culture believe, then Bible doctrine cannot say something is absolute, objective and true for everyone. If Bible doctrine says God is one or the Bible is inerrant or Jesus is the only savior, and truth is not absolute, then these cannot be held as objective and true for everyone. Hence, our prolegomena must settle the question of truth as well as many other areas that Bible doctrine depends upon.

Christian apologetics is a defense of the faith that shows Christianity is true. Our prolegomena to Bible doctrine depends on many reasons and arguments from apologetics. However, the goal of our study is different from apologetics. In apologetics we establish the truth of Christianity and show that all which is opposed to it is false. In prolegomena we establish the truth of the preconditions that make Bible doctrine true and show that all opposing approaches are false.

The study of biblical doctrine is the attempt to correctly think about God and His revelation; so it is very important to our lives. However, only a systematic study of biblical doctrine organizes all knowledge, in and outside the Bible, in relation to God. It establishes what the Christian faith is, hence making known the faith to be defended by apologetics. The Bible considers knowledge of God essential to maturity and growth (2 Tim. 3:16–17). It is able to protect us from wrong thinking about God and ultimately provides the foundation for the development of a Christian worldview.

Evangelical Theologians believe the Bible is the infallible and inerrant, absolutely true communication in human language that came from the infinite, personal and morally perfect God. For us to show the preconditions to this statement are true we must cover five areas: 1) Creation and God, 2) Revelation and Miracles, 3) Truth and Knowledge, 4) Meaning and Language and finally 5) Methodology. All of these areas serve to establish truth that is compatible with Scripture and shows the Bible and our Doctrine to be true.

CREATION AND GOD

God's creation constantly changes. Change in creation or existence is accounted for by two principles called actuality and potentiality. *Actuality* is that something exists and *potentiality* is that something can become other than what it is or can change. To account for anything that could come into and out of existence, there must be a principle to show that what something is (*essence*) is different from the fact that it is (*existence*). As such, no changing thing can account for its own existence since its nature does not necessitate its existence, since it could not exist. Hence, there cannot be one thing causing another thing forever, an infinite regress, since one thing in the regress would need to cause another thing and be the cause of itself, which is impossible. Therefore, there must be something that cannot change or is *pure actuality* with no potentiality to change; one Being whose essence and existence are identical (=God).

God's creation can be understood in terms of six kinds of causes. There is first a cause *by which* something comes into existence and stays in existence which is called an *efficient cause* (=God). Second, there is a *formal cause* that accounts for something's nature or form, namely, that *of which* something is, for example a tree. Third there must be a *material cause* that accounts for that *out of* which something is made, for example, wood. Fourth, there is an *instrumental cause*, that through which something exists which the Bible calls the Logos (John 1:3). Fifth, there is an *exemplar cause*, or pattern, namely, that *after which* something is made, namely the ideas in the Mind of God. And finally, all created things have a *final cause*, that *for which* something is made, namely, a goal or purpose for which something is made, that is the glory of God.

God is the ultimate reality or ground of all existence or being. As such, His creation is like Him. For an efficient cause cannot produce what it does not possess. The Apostle Paul acknowledged this in Romans 1:19–20. While there are many arguments for the existence of God, the following brief argument from creation to a Creator, also known as a cosmological argument, serves our purposes in establishing God's existence and nature.

1. Something Exists (e.g., I do).
2. Nothing cannot produce something.
3. Therefore something exists eternally and necessarily.
4. I am not a necessary and eternal being (since I change).
5. Therefore both God (a Necessary Being) and I (a contingent being) exist (=theism).

One thing that is inescapable or undeniable is that something exists. If we deny that we exist, then we affirm our own existence in the act of trying to deny it. Hence, existence is an undeniable and inescapable truth. The second and third points show something must be eternal. If there ever was absolutely nothing, then there would always be absolutely nothing because nothing cannot produce something. Something must exist necessarily because everything cannot be a contingent being. All contingent beings could change or cease to exist; therefore they need a cause of their existence. And there cannot be an infinite regress of contingent beings, one being causing another forever. There must be one being that is not caused or uncaused which is the Cause of all contingent beings. The fourth point is true because "I change" and as we have shown everything that changes needs a cause and therefore cannot be necessary and eternal. The conclusion follows, therefore both God (a Necessary Being) and I (a contingent being) exist. This of course is what we mean by Theism, that there is one transcendent, uncaused, unchanging, eternal being. All perfections must be attributed to the all perfect being. Therefore, One infinite, uncaused, personal, morally perfect, all–knowing, all–powerful Being is what we mean by theism. Hence, the theistic God exists who caused finite being(s) similar to himself to exist.

The God of our argument must be the same God of the Bible. Since the same God of Scripture is pure existence – Ex. 3:14, One – Deut. 6:4, Infinite – Ps. 147:5, Personal – Gen. 1:26; 2 Cor. 6:18, All Good (Morally Perfect) – Ps. 86:5; Luke 18:19, All knowing (omniscience) – Ps. 147:5; Rom. 11:33, All Powerful (omnipotent) – Gen. 1:1; Matt. 19:26, Eternal (Necessary) – Ps. 90:2; Heb. 1:2, Unchanging (Immutable) – Mal. 3:6; Heb. 6:18, Infinite and present everywhere (omnipresent) – 1 Kings 8:27; Col. 1:17. There can only be one being of pure actuality. There cannot be two infinite beings or two absolutely perfect beings because in order to tell them apart they would have to differ. But if they differed, one would lack a perfection the other had. But if one lacked what the other had it would not be an ultimate being. Hence, there can be only one ultimate Being (=God).

We have argued for the true God of the Bible, but not everyone studying biblical doctrine has the same view of God. So it is important to distinguish the correct view form incorrect views of God. The only correct view of God: *Theism* says there is an infinite personal creator who exists beyond the world who created the world out of nothing and can intervene in it.

Deism says that God created the world but denies miracles. It is God minus miracles. In Deism, God does not do miracles either because He can't or He won't. But certainly any being that can create the universe can intervene supernaturally in any way. Which is harder, creating something from nothing or making something from something? If God can create from nothing, He certainly can immediately change water into wine. If God won't do miracles, then we must ask why God would not intervene to reveal himself to a lost creation as any father would to save his children.

Finite godism says there is one limited god, or polytheism says there are many limited gods. The problem here is that any finite being needs a Creator and this god(s) is just a finite changing being. Hence, one finite god or many are not ultimate and need a Creator to account for their existence.

Pantheism (*Pan*–all and *theism*–God) says God *is* all and all is God. The problem with Pantheism is that all Pantheists believe they changed from not knowing they (and everything else) is God to knowing they (and everything else is God) through enlightenment. But Pantheists believe God does not change. Hence, one thing the pantheists should understand, if he wakes up one morning believing he is God, he is not!

Panentheism (*Pan*–all *en*–in *theism*–God) says God is *in* creation as a soul is in a body. Panentheists say God has two poles: one that is unchanging (soul) and another that changes (body). God, according to Panentheists, is learning and changing; literally God has a body (=the world) that grows. But if that is the case, as we have pointed out, the God of Panentheism cannot be ultimate because God is in the universe needs a cause outside himself.

Atheism says there is only a world and no God or gods. The problem with this is that it gives no explanation for the Universe. Not only for its initial beginning but also its continued existence. Why is there something rather than nothing?

As was shown above, there must be an unchanging Being that is *pure Act* to account for a changing world. Hence, only Theism can account for *what is* Being, since it is impossible for there to be more than one eternal unchanging being that is pure actuality. The theistic understanding of God equated with pure actuality is the basis for understanding the biblical nature of God (Chapter 3).

REVELATION AND MIRACLES

For there to be revelation, there must be a Revealer, a being capable of giving it (God), a being capable of receiving it (humans), and a medium through which it can be transmitted (language). God has revealed truth about himself in two realms: 1) General revelation concerns all truth discoverable outside the Bible in creation (Rom. 1:19–20). General revelation concerns knowledge about creation and moral instruction given to all humanity. 2) Special revelation concerns all truth discoverable inside the Bible (2 Tim. 3:16–17). Special revelation is God's word given through prophets, chosen men of God, who were moved by the Holy Spirit (2 Peter 1:21) to write the 66 books of the Bible (Chapter 2). Ultimately, both revelations must agree since their source is the same unchanging and unerring God. However, humans, who are subject to error, must strive to properly understand the world and interpret the Word. While the Bible is infallible human understanding and interpretation is not.

As C. S. Lewis once pointed out, if a supernatural God exists, then supernatural acts of God are possible. If there is a creation of God, then there can be intervention by God, otherwise the effect is greater than the Cause. To disprove miracles one must disprove God, not just dislike God. If God exists, miracles are possible. So to disprove miracles one must disprove God. Those that have attempted to disprove miracles usually assume there is no God. They also weigh evidence of all normal acts against supernatural ones. Instead, they should examine the evidence for the supernatural, such as the resurrection of Jesus. Also, the Bible is full of genuine miracles that cannot be mistaken for just unusual natural events.

A miracle is a divine intervention in the natural world that produces an event that would not have resulted from purely natural causes. Miracles are *not* an unusual event or an unknown natural cause (=anomaly); such as why water expands when frozen, when other liquids contract. Miracles are *not* providence which is an unusual but a known natural cause, such as surviving an accident that should have resulted in death. Miracles are *not* magic which is an unusual but a secret natural cause that fools the eye or mind. Miracles *cannot* have a Satanic or evil spiritual cause, since God is an absolutely good Being. A miracle is, for example, being able to divide the Red Sea, healing the blind, multiplying loaves, turning water into wine, walking on water, and resurrecting the dead. The primary purpose, not exclusive purpose, of miracles is to confirm a message from God (John 3:2, Acts 2:22; Heb. 2:3). As such miracles must be immediate (Matt. 8:3; 8:13), multiple (Matt. 9:35; Acts 1:3), contain a predictive element (Matt. 12:40) and connect with a truth claim in the name of God (Mark 2:10–11). This is indeed what we find in the Bible with 250 miracles and 60 in the Gospels alone.

Truth and Knowledge

What is truth? Truth is a statement that corresponds to reality. As the Greek philosopher Aristotle once said, "To say of what is, that it is not, or of what is not, that it is, is false; while to say of what is, that it is, and of what is not, that it is not, is true." There is no other adequate explanation of what is truth. Hence, truth is not that which works, not that which coheres, not that which was intended, not that which is comprehensive, not that which is relevant, and not that which feels good. Any of these views of truth would expect truth to correspond to their view, which makes the view of truth self–defeating since it depends on the correspondence view to assert itself.

Is truth relative? By relative we mean something is true with respect to space, time or persons. True here, but not there, true now but not then, true to you but not me. By absolute we mean that something is true for all time, places and people. Any truth claim cannot be relative. Consider the truth claim that "all truth is relative." The relativists must answer if this is true everywhere, all the time for all people. If they answer yes, it is false, if they answer no, then it is not always true. Hence, the relativist is forced to hold to absolute truth or hold his view of truth is not always right. Truth must be absolute because relative truth is self–defeating and results in an impossible world. In a relativistic world, learning would be impossible, since what we learn is true today may be false tomorrow or not true somewhere else. There would be no wrong answer and no true facts.

At this point it is important to distinguish a belief from a truth claim. People may believe all kinds of things that are not true, such as believing the world is flat at one time. Beliefs cannot alter truth, since it never was the case that the world is flat. We should also clarify comparisons and tastes. If you feel warm and I feel cold at the same time in the same room it is not a relative truth. It is absolute for all time, places, and persons that we feel differently at the same time. Likewise, the comparisons of short or tall are not relative, Wilt is always taller than Willie is true for everyone. Likes and dislikes or tastes also are not relative. If you like chocolate and I like vanilla it is true for everyone that you like chocolate. Our tastes and comparisons may change, but not the nature of the truth claims involved.

Do we know truth? It is undeniable that we know truth. For if someone says, "Truth is unknowable" we have to ask if that statement is true. If they say yes, then it is false, since we at least know that truth. If they say no, then why hold it? This stands also for historical knowledge and truth. If someone says, "historical truth is unknowable" we have to ask how that historical truth is knowable. Also, we do not have to have comprehensive knowledge, evidence or proof to conclude something is true or not true. Only God can have that, all we need is an argument with correct reasoning and/or sufficient evidence for support.

The truth is there is no such thing as a relative truth. All truth must be absolute and objective. Truth by its very nature is narrow since it excludes every view opposed to it. This we will find to be the case in every area of inquiry, including Bible doctrine.

MEANING AND LANGUAGE

If truth cannot be relative, if follows that meaning also cannot be relative. For example, if someone says "all meaning is relative," clearly it is self–defeating. Is that meaning relative? If no, it is not true, if yes, why hold it? We might at first think meaning is absolute because individual words have correspondence to things in the world. However, the same words can be used for the different things (e.g., "bark" on a tree or "bark" of a dog) or they change over time (e.g., the term "idiot" use to be used for just a layman or person without skill). Words can change their meaning over time and this is true in all languages. But meaning is something that is objective and able to be transmitted through language. Hence it is objective in that it corresponds to things in the world and is expressed in symbols or "words." Although language can vary in expression, there can be only one meaning for any given unit, such as a sentence, of expression in a text. This is because words describe our world. Hence, our method of understanding a text must consider the historical background of the text, its words, grammar and literary nature. This is known as the historical grammatical method of interpretation which alone can result in an objective understanding of any given text or unit of meaning.

All this is important because meaningful language is used of God. But God as we have seen is completely different from anything else; hence our language is limited when used to describe God. Some say that language applied to God cannot say anything meaningful about him. That is, whatever we say about God is entirely different then the way He really is. However, if that is the case it would result in complete skepticism. The other extreme, some hold, is that what we say about God means entirely the same thing as it does for us. The problem with this is it makes what we say about God to be only on the level of a creature. Our talk about God or God–Talk therefore must be similar or analogous. It must combine our definition of words with a different application when applied to God. When this is done it results in analogy. For example, when we say "God is good," there is something in the definition of "good" that is the same for humans and God, but when applied to God it is completely different. Since God is infinite goodness and humans are only finitely good. Hence, language is an adequate medium for expressing truth about God (Rom. 11:33; John 1:18), but it is not comprehensive or exhaustive.

METHODOLOGY

Biblical doctrine is a human attempt to understand God's revelation. As such it must follow a method that will allow that to happen. This naturally begins with an inductive study of all Scripture relevant to a biblical doctrine according to the historical grammatical method. Once all relevant Scripture is examined a conclusion is made regarding its teaching about the subject. We then must consider any true knowledge or science outside of Scripture that would have bearing on our subject. Then the two must be integrated and systematized. Only then, can we formulate a biblical doctrine of both revealed areas to makes an application to life.

For example, we can illustrate this with the doctrine of inerrancy. Our inductive biblical study shows that, as Hebrews 6:18 says, "It is impossible for God to lie" (cf. Titus 1:2). Second Timothy 3:16 says, "All Scripture is inspired by God." From this we can reason:

1) It is impossible for God to err.
2) The Bible is the word of God.
3) Therefore, it is impossible for the Bible to err.

Outside of the Bible we know from our philosophical argument that God cannot err since He is unchanging perfection. We would also discover that only reliable copies of the original manuscripts of the Bible have survived. These reflect human literary forms and the current culture at the time of writing. Hence, we can now formulate a teaching that says, "The Bible is God's inerrant word in the original manuscripts in terms of the culture and literary forms of its day." Hence, our application to life is that we can have confidence that the Bible is God's word and cannot err as we approach its study. This in short, is how Bible doctrine is done for every area.

SUMMARY

Bible doctrine presupposes many things that are able to be defended or shown true. That God exists and has revealed truth outside the Bible in creation and inside the Bible. Miracles are possible and distinguishable from natural events. Truth and meaning are absolute, objective and able to be expressed in language. Even talk about God, while not exhaustive, is adequate to give us truth about God. Finally, given God's revelation a method must be followed to adequately systematize God's revelation to give us knowledge for life.

QUESTIONS TO ANSWER

1. What are the different doctrinal subjects and what do they study?
2. What Scripture supports the distinction between general and special revelation?
3. Why must the God of our philosophical argument be the same God of the Bible?
4. What are the different views of God and their understanding of God's nature?
5. What is a true miracle and identify biblical verses that describe miracles?
6. Why must truth be absolute as opposed to relative?

Inspiration of the Bible

All Scripture is inspired by God and profitable for teaching,
for reproof, for correction, for training in righteousness;
so that the man of God may be adequate,
equipped for every good work.
2 Timothy 3:16–17

HAVING established the preconditions to studying Bible doctrine (Chapter 1) we now turn to the nature of the Bible's inspiration (Bibliology) by considering what the Bible has to say about its own prophetic inspiration, what Jesus taught about the Bible, and how and what inspired books are recognized as belonging to the canon of Scripture.

INSPIRATION

God has revealed truth in two realms. The first is general revelation that serves as truth discovered outside the Bible, from creation. Truth found here serves as a precondition to doing Bible doctrine (Chapter 1). Special revelation concerns truth found in Scripture and is the only infallible written revelation from God. The inspiration of the Bible entails at least seven things: 1) It has a Divine origin or is from God; 2) A human prophetic agency or through men; 3) In a written human language that is verbal or in words, 4) It is to be found in the original written text or autographs; 5) It is the final authority and normative for believers; 6) It is inerrant or without error in all it affirms or teaches, and finally 7) It is limited and complete in only the 66 books of the canon.

The Apostle Paul's use of the word "inspired" in 2 Timothy 3:16 does not mean inspired like Shakespeare was an inspiring author. This word literally means God inspired or breathed out through prophets who expressed in their own vocabulary and cultural setting the very word of God in a written text (2 Tim. 3:16; 2 Peter 1:20–21). As such when Scripture speaks (Gal. 3:8) so does God (Gen. 12:3) since it is the Word of God. The locus of inspiration is in the complete or plenary written text of Scripture (Jer. 26:2). Properly speaking, inspiration applies only to the autograph which is the original written text. It is authoritative and normative for all believers. It alone is the only *written* source of *infallible* truth from God. While some inspired truths may be more important than others, there are no degrees of inspiration. All parts of Scripture are equally inspired by God.

Inerrancy

Inerrancy is implicit in the term "inspiration" (2 Tim. 3:16; 2 Peter 1:20) since the doctrine begins with God's unerring (Heb. 6:18) and immutable nature as understood from general and special revelation. If God cannot err and the Bible is the word of God, then it follows that the Bible cannot err. Hence, the Bible must be true in all that it affirms and teaches, whether spiritual, doctrinal (e.g., 1 Cor. 15:13–19) or factual including history and science (e.g., Rom. 5:12).

Negative higher criticism that arose in the late 1800s undermined the inspiration and inerrancy of Scripture. Reactions produced at least three incorrect views of inspiration: 1) Liberalism while denying essential doctrines, only affirmed a religious nature of the books to *contain* the word of God. 2) Neo–orthodoxy, reacted to Liberal doctrinal denials but still accepting the results of negative criticism. Neo–orthodoxy sees the Bible as *becoming* the word of God under a personal encounter with Jesus Christ. 3) Neo–Evangelicals, to allow for higher criticism and inspiration, moved inspiration away from the text to the *ideas* or *concepts* generated by the Bible or to just the so-called essentials (i.e., redemptive matters). The evangelical or orthodox (correct) view of inspiration has always been and is that the Bible, the original text *is* the word of God.

Jesus' View of the Bible

Jesus affirmed seven things about the Bible, the Old Testament, that are true.

1. It is divinely authoritative. Jesus use of the statement "It is written . . ." is a present imperative, still existing written authority. "It is written: 'Man does not live on bread alone, but on every word that comes from the mouth of God.'. . . It is also written: 'Do not put the

Lord your God to the test. . . .' Away from me, Satan! For it is written: 'Worship the Lord your God, and serve him only'" (Matt. 4:4, 7, 10).

2. It is imperishable. Matthew 5:17–18: "Do not think that I have come to abolish the Law or the Prophets; I have not come to abolish them but to fulfill them. I tell you the truth, until heaven and earth disappear, not the smallest letter, not the least stroke of a pen, will by any means disappear from the Law until everything is accomplished." This is not hyperbole: even the least commandment is signification.

3. It is infallible. If he called them 'gods,' to whom the word of God came—and the Scripture cannot be broken . . ." (John 10:35). Nothing else is infallible or unbreakable. It will break us but we cannot break it.

4. It is inerrant (without error). Jesus replied: "You are in error because you do not know the Scriptures or the power of God" (Matt. 22:29). "Thy Word is truth" (John 17:17). "You are in error," implies the Scripture are not in error. The Bible must be inerrant because,

1) The Bible is the word of God.
2) God cannot err.
3) Therefore, the Bible cannot err.

To deny this reasoning you must either hold 1) that the Bible is not the word of God or 2) that God can err (Matt. 4:4; Rom. 3:4; John 10:35; 17:17). But if you do not hold either of these, then you must conclude that the Bible cannot err.

5. It is historically reliable (Matt. 12:40; 24:37–38). Matthew 12:40: "For as Jonah was three days and three nights in the belly of a huge fish, so the Son of Man will be three days and three nights in the heart of the earth." Matthew 24:37–38: "As it was in the days of Noah, so it will be at the coming of the Son of Man. For in the days before the flood, people were eating and drinking, marrying and giving in marriage, up to the day Noah entered the ark." Jesus affirmed the existence of Jonah and Noah. This truth puts the critics in a dilemma. The first 11 chapters of Genesis as well as other parts of the Old Testament are doubted by many critics. Yet, they are affirmed in the New Testament. If one has a problem affirming their historicity then they have a problem with Jesus. Consider all that Jesus and His Apostles affirmed about the Old Testament:

1. Creation of the universe (Gen. 1)	John 1:3; Col. 1:16
2. Creation of Adam and Eve (Gen. 1–2)	1 Tim. 2:13–14
3. Marriage of Adam and Eve (Gen. 1–2)	1 Tim. 2:13
4. Temptation of the woman (Gen. 3)	1 Tim. 2:14
5. Disobedience / sin of Adam (Gen. 3)	Rom. 5:12; 1 Cor. 15:22
6. Sacrifices of Abel and Cain (Gen. 4)	Heb. 11:4
7. Murder of Abel by Cain (Gen. 4)	1 John 3:12

8. Birth of Seth (Gen. 4)	Luke 3:38
9. Translation of Enoch (Gen. 5)	Heb. 11:5
10. Marriage before the flood (Gen. 6)	Luke 17:27
11. The flood and destruction of man (Gen. 7)	Matt. 24:39
12. Preservation of Noah and his family (Gen. 8–9)	2 Peter 2:5
13. Genealogy of Shem (Gen. 10)	Luke 3:35–36
14. Birth of Abraham (Gen. 11)	Luke 3:34
15. Call of Abraham (Gen. 12–13)	Heb. 11:8
16. Tithes to Melchizedek (Gen. 14)	Heb. 7:1–3
17. Justification of Abraham (Gen. 15)	Rom. 4:3
18. Ishmael (Gen. 16)	Gal. 4:21–24
19. Promise of Isaac (Gen. 17)	Heb. 11:18
20. Lot and Sodom (Gen. 18–19)	Luke 17:29
21. Birth of Isaac (Gen. 21)	Acts 7:9–10
22. Offering of Isaac (Gen. 22)	Heb. 11:17
23. The burning bush (Ex. 3:6)	Luke 20:32
24. Exodus through the Red Sea (Ex. 14:22)	1 Cor. 10:1–2
25. Provision of water and manna (Ex. 16:4; 17:6)	1 Cor. 10:3–5
26. Lifting up serpent in wilderness (Num. 21:9)	John 3:14
27. Fall of Jericho (Joshua 6:22–25)	Heb. 11:30
28. Miracles of Elijah (1 Kings 17:1; 18:1)	Jas. 5:17
29. Jonah in the great fish (Jonah 2)	Matt. 12:40
30. Three Hebrew youths in furnace (Dan. 3)	Heb. 11:34
31. Daniel in lion's den (Dan. 6)	Heb. 11:33
32. Slaying of Zechariah (2 Chron. 24:20–22)	Matt. 23:35

6. It is scientifically accurate (Matt. 19:4–5). Jesus is asked a moral question about actual people, and answers, "have you not read that He who created them from the beginning made them male and female." Hence, if one does not believe the creation account is scientifically accurate then they do not hold Jesus' view, since a denial of God creating man and women undermines Jesus' moral teaching.

7. It has ultimate supremacy. Matthew 15:3, 6: "Jesus replied, 'And why do you break the command of God for the sake of your tradition? . . . Thus you nullify the word of God for the sake of your tradition.'"

Some have said Jesus' view was just an accommodation to the view of the Bible in His day. However, Jesus was no accommodator to the times in which He lived. In fact He affirmed the Old Testament's Christ centered meaning. "Beginning at Moses, he expounded to them all the scriptures the things concerning himself" (Luke 24:27). In fact, Jesus condemned teaching that was contrary to the Bible (Matt. 15:3–6; 22:29). Further, Jesus promised the Holy Spirit would teach the Apostles "all things" and lead them into "all truth." "But the Helper, the Holy Spirit, whom the Father will send in My name, He will teach you all things, and bring to your remembrance all things that I said to you" (John 14:26). "However, when He, the Spirit of truth, has come, He will guide you into all truth; for He will not speak on His own authority, but whatever He hears He will speak; and He will tell you things to come" (John 16:13).

Others have suggested that Jesus' human limitations caused him to err in His teaching. Jesus was limited in His human knowledge. "He grew in wisdom and knowledge" (Luke 2:52) and He did not know the time of His return, "No one knows about that day or hour, not even . . . the Son, but only the Father" (Matt. 24:36). Furthermore, He did not know what was on the fig tree (Mark 11:13). But He did not err in His teaching. Jesus did not teach about what He did not know and what He taught about He did know. This is because what He did know, the Father taught Him and what the Father taught Him was completely true. For it says, "It is impossible for God to lie" (Heb. 6:18) and "the God who cannot lie" (Titus 1:2). "Let God be true and every man a liar" (Rom. 3:4). Hence, what the Father taught Him was completely true. When Jesus spoke on any topic it was with the authority of God (Chapter 5).

Jesus did not err in His words. Jesus said, "Heaven and earth will pass away but My word will not pass away" (Matt. 24:35). "All authority in heaven and earth has been given to me" (Matt. 28:18). "All things have been delivered to me by my Father" (Matt. 11:27). "Observe all things I have commanded you" (Matt. 28:20). "He who sent me is true; and I speak to the world those things which I heard from Him" (John 8:26). "The words that I have spoken to you will judge you in the last day" (John 12:48).

Jesus confirmed the Old Testament and promised the New Testament. Therefore, Jesus taught the whole Bible is the word of God: The Old Testament explicitly and the New Testament implicitly since Jesus promised the Holy Spirit would teach the Apostles "all things" and lead them into "all truth." "But the Helper, the Holy Spirit, whom the Father will send in My name, He will teach you all things and bring to your remembrance all things I said to you" (John 14:26). "However, when He, the Spirit of truth, has come, He will guide you into all truth; for He will not speak on His own authority, but whatever He hears He will speak; and He will tell you things to come" (John 16:13).

Canonicity of the Bible

How do we know what books belong in the Bible? There is a test for what books belong in the Bible or canonicity. This test is spelled out in our prolegomena (Chapter 1). There we showed that God exists, miracles and prophecy are possible, human language is an adequate medium of communication and humans can recognize and know truth. Out of that the following questions help us recognize Scripture:

1) Was it written by a prophet of God?
2) Was the writer confirmed by acts of God?
3) Does the message tell the truth about God?
4) Did it come with the power of God?
5) Was it accepted by the people of God?

All Christians recognize the following 66 books (Table 2.1) meet this test.

These books are recognized as Scripture because they pass the test of canonicity or they are recognized by another inspired book as being Scripture and does not teach or affirm anything opposed to the other books of Scripture.

Some have suggested other books should be included. The term used for these books is "apocrypha" which means hidden or doubtful. There are 14 apocryphal books (or 15 if the letter of Jeremiah is separated out from Baruch, thus making two books of it).

1) The Wisdom of Solomon (c. 30 B.C.)
2) Ecclesiasticus (Sirach) (c. 132 B.C.)
3) Tobit (c. 200 B.C.)
4) Judith (c. 150 B.C.)
5) 2 Esdras (c. 100 A.D.) [4 Esdras in Catholic Bible]
6) 1 Esdras (c. 150–100 B.C.) [3 Esdras in Catholic Bible]
7) 1 Maccabees (c. 110 B.C.)
8) 2 Maccabees (c. 110–70 B.C.)
9) Baruch (c. 150–50 B.C.)—Baruch 1–5
(Letter of Jeremiah [c. 300–100 B.C.])—Baruch 6
10) Addition to Esther (140–130 B.C.)
11) Prayer of Azariah (2nd or 1st cent B.C.)—Daniel 3:24–90
12) Susanna (2nd or 1st cent B.C.)—Daniel 13
13) Bel and the Dragon (c. 100 B.C.)—Daniel 14
14) Prayer of Manasseh (2nd or 1st cent B.C.)

Eleven of these books were added by the Roman Catholic Church in 1546 at the Council of Trent. Seven are listed as extra books in their table of contents. Four books are amended to other books (Daniel and Ester).

BOOKS OF THE OLD TESTAMENT		
The Law (Pentateuch) – 5 books	Poetry – 5 books	
1. Genesis 2. Exodus 3. Leviticus 4. Numbers 5. Deuteronomy	1. Job 2. Psalms 3. Proverbs 4. Ecclesiastes 5. Song of Solomon	
History – 12 books	Prophets – 17 books	
1. Joshua 2. Judges 3. Ruth 4. 1 Samuel 5. 2 Samuel 6. 1 Kings 7. 2 Kings 8. 1 Chronicles 9. 2 Chronicles 10. Ezra 11. Nehemiah 12. Esther	Major	Minor
	1. Isaiah 2. Jeremiah 3. Lamentations 4. Ezekiel 5. Daniel	1. Hosea 2. Joel 3. Amos 4. Obadiah 5. Jonah 6. Micah 7. Nahum 8. Habakkuk 9. Zephaniah 10. Haggai 11. Zechariah 12. Malachi

BOOKS OF THE NEW TESTAMENT	
Gospels	History
1. Matthew 2. Mark 3. Luke 4. John	Acts of the Apostles
Epistles	
1. Romans 2. 1 Corinthians 3. 2 Corinthians 4. Galatians 5. Ephesians 6. Philippians 7. Colossians 8. 1 Thessalonians 9. 2 Thessalonians 10. 1 Timothy 11. 2 Timothy	12. Titus 13. Philemon 14. Hebrews 15. James 16. 1 Peter 17. 2 Peter 18. 1 John 19. 2 John 20. 3 John 21. Jude
Prophecy	
Revelation	

Table 2.1 Biblical Canon

Extra books added to the Roman Catholic Old Testament:
1) The Wisdom of Solomon (c. 30 B.C.)
2) Ecclesiasticus (Sirach) (c. 132 B.C.)
3) Tobit (c. 200 B.C.)
4) Judith (c. 150 B.C.)
5) 1 Maccabees (c. 110 B.C.)
6) 2 Maccabees (c. 110–70 B.C.)
7) Baruch (c. 150–50 B.C.)—Baruch 1–5 (Letter of Jeremiah [c. 300–100 B.C.])—Baruch 6

Four are added to other books:
8) Addition to Esther (140–130 B.C.)—Esther 10:4–16:24
9) Prayer of Azariah (2nd or 1st cent B.C.)—Daniel 3:24–90
10) Susanna (2nd or 1st cent B.C.)—Daniel 13
11) Bel and the Dragon (c. 100 B.C.)—Daniel 14

One reason Roman Catholicism did not add all the Apocrypha books is because they contradict each other. For example, 2 Esdras (called 4 Esdras by Roman Catholics since Ezra and Nehemiah are called I and II Esdras) 7:105 is against praying for the dead while 2 Maccabees 12:45–46 is for praying for the dead.

There are ten reasons why evangelical Protestants do not accept the Apocrypha as inspired by God.
1) It does not claim to be inspired by God.
2) It was not written by prophets of God (1 Mac. 9:27).
3) It was not confirmed by supernatural acts of God (Heb. 2:3–4).
4) It does not always tell the truth of God: On praying for the dead (2 Mac. 12:46); On working for salvation (Tobit 12:9).
5) It was not accepted by the people of God (to whom it was given).
6) It was not accepted by Jesus the Son of God (Luke 24:27).
7) It was not accepted as inspired by the Apostles of God.
8) It was not accepted by the Early Church of God.
9) It was not accepted by the Catholic translator of Word of God (Jerome).
10) It was not written during the period of prophets of God.

There is no claim to be inspired by God in the Apocrypha and there is no prophet of God in the land according to 1 Maccabees 9:27. There are no supernatural acts of God to confirm a message from God and they do not tell truth about God. Second Maccabees teaches praying for the dead (2 Mac. 12:46) and Fourth Esdras (7:105) rejects praying for the dead. Tobit teaches salvation by works (Tobit 12:9). Also, they were not accepted by the Jews who were the people of God when they were written. Instead, they were not added to the Bible officially by Rome until 29 years after Martin Luther at the Council of Trent to support the doctrine of purgatory. Roman Catholicism infallibly pronounced at the Council of Trent Anathema (which means repent or you will go to hell) to anyone who says works are not a condition of salvation for receiving justification. They were never accepted by the Jewish people of God. There is no acceptance by Jesus (Luke 24:27) who referenced the Old Testament by the phrase "Law and Prophets" that covered only the Hebrew Bible. Also, no Apostle quoted from the Apocrypha. In fact, allusions are made from other non–biblical books, but not the Apocrypha. They were not accepted as Scripture by the early Church. Even the great Roman Catholic scholar Jerome, who translated the Greek/Hebrew Bible into the Latin Vulgate in 400 A.D., rejected the Apocrypha as inspired.

Finally, the Apocrypha was not written during the period of the prophets of God. Jewish teaching ceased after Malachi. This is according to Jewish teaching: The Jewish historian Josephus says, "From Artaxerxes [4th cent B.C.] until our time everything has been recorded, but has not been deemed worthy of like credit with what preceded, because the exact succession of the prophets ceased" (*Contra Apion* 1.8). The Jewish Talmud also teaches: "With the death of Haggai, Zechariah and Malachi the latter prophets, the Holy Spirit ceased out of Israel" (*Tosephta Sotah* 13:2).

Some claim that there are 80 other Gospels that should be considered. However, there are only four Gospels from the first century: Matthew, Mark, Luke, and John. These other so called "Gospels" were written later in the 2nd–3rd century. They are not earlier, and were never considered for inclusion in the New Testament. How many? There are dozens of fragments but only about 15–20 apocryphal Gospels worth noting:

- The Gospel of Thomas
- The Gospel of Peter
- The Gospel of James
- The Gospel of Judas
- The Gospel of Truth
- The Gospel of Matthias
- The Gospel of Eve
- The Gospel of the Ebionites
- The Gospel of the Egyptians
- The Gospel of Philip
- The Gospel according to Mary (Magdalene)
- The Gospel of the Hebrews
- The Gospel of the Twelve
- The Gospel of Perfection

All of these Gospels contain false teachings. We know these are false Gospels because they make false claims such, as being written by an Apostle who were long dead by that time. They had false miracle claims about Jesus' infancy, but this does not agree with John 2:11 that records Jesus' first miracle. They had false claims about biblical events and at least 14 false teachings throughout their pages.

1) On God: Pantheism.
2) On Creation: Emanationalism
3) On the Soul: Preexistence
4) On the Body: Platonism
5) On Matter: Dualism
6) On Human Nature: Perfectionism
7) On Salvation: Gnosticism
8) On Jesus' Heavenly Nature: Arianism
9) On Jesus' Earthly Nature: Docetisim
10) On Jesus' Sonship: Adoptionism
11) On Jesus' Miracles: Mythologism (cf. John 2:11)
12) On Jesus' Disciples: Mysticism
13) On Interpretation of Jesus' Words: Allegorism
14) On Morality: Asceticism

Furthermore, the Church Fathers clearly rejected these false Gospels; Irenaeus in the 2nd century said: "It is not possible that the Gospels can be either more or fewer in number than they are. For . . . while the Church is scattered throughout all the world, and the "pillar and ground" of the Church is the Gospel and the spirit of life; it is fitting that she have four pillars, breathing out immortality on ever side, and vivifying men afresh" (*Against Heresies* 3.11.8). He continued: "Indeed, they have arrived at such a pitch of audacity, as to entitle their comparatively recent writing, 'the Gospel of Truth,' though it agrees in nothing with the Gospels of the Apostles, so that they have really no Gospel, which is not full of blasphemy. . . . But that these Gospels [of the Apostles] alone are true and reliable, and admit neither an increase nor diminution of the aforesaid number [four], I have proved by so many and such arguments" (*Against Heresies* 3.11.9). Eusebius the early church historian called them "totally impious and absurd" (*Ecclesiastical History*). Likewise, many contemporary historians have also noted that they can hardly compare to the canonical Gospels since they contain legendary characteristics that bear the clear marks of forgery.

SUMMARY

The study of the Bible (Bibliology) shows it is inspired in that it was breathed out by God and therefore must be inerrant or without error in all that it affirms or says. Jesus, who is God, clearly taught that the Bible (Old Testament) was divinely inspired, authoritative, infallible, without error (inerrant), scientifically and historically accurate in all that it affirms or teaches. Jesus never accommodated His teaching and His human limitations never caused him to err, because He always taught what the Father (God) told him. Jesus explicitly affirmed the inspiration and historicity of the Old Testament and implicitly promised the New Testament. Only the sixty–six books of the Protestant Bible pass the tests of canonicity. The Apocrypha was never accepted by the Jews and Jesus, as well as the Apostles who never quoted from it. The other so–called Gospels written well after the 1st century have false teaching and false miracles, and were rejected by early Church Fathers. Hence, only the 66 books accepted by all Christians are canonical Scripture.

QUESTIONS TO ANSWER

1. What is a good definition of the inspiration of the Bible?
2. What do each of the following mean with respect to inspiration: Verbal, Plenary, infallible and Inerrant?
3. What are some incorrect views of the inspiration of the Bible?
4. What does the inerrancy of the Bible include and exclude?
5. How do the principles of canonicity help us discover what books are inspired?

The Nature of God

*I am the L*ORD*, and there is no other; Besides Me there is no*
God. I will gird you, though you have not known Me;
That men may know from the rising to the setting of the sun
*That there is no one besides Me. I am the L*ORD*, and there is*
no other, The One forming light and creating darkness,
Causing well–being and creating calamity;
*I am the L*ORD *who does all these.*
Isaiah 45:5–7

GIVEN the foundation for studying Bible doctrine that includes truth about God from creation and the Bible (Chapter 1 & 2), we now turn to a study of the nature of God (Theology Proper). Almost all of one's study of the Bible is an outworking of their understanding of the nature of God. Hence, a mistake here can have drastic consequences in other areas of Bible doctrine. We first examine the attributes, characteristics and activity of God as given in Scripture. We then turn to the Triune nature of God and conclude with what our response should be towards this discovery of God's nature.

ATTRIBUTES OF GOD

An attribute is a property attributed to God because of His nature. It is true of God because of His very nature. For example, God is Holy, is an attribute of God because of His very nature. Other things said of God may only be a characteristic or activity said of God because of His relation to creatures, and while true, is not something directly attributed to His nature. For example, God can only have mercy because He created beings upon which He can act. Characteristics or activates are usually closely tied to attributes, but exist because God created. Attributes, on the other hand, are true of God's nature regardless of creation. While there are multiple attributes given to the nature of God, it is important to keep in mind that God is one simple undivided being. Hence, these are just many things that can be said about the one simple nature of God. For example, the many things that can be said about one rock that is it is gray, round, heavy, etc. For example, there are many radii of a circle, but they are all one at the center.

As indicated previously (Chapter 1), since we do not know God directly and only know him through His effects (i.e., creation), all proper statements about God must be analogical or similar. More specifically the definition, such as goodness, is the same for us and God, but the predication or application is completely different. This is because God is infinite and we are finite and while the definition of goodness is the same, the application of goodness must be completely different for God than for humans. Also, we must recognize that the Bible as well as our common language used to speak about God is filled with metaphors and anthropomorphism (Heb. 4:13; 2 Chron. 6:40; Deut. 5:15; Eph. 4:30; Gen. 6:6; Isa. 43:25; Job 11:6). That is, the Bible will often describe God by using figures of speech and in human terms (Table 3.1).

Metaphysical Description	Biblical Description
God is the uncaused cause of our being	"The eternal God is a dwelling place, And underneath are the everlasting arms" Deut. 33:27
God is omniscient (all–knowing)	"And there is no creature hidden from His sight, but all things are open and laid bare to the eyes of Him with whom we have to do" Heb. 4:13

Table 3.1 Anthropomorphic Descriptions

Anthropomorphisms and metaphors are used because they are easier to understand and invoke a response to who God is. They point us to what is true of God, but often in a devotional manner not achieved by technical theological language. One danger is to never take metaphors as literal descriptions of God, for this will result in a wrong understanding of God's nature.

There are important areas to consider in our study of God's nature. First we consider metaphysical (sometimes called non–moral) attributes of God. These are attributable only to God because of His divine nature. Second, we consider non–moral characteristics, moral attributes attributable to His nature and moral activities that are true because of His relation to creation. Finally, we will gain our greatest insight into God by exploring His Triune nature.

METAPHYSICAL ATTRIBUTES (INTRINSIC TO HIS NATURE)

Pure actuality
Simplicity
Aseity
Necessity
Immutability
Eternality
Impassibility
Infinity
Immateriality
Immensity
Omnipotence
Omnipresence
Omniscience
Omnisapience (Wisdom)
Majesty–Beauty
Life–Immortality
Unity

NON–MORAL CHARACTERISTICS (BECAUSE OF HIS RELATION TO CREATION)

Sovereignty
Transcendence
Immanence
Ineffability

MORAL ATTRIBUTES (INTRINSIC TO HIS NATURE)

Holiness
Righteousness
Truthfulness
Love (Goodness)
Jealousy
Perfection

MORAL ACTIVITIES (BECAUSE OF HIS RELATION TO CREATION)

Mercy
Wrath

TRINITY (TRI UNITY OF GOD)

METAPHYSICAL ATTRIBUTES

After God's pure actuality is demonstrated from reason (Chapter 1), it is clear that this is the same God of Scripture who is pure existence (Ex. 3:14 "I AM WHO I AM"). Some object that God could not be Creator of anything if He is pure actuality with no potentiality. However, a distinction should be made between passive and active potency. God has no *passive* potency that is changeability or ability to become what He is not. But God does have *active* potency. Active potency is being able to cause what has no existence to exist. So while God has no passive potency (mere capacity), He surely has active potency, the power to create anything possible. It follows from pure actuality that God is simple or not composed. Deuteronomy 6:4 says, "Hear, O Israel! The Lord is our God, the Lord is one!" Because God is simple, all that is attributed to His nature must be true of all of Him. God cannot be partly anything. If God is love, He is love completely and not partially. Some object that God cannot be simple if He has multiple attributes. However, as we have already indicated, the attributes are ascribed to God in the way many things can be said about something that is one. They are not to be taken as describing different properties. Such an objection assumes the attributes to be Platonic properties or distinct realities existing eternally in themselves. But this fails to see the analogous sense in which we are using these terms (Chapter 1).

The following metaphysical attributes of God are known because of God's simplicity and Scripture. God is completely independent self-existence (Aseity). Romans 11:36 says "from Him [God] and through Him and to Him are all things. To Him be the glory forever. Amen." (cf. Gen. 1:1; Col. 1:17). As such God is Necessary existence. That is a Being whose existence is essential, whose non-existence is impossible; a Being whose essence is to exist, whose essence (what He is) and existence (that He is) are identical. God is unchanging and unchangeable (Immutable). Malachi 3:6 says "'For I, the Lord, do not change . . .'" (cf. Num. 23:19; 1 Sam. 15:29; Titus 1:2; James 1:17). This entails that God's will, mind and purpose cannot change. Nothing a creature does can change God in any way. God cannot break His unconditional promises. God alone is Eternal. He is eternally now (with no past or future) as opposed to in time or a measurable duration. Psalm 90:2 says, "Before the mountains were born Or You gave birth to the earth and the world, Even from everlasting to everlasting, You are God." God does not fore-see the future; He sees it and everything else (all of time) in His eternal present. Because God is eternal, does not change or lack anything, it follows that He does not and cannot undergo passion or suffering (Impassible). He cannot change in emotions or feelings. The creature will change with respect to God, as a sinner repents and moves to be under another unchangeable attribute. Just as a pillar does not move, but the person moves to the right or left of the pillar, so God does not move or change (cf. Job 22:2–3; Rom. 11:35–36; Acts 17:25). God is actually infinite. Psalm 147:5 says, "Great is our Lord and abundant in strength; His understanding is infinite." This actual or real infinite is opposed to a potential or numerical infinite in which we can imagine something being added to it forever. Nothing can be added or taken away from God's infinity. God is immaterial and not measurable (Immensity). John 4:24 says, "God is spirit, and those who worship Him must worship in spirit and truth." This is completely opposite to having matter, extension in space or energy.

God is all powerful and therefore has the ability to do anything possible (omnipotent). Jeremiah 32:17 say, "Ah Lord God! Behold, You have made the heavens and the earth by Your great power and by Your outstretched arm! Nothing is too difficult for You" (cf. Job 11:7; Luke 1:37). This does not entail that God can do something against His nature or do the contradictory. He cannot for example, make square circles or force freedom (Matt. 23:37). Furthermore, God does not have to do all that He can do. God is free to limit the use of His power, but He is not free to limit the extent of His power.

God is also everywhere present (omnipresent) as in Psalm 139:7–10: "Where can I go from Your Spirit? Or where can I flee from Your presence? If I ascend to heaven, You are there; If I make my bed in Sheol, behold, You are there. If I take the wings of the dawn, If I dwell in the remotest part of the sea, Even there Your hand will lead me, And Your right hand will lay hold of me" (cf. 1 Kings 8:27). This means, all of God is everywhere at once. God does not have one part here and another part there (since He is simple or has no parts). God is present to but not part of creation. God is everywhere, but He is not identical to anything(s). God is at every point in space, but He is not spatial. He is at every point in space but He is not identical to any point in space. God is in the universe as its cause (Col. 1:17), but He is not a part of it. All of God is everywhere, yet no part of God is anywhere (since He has no parts). God in His eternity knows all things possible and actual (omniscience). This does *not* mean that God's knowledge is merely greater than ours or God's knowledge is merely the greatest actual knowledge of any being. It is the greatest possible knowledge of any being. Of course, God cannot know what is impossible to know. For example, He cannot know what a square circle is or know that good is evil.

God knows all our future choices related to free will for it is His understanding that is infinite (Ps. 147:5). From eternity God brings about everything in accordance with all His knowledge that ensures human free will. As 1 Peter 1:2 says, "Who are chosen according to the foreknowledge of God the Father." God only causes what is good. Evil is not a thing or a substance in and of itself, but a privation of essentially good things. God is responsible for the fact of human freedom; we are responsible for the acts of freedom.

God is infinite wisdom (omnisapience) which entails God's unerring ability to choose the best means to accomplish the best of all possible ends. Job 12:13 says, "With Him are wisdom and might; To Him belong counsel and understanding." God is the most pleasing thing to be seen; hence He is majesty and beauty (Ps. 96:9). God alone possesses immortal life. God possesses life intrinsically and eternally. God is Life; all else merely has life (1 Tim. 6:16). Finally, God is Unity (1 Tim. 2:5; cf. Deut. 6:4). This entails not only God's simplicity but also that there is no other god or gods. Hence, anything else that is worshiped is a false god.

Non–Moral Attributes and Characteristics

Because God created, He is sovereign or in complete control of all things. Christian theism also uniquely affirms God is transcendence and immanent. Transcendent means God is above and beyond all creation or not identical with creation and is immanent meaning God is present to or within creation or the entire universe. We must also see that God is ineffable. This means the transcendent attributes and characteristics of God cannot be exhaustedly expressed in human language. This does not mean, however, we cannot understand God's attributes at all; nor does it mean that we cannot express truth about God, since both of these would be self–defeating. God certainly is infinitely more than can be said of Him (ineffability).

Moral Attributes

God alone is absolutely Holy. Exodus 15:11 says, "Who is like You among the gods, O Lord? Who is like You, majestic in holiness" (cf. Lev. 11:45; 19:2). God is totally and utterly set apart from all creation and evil. God's essence is Love since 1 John 4:16 says, "God is love." To love is to will the good of another. So added to this is Goodness (omnibenevolence), which is interchangeable with love. This entails that God can only and completely will the good of all (cf. Jer. 31:3; Rom. 8:35–39; Eph. 3:19). The implications for the rest of Bible doctrine are very significant. For example, the atonement of Christ's death on the cross must be unlimited. Christ died for all, not just the elect (John. 3:16–19; Rom. 5:6–8; 2 Cor. 5:15; 1 John 2:1–2; 2 Peter 2:1). God's grace cannot be forced on someone unwilling to receive it (Chapters 9 and 12). Also, we should be compelled by the love of God to evangelize every sinner who can be told Christ died for them. For John 3:16 says, "For God so loved the world, that He gave His only begotten Son, that whoever believes in Him shall not perish, but have eternal life."

God alone is absolutely and completely righteous or just (Ps. 89:14) and truthful (Ex. 34:6). God is truth (Ex. 34:6; 1 Thess. 1:9), He does not lie or change His mind (Num. 23:19; 1 Sam. 15:29). He cannot lie (Heb. 6:18). God is the God of truth (Deut. 32:4; Ps. 31:5). Jesus is the truth (John 14:6). The Holy Spirit is the Spirit of truth (John 15:26). God's works are done in truth (Ps. 33:4). God is characterized in Scripture as a jealous God (Ex. 34:14). God's jealousness is a holy zeal to protect His supremacy and display His anger and wrath toward idolatry and other sins. God is absolute perfection, morally flawless and the ultimate standard for what is morally right. God's judgment is done in truth (Ps. 96:13) and God joins both mercy and truth together (Ps. 85:10).

Moral Activities

God is merciful in all that He does. Mercy is *not* giving someone what they deserve. Grace is giving them what they do not deserve. Mercy and grace flow from God's goodness and justice. Everything God does (works) involves mercy. By creating creatures, God shows mercy. Micah 7:18 says, "Who is a God like You, who pardons iniquity and passes over the rebellious act of the remnant of His possession? He does not retain His anger forever, Because He delights in unchanging love." Luke 1:50 says, "And His mercy is upon generation after generation toward those who fear Him." God's mercy flows from His goodness and justice. As such, God may be characterized as wrathful (Rom. 1:18); angry against all that is opposed to His holiness, goodness and justice, including unrepentant sinful humans.

The Trinity

The Trinity or tri-unity of God is a theological mystery arrived at through a study of Scripture. It is known only through God's special revelation (the Bible) alone and not through nature. However, it is a teaching of Jesus Christ who prayed to the Father (John 17) and promised the Holy Spirit (John 14–16). It is arrived at completely through a study of the Scripture. From Scripture, we read that there is only one God (Deut. 6:4), that the Father (John 6:27), the Son (John 8:58), and the Holy Spirit (Acts 5:3–4) are assigned the names, the attributes, and the acts that can only belong to God (John 1:1–18). For example, the Son claims to be Yahweh (Jehovah) (John 8:58), be equal with God (John 5:18), to accepted worship as God (John 9:38;

20:28), equal authority with God (Matt. 24:35) and accept prayer as God (John 14:13–14). Likewise, the Holy Spirit, is synonymous with the name "God" (Acts 5:3–4; 1 Cor. 3:16; 6:19), has all the attributes of Deity (omniscience, 1 Cor. 2:11; omnipresence, Ps. 139:7; holiness, Eph. 4:30; truth, John 16:13; life, Rom. 8:2) and performs the acts of God (creation, Gen. 1:2; redemption, Eph. 4:30; miracles, Gal. 3:2–5; cf. Heb. 2:4). In the Old Testament all three are implicit: Isaiah 63:7–10 says,

> I shall make mention of the loving kindnesses of the Lord, the praises of the Lord, According to all that the Lord [Father] has granted us, . . . So He became their Savior [Son]. In all their affliction He was afflicted, And the angel of His presence saved them; In His love and in His mercy He redeemed them, . . . But they rebelled And grieved His Holy Spirit.

At Jesus' baptism Matthew 3:16–17 says,

> After being baptized, Jesus [Son] came up immediately from the water; and behold, the heavens were opened, and he saw the Spirit of God [Holy Spirit] descending as a dove and lighting on Him, and behold, a voice out of the heavens [Father] said, "This is My beloved Son, in whom I am well–pleased."

Likewise, Jesus gives the baptismal formula "Go therefore and make disciples of all the nations, baptizing them in the name of the Father and the Son and the Holy Spirit" (Matt. 28:19).

Hence, all three must be the one (undivided) divine nature. The argument goes as follows:

1) There is only One God.
2) Three different Persons are God: Father, Son, and Holy Spirit.
3) Therefore, all three are the One God.

This does not mean that there are three gods (Tritheism), and this does not mean that God has three modes of existence (Modalism). It does mean that God is triune or plurality within unity: three persons in one essense or nature. The term essense (or nature) is appropriately used of God's divinity, since it answers "what" God is. A nature is an objective center of essential attributes. The term person is appropriately applied to God's relations, since it answers "who" God is. A person, as applied to the Trinity, is a subjective center or subsistence of intellect and will. While there can be no differences in God's essence because of unity, there can be a relational differences in God's subsistence or intentions. Hence, God is tri–personal. The three persons are distinct (Matt. 3:16–17, 28:19) from each other via a relation and therefore the Father is not the Son, and the Son is not

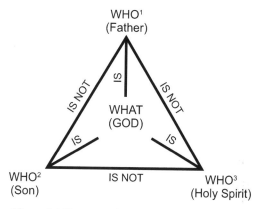

Figure 3.1 Nature and Persons of the Trinity

the Holy Spirit, etc. However, the three persons are the one divine nature and not distinguished from it so it can be said the Father is God, the Son is God and the Holy Spirit is God. God is one "What" and three "Whos." That is, God is one Nature consisting of three co-equal Persons is not contradictory. To illustrate this, it is like an equilateral triangle that has three distinct angles from each other but not distinct from the triangle. It is like 1^3 (1 x 1 x 1) = 1 or the relation of my intellect (mind) to its ideas, thoughts and words.

The Trinitarian view is that there are three persons that subsist in the one nature. The Trinity should be distinguished from heretical views. These include Tritheism that says there are three separate gods in the Godhead; Modalism (or Sabellianism) says God is one person in three roles or modes; Binitarianism says there are only two persons in the Godhead.

	PERSON(S)	NATURE(S)
Trinitarianism	Three	One
Tritheism	Three	Three
Modalism	One	One
Binitarianism	Two	One

Table 3.2 Trinity vs. Heretical Views

Other heresies that involve the Trinity and deity of Jesus Christ (Chapter 5) include Patripassianism that says the Father suffered on the cross and not just the Son. Monotholitism says there is only "one will" in Christ which confuses His two natures, human and divine, of the Son. Subordinationism says the Son is subordinate or a lesser nature than the Father. Monarchianism denies the deity of the Son to supposedly save the unity of God. Adoptionism says Jesus, the son, was adopted by God to achieve the status of deity. The Apostles' Creed, the Nicene Creed, the Definition of Chalcedon and the Athanasian Creed preserve the orthodox or correct view of which all of orthodox Christendom agrees.

Our Response to God

Our response to God should be one of awe, exaltation and worship. Entire chapters of the Bible are dedicated to God's attributes (see Psalm 139). God's simplicity should cause us to rest in His imperishableness (Rom. 1:23). God's aseity should cause us to realize our utter dependence upon Him for our moment–by–moment existence (John 1:3; Col. 1:17). God's immutability should cause us to trust His word (Num. 23:19, 20; Heb. 13:7, 8) that contains His promises and prophecy that will come to fulfillment (Heb. 6:17, 18). His impassibility means God never changes His feelings; He always feels happy about our righteousness and sad about our sin. His infinity should cause us to be assured and humbled that God is infinitely sufficient to meet our every need (1 Kings 8:27–30). His immateriality directs us to that which is unseen by faith is more real than that which is seen in the material world (Rom. 1:20; 1 Tim. 1:17). Hence, we should avoid all forms of idolatry and worship God alone in our spirit (John 4:24).

God's omnipotence should cause us to humble ourselves before Him in adoration and servitude. We should be certain about God's power to solve our problems and provide our future assurance of salvation through the fulfillment of His word. This is the power that saves us and is available to us through Christ (Eph. 1:19). God's omnipresence means He is with us in good times and bad. God is always nearer to us than anyone else (Ps. 139:7–10). God's omniscience should encourage us to think and act as if we always lived in public. Nothing can be hidden from God. He supports our good actions and knows our secret sins. He is the rewarded of our secret good works (2 Chron. 16:9; Ps. 90:8). We should be humble and realize our need for instruction and correction (Job 42:3–6). God's majesty and beauty shows us He alone is worthy of our worship, praise and adoration. All beauty is a gift from God, but His beauty, seeing God face–to–face, should be our anticipation. God can provide all we need for life because He is the source of all life who alone can give immortality. God's unity should be emulated in the body of Christ (Eph. 4:1–6).

Given God's sovereignty we should live with assurance that He is in control and be grateful that God includes us in what He does (Ps. 115:12–13). We should be holy because God is Holy (Lev. 11:44; 1 Peter 1:14–16). We should also be just and assured that we will not be unjustly treated by God (Ps. 19:9; Rom. 2:6–8). God's truthfulness should cause us to recognize its absolute nature (Mark 13:31;

Heb. 6:18) and to purse truth (Phil. 4:8). God's love and goodness should cause us to do good to all men (John 15:12, 13; Gal. 6:10; 1 John 4:7). God's jealously should cause us to make Him our ultimate devotion and love (Ex. 20:5). God's perfection should cause us to strive for God–like moral excellence in His power (Matt. 5:48) and give us assurance that He will bring us to perfection (Phil. 1:6; Heb. 10:14).

SUMMARY

This study of God's nature (Theology Proper) shows that there is no one like God. There is only one simple, self–existing, necessary, unchangeable, infinite spirit, who is eternal, all powerful, always present, all knowing and wise Being: who the creature must describe as sovereign, transcendent, immanent and ineffable. God alone is holy, righteous, truthful, all loving and all good who acts upon His creation with mercy and wrath. God is triune, being one divine nature subsisting in three distinct co–equal, co–eternal persons, Father, Son and Holy Spirit. There is no one else we can turn to for salvation. He, alone is our beginning and end (Rev. 22:13).

QUESTIONS TO ANSWER

1. How can God be simple and yet have many attributes that describe Him?
2. What are the attributes of God and what biblical verses support them?
3. How can God remain the same and yet show mercy and wrath?
4. What is the Trinity and how is it taught in Scripture?
5. What response should we have to the study of God's attributes?

Creation

God saw all that He had made, and behold, it was very good.
And there was evening and there was morning, the sixth day.
Thus the heavens and the earth were completed,
and all their hosts.
Genesis 1:31; 2:1

GIVEN the theistic understanding of God (Chapter 3), we now turn to a study of God's creation. Here we examine the biblical basis and understanding of creation. We will also examine issues related to the age of the earth and the challenge posed by evolution.

BIBLICAL BASIS OF CREATION

The Genesis creation account (1–2) answers basic questions about creation. First the account answers the question: **who** is the creator? "God created..." (Gen. 1:1): By "God" this asserts the theistic understanding of God. God alone is the creator (Gen. 1:1) and by implication rejects all views opposed to Theism, such as Deism, Pantheism, Panentheism, Finite Godism, Polytheism, and Atheism (see Chapter 1). The account answers the question **when** was creation? Creation is "In the beginning" (Gen. 1:1) and this is "in six days" (Gen. 2:1, 2; Ex. 20:11). Creation is also finished or completed (Gen. 2:1; Heb. 4:3). The account answers the question **what** was created? God by His power alone *created* the beginning (Gen. 1:1), matter (v. 1), life (v. 21), every living creature (v. 21) and man (v. 27). God *made* the grass (v. 11), herbs, fruit, fish, fowl (v. 20), sea monsters (v. 21), cattle, creepers and beasts (v. 24). Creation, in the account, is given a sequence or order of six days (Gen. 2:1, 2; Ex. 20:11): 1. Universe (Gen. 1:1a), 2. Earth (v. 1b), 3. Sea (v. 6), 4. Land (v. 9), 5. Plants (v. 11), 6. Sea animals (v. 20), 7. Land animals (v. 24), 8. Man (v. 27). After this order, God ceased from His creation.

The account describes **how** man was created:

> Then God said, "Let Us make man in Our image, according to Our likeness; and let them rule over the fish of the sea and over the birds of the sky and over the cattle and over all the earth, and over every creeping thing that creeps on the earth." God created man in His own image, in the image of God He created him; male and female He created them. (Gen. 1:26–27)

Note that only humans received the image of God. This is what distinguishes us from the animals (Chapter 9). The account describes **where** man was created: "Then the Lord God formed man of dust from the ground, and breathed into his nostrils the breath of life; and man became a living being. The Lord God planted a garden toward the east, in Eden; and there He placed the man whom He had formed" (Gen. 2:7–8).

Also note that man is not created from the animals, but from dust and He is placed in a specific geographic location (Gen. 2:10–14).

Why did God create? God did not create because He was lonely or in need of companionship. The Triune God is perfect love and has no lack or need for fellowship. God did not create because He needed anything. God, as we have seen, is perfect and lacks nothing (Chapter 3). The Scripture implies two reasons that God created. One is to declare His glory. Psalm 19:1 says, "The heavens are telling of the glory of God; And their expanse is declaring the work of His hands" (cf. Col. 1:16; Rev. 4:11). The second reason is to provide for our good. First Timothy 6:17 says, "Instruct those who are rich in this present world not to be conceited or to fix their hope on the uncertainty of riches, but on God, who richly supplies us with all things to enjoy" (cf. James 1:17).

Genesis is not the only book in the Bible that speaks of God's creation. Many aspects of the Genesis account are acknowledged throughout Scripture. This gives further support for the account to be taken as historical, since the rest of Scripture does. There is a beginning of creation (Mark 13:19; Rom. 1:20; 2 Peter 3:4). Creation is of all things (Acts 17:24; Eph. 3:9; Col. 1:16; Rev. 4:11) and is described as heaven and earth (Ex. 20:11; Ps. 33:6; Isa. 42:5; 45:18; Jer. 32:17; 51:15). Angels are created by God (Ps. 148:2, 5; Col. 1:16). Light and darkness are created, as well as the Sun, Moon, and Stars

(Ps. 148:3–5; 8:3; Isa. 40:26). The earth, sea, and all living things are created (Prov. 8:25–29; Jer. 27:5; Amos 4:13). The first man is created with dust and with breath (Eccl. 12:7; Job 34:15). It is only Man that is created in God's image (Gen. 5:1; 9:6; Ps. 8:5; Eccl. 7:29; Col. 3:10; James 3:9). Male is created first, then female (Matt. 19:4; 1 Cor. 11:9; 1 Cor. 15:25; 1 Tim. 2:13). God is the sustainer and preserver of all creation (Col. 1:17; Neh. 9:6; Ps. 66:9; Acts 17:28). All of this reinforces the necessity and importance of taking the Genesis creation account as historical rather than mythical.

PRESERVATION

God is the creator and preserver of all things. God is the originating Cause as well as the sustaining Cause of everything that exists. That is there is a distinction between God's work in the origin of the world and His work in the operation of it. In the Bible this is seen by the use of the word *creation* for the past event of origin (Gen. 1:1, 21–27; Ps. 89:11–12; Mark 10:6; Rom. 1:20). God is also at work *in* creation. God created in the past (Gen. 1:1) and is later at work operating in the world *producing* vegetation (Gen. 1:11) or bringing forth food from the earth (Ps. 104:5, 14). God rested from creation in the past (Gen. 2:3) but Jesus affirmed that the Father [God] "is always at his work" (John 5:17). Paul said, God made the world and keeps it in existence (Acts 17:24; 28). Hence God makes and sustains the world (Heb. 1:2, 3).

God is sovereign over all things. This not only includes God's right to control all, but also His actual dominion over all things. Biblically this is seen in the attributes of God (Chapter 3) and entails that God is not only in charge of all things, but in control of all things, nothing happens apart from God's Will (Job 42:2; Ps. 115:3, 135:6). All of creation is under His control, including kings (Prov. 21:1), human events (Dan. 2, 7; Isa. 55:11), Angels, good and evil (Col. 1:15–16; Eph. 1:21) and human decisions (Eph. 1:11; Rom. 8:29–30) and this even includes those who are against God (1 Peter 2:8; Rom. 9:22–23).

PROVIDENCE

Providence is the means of control. Such control is both general and particular. This is so because God cannot control the general without controlling the particular. God's love for all extents to the smallest detail that affects the general and this is affirmed in Scripture (Job 23:10; 2 Cor. 2:14; Eph. 3:1). Psalm 104:1–23 speaks of God's complete and meticulous providence for every minute part of creation. It begins with His prearrangement of the universe (vv. 1–9) and extends to every operation of natural processes for the perpetuation of life (vv. 10–23). Matthew 6:25–33 speaks to His providence towards subhuman creation and humankind. God's providence is over the natural and animal world (Job 9:5–6; Ps. 104:21, 27–28) and the human world. God's providence is over human affairs in general (Dan. 4:35), affairs of nations (Ps. 22:28, Prov. 21:1), and humankind's lot in life (1 Sam. 2:6; James 4:14–15). Nothing happens by chance in God's universe, seemingly fortuitous events, and even "accidental" deaths (Ex. 21:13) are under His control. Everything is planned by God (Prov. 16:33). Even evil events are permitted in God's providence for a greater good (Gen. 50:20). God's providence extends over human free acts, good (Phil. 2:13) and permitting evil acts (2 Sam. 16:10). God restrains and controls evil acts (Ps. 66:10–12). Nothing is beyond His cognizance and ultimate control. He protects the righteous (Ps. 4:8), provides the needs of His people (Ps. 37:25; Phil. 4:19) and punishes the wicked (Ps. 11:6). God's providence is present in answers prayer (Isa. 65:24; Matt. 6:8). This should not be confused with miracles. Special providence involves no direct supernatural intervention. No natural law is suspended. Rather, this is often manifesting in His pre–timing of events to bring about unusual occurrences in response to our requests He wishes to honor. Even speedy or unusual recoveries from sickness are usually acts of special providence by which God uses health and natural regenerative process of the body. There are times when God deems it necessary to transcend a law of nature and exercise providential care for His creatures (Gen. 19:1–29).

Two cautions with respect to God's providence are important: 1) We can trust God's providence to care for us if we live reasonable lives according to His laws, but we should not presume upon God's providence to protect us if we take unnecessary risks. Jesus didn't (Matt. 4:9–10). 2) That many worldwide suffer for lack of food, drink, cloths and shelter is not a lack in God's providence for humanity. God has provided enough for everyone on earth. Instead, Human depravity, sinful greed and the quest for power as well as inefficiency results in such conditions.

BIBLICAL UNDERSTANDING OF CREATION

God's creation is ex *nihilo* which means creation out of nothing. When we declare that God created "out of nothing" we do not mean that "nothing" is some kind of invisible, immaterial thing. "Nothing" means absolutely nothing, before creation only God exists and utterly nothing else. Only after God created did something else exist. This view is opposed to *ex materia* which is creation out of already existing matter or *ex deo* which is creation out of God. Creation from nothing does not mean creation *by* nothing. All things are created *by* Someone (God); Someone who used absolutely nothing else caused the entire creation to come into being "by his powerful word" (Heb. 1:3). There is a fundamental and real difference between the Creator and creation. God is the Maker, and creation is the made. God is the cause and creation is the effect. God is unlimited and the world is limited. The Creator is self–existing, but creation is entirely dependent on Him for its existence.

CREATOR	CREATION
Uncreated	Created
Infinite	Finite
Eternal	Temporal
Necessary	Contingent
Changeless	Changing

Table 4.1 Creator Compared to Creation

God is to the world as a painter is to a painting. That is to say, while the artist is in some sense manifested in his art, he is also beyond it. The painter is not the painting; He is beyond, over, and above it. Likewise, God is the Creator of the world which He causes to exist and who is revealed in it, but He is not identical to the world.

The source of creation is God and God alone. Only God can cause existence. His act of creation is voluntary from eternity. Each member of the Trinity, since they are identical with His essence, is involved in creation (Col. 1:16–17). God created everything that exists (Gen. 1:1, 20–27). No creature, human or angelic, can create existence from nothing; this superior cause belongs to God alone. All that a creature can do is work instrumentally with creation to reduplicate what God made.

God created everything that exists (Gen. 1:1, 20–27). God created existence out of nonexistence. He made something out of nothing. All things are *from* God but they are not *of* God. By "from" we do not mean that creation comes *from* something, but *after* nothing. God is Pure Existence ("I AM THAT I AM" Ex. 3:14). God, who is uncaused Existence, brought all else into existence. God is the unmoved Mover, but He is not the unmoving Mover. He is unmovable, but not immobile. God does not change, but He is the unchanging Changer of the changing world.

His method of creation is simply by His Word, with no instrumental or intermediate cause. There is no medium between nothing (nonbeing) and something (being). Since God is infinite power, He can do anything that is possible. It is not impossible for the infinite Creator to produce a finite creature. Unlimited power is not limited in its ability to create limited powers. And this creation is not only by His power but also by His will. God is not bound or limited by any obligation.

God created "in the beginning." God is eternal, but the world is not. The world came to be, but God always was and actually always, is. But the world had a point of beginning—that is temporal, not eternal. God is prior to the universe in order, but not in time. There was no time before creation, since time measures change or physical motion, and there was no change before creation. Space and time itself are created aspects of creation. God did not need time to create nor did He have to move to create motion. What was God doing before He created? Or why did God not create earlier? These ultimately are meaningless questions. To speak of "doing" and "before" or "earlier" imply time and there is no time before time. It is like asking, what time is it for a timeless Being? There is no time before time began, only eternity. God did not create *in* time or space; rather, it was a creation *of* time. He created time with the changing universe.

If God created from eternity, why is the world not eternal? Everything preexisted in God according to His will. But God willed eternally that created things have a beginning. Similar to a doctor who decrees (prescribes) medication from the beginning for an illness to be treated over time. Likewise, God wills events from eternity that occur in time.

Why, if God is free, did He create rather than not create? God did not create because He *had* to, but because He *wants* to do so. God is infinitely good; as such He desires to share His goodness. God created simply because it is good and the purpose of creation is to manifest the goodness of God. It is a rational response for a creature to recognize His Creator (God) and have it result in their worth–ship (worship) of Him. In acknowledging His good as the highest good, we find our highest good.

God is the creator and preserver. This is necessary for the world to come to be and to continue to be. He brings it into existence in the past from nothing and keeps it from returning to nothing in the present. God is the primary cause of all things, but He also works through secondary causes such as natural processes and causes found in creation that we describe in natural laws. This is needed for creation because creation is contingent (something that could not be) and only God is a necessary Being. Once it is a contingent being it always remains a contingent being and is therefore dependent for its existence at all times. God also acts in creation either directly or indirectly. Direct intervention is always immediate and instantaneous, as in *ex nihilo* Creation or *de nova* (brand–new) making life from non–life.

Indirect action is mediate and involves a process as in preserving the operation of the natural world observed today.

God's sovereignty is based on His attributes, especially since He is all–powerful, all–good, all–knowing, and all–wise (Chapter 3). Some may object that God cannot be sovereign and humans have free choice. But this is a failure to see that God's infallible foreknowledge can sovereignly will to accomplish things through the free will that He gives to His creatures. That God infallible knows what each creature will do with his freedom in advance is sufficient to assure that He has complete sovereign control over every event and the final outcome. Furthermore, there is no contradiction between 1) a future free act is determined from the relationship of God's infallible foreknowledge, and 2) also free when viewed from the relationship of our free choice (in the sense of the power to do otherwise). There is no contradiction since, the law of non–contradiction demands that to be contradictory two propositions must affirm and deny the same thing at the same time in the same relationship. So the same event can be determined in relationship to God's knowledge, and free in relationship to our free choice.

THE AGE OF THE EARTH AND THE "DAYS" OF GENESIS

A point of contention, especially since the rise of modern geology (1800s), concerns the interpretation of the Genesis creation account with respect to the age of the earth. However, this problem exists only if one assumes there are no gaps in the Genesis record (Gen. 1–11). It also rests on some unproven presuppositions. How much time and how many gaps are in the genealogies is not known, but even Jesus' genealogy that overlaps Genesis clearly contains gaps (Gen. 11:12; cf. Luke 3:35–36). Further, Matthew 1:8 omits three generations between Joram and Uzziah (see 1 Chron. 3:11–14). Genesis is not a complete chronology, even though it is an accurate genealogy (lines of descent).

What is more, science considers the speed of light (186,000 miles per second) to be constant which is used in arguments for an old earth/universe. If so, the universe is billions of years old since there are stars that are billions of light years away. There is nothing in Scripture that contradicts this since all the Bible affirms is that there was a "beginning" (Gen. 1:1), not how many years ago this happened. Hence there is no demonstrated conflict between Genesis 1–2 and scientific fact.

The two major views regarding time and the Creation account is the young–earth view (sees the universe as about 15,000 years old) that interprets the "days" as six successive literal solar days of twenty–four hours each (144 hours of Creation). The other view is the old–earth view (sees the universe as about 15 billion years old) that accepts the "days" as significant periods of time. Since God is the creator of the world and inspired His Word, there can be no conflict between creation and the Bible. The conflict must be between human interpretation and scientific theories. Science has not proven that a six–successive–twenty–four–hour day view is impossible nor is a literal–historical interpretation of Genesis inconsistent with an earth/universe that is billions of years old. The Bible does not say how old the universe is, and the age of the earth should not be a test for orthodoxy. Many scholars today and throughout church history have held the earth/universes to be quite old and such is not incompatible with the inerrancy of the Bible (Chapter 3).

Other views have been put forward that allow for a twenty–four hour interpretation of "days" in Genesis and an old earth. These include the Revelatory–Day view that says Adam or Moses was given revelation over the days of Genesis. Gap Theories see a gap or lapse of time before the six–twenty–four–hour days begin. The Alternate–Day–Age view says the days are twenty–four–hours but there are long periods of time between the days. The Ideal–time view says the earth and life was given the appearance of age (however, this view does charge God with deception). Finally, the Literary–Framework view says "days" "evening and morning" are used as ancient literary devices to cover certain periods of time. Whatever view or interpretation of Genesis is accepted it must preserve: 1) the historical–grammatical interpretation, 2) the historicity and context of the Genesis account and 3) the inerrancy and infallibility of Scripture.

Creation and Evolution

In 1859 Charles Darwin wrote his well–known *On the Origin of Species*. Since then Neo–Darwinian evolution theorizes that every form of life, existing and extinct, developed over time gradually or maybe rapidly by natural processes from a single living structure. Regardless if God is thought to initiate evolution, which is known as Theistic Evolution, this theory is fundamentally in conflict with the Genesis creation account that demands the special creation of animal "kinds" (Gen. 1:24–25) and the special creation of man (male and female 1:27) from the dust of the earth; as opposed to creation from other animals. The account of creation can allow for genetic changes within created kinds. This in science is known as microevolution which is observed among the different species existing today. However, the Bible does not allow for changes between kinds or types which is known as macroevolution.

Imposing Neo–Darwinian evolution upon the creation account violates its historicity and grammar. Christian's may disagree on the timing of creation, but they should not disagree on the historicity of the biblical account of creation. To do so, would violate the normal understanding everyone uses to know the meaning of a written text. Such would contradict the special creation of man and woman affirmed by Jesus, the son of God who said in Matthew 19:4 "Have you not read that He who created them from the beginning made them male and female" (cf. Mark 13:19 cf. 1 Cor. 11:8–9). It would also violate the numerous biblical references cited elsewhere in Scripture that references the literal creation of man and woman (see above). The historical creation account serves as a connection to redemption. Paul makes this point in Romans 5:12, 14–15:

> Therefore, just as through one man sin entered into the world, and death through sin, and so death spread to all men, because all sinned– . . . Nevertheless death reigned from Adam until Moses, even over those who had not sinned in the likeness of the offense of Adam, who is a type of Him who was to come But the free gift is not like the transgression. For if by the transgression of the one the many died, much more did the grace of God and the gift by the grace of the one Man, Jesus Christ, abound to the many.

Likewise, Jesus makes an inseparable connection between the historical creation account and ethics when He answers a moral question involving marriage: "And He answered and said, 'Have you not read that He who created them from the beginning made them male and female.'" (cf. James 3:9). Paul makes an inseparable connection between Adam and Christ in 1 Corinthians 15:45: "So also it is written, 'The first man, Adam, became a living soul.' The last Adam became a life–giving spirit." Hence, Adam must be just as historical as Jesus for redemption to have been accomplished.

Neo–Darwinian macroevolution also violates fundamental philosophical principles. First, it is an undeniable truth that nothing cannot produce something. Hence, total cosmic evolution is impossible. Second, the non–living cannot produce the living. It is impossible for life to have arisen from non–life. As such, biological evolution that theorizes life arising by chance from non–life is impossible. Third, the impersonal cannot produce the personal. Hence, evolution that theorizes human consciousness, intellect and will arose from that which lacks it is not credible.

Scientifically there are several problems with Neo–Darwinian evolution. First, it confuses the results of two distinct sciences. Origin Science studies past singularities, such as the origin of the universe and first life that cannot be directly observed or repeated today. Only their effects can be studied. It is similar to a forensic science which does not observe the past but only what remains in the present. Operation Science studies observable regularities. That is, things that happen over and over again today that can be directly observed and tested. The fundamental flaw of Neo–Darwinian evolution is it has taken the results of Operation Science that studies genetic changes within species and wrongfully applied them to the domain of Origin Science. They assume that the same mechanism that accounts for genetic changes within species accounts for the development of new species.

Another problem is that Origin Science shows from the fossil record that the basic forms of life appear suddenly and producing after their kind, which is known as stasis. If Neo–Darwinian evolution were true, the fossil record would contain millions of intermediate transitional forms showing a change from one species to another. Without these intermediate forms, Neo–Darwinian evolution has no explanation for such gaps in the fossil record. Another problem with Neo–Darwinian evolution is the well–established second law of thermodynamics. This law states that in a closed isolated system, the amount of usable energy is decreasing. But the universe does not have an infinite amount of energy, and it has not all been depleted yet. Hence, the universe must have had a beginning, just as Genesis 1:1 states: "In the beginning God created . . ."

Many scientists have shown that life shows clear signs of intelligent design. This is evidence at the molecular biological level and information found in the nucleus of living cells. Some biological mechanisms such as the motor that runs the flagellum found in some bacteria cannot function without all of its parts present. Furthermore, information content found in the DNA of cells has been compared to the amount of information found in a multi volume set of encyclopedias. Given these findings, intelligent design is a valid scientific inference. Finally, the simplest conceivable form of life still requires so many protein molecules all in the right sequence that the possibility that such would arise by chance is mathematically impossible. Given these reasons against Neo–Darwinian evolution, a historical understanding of the creation account of Genesis (1–2) and the rest of the Bible remains credible.

Summary

This study of Creation shows that the Bible answers basic questions about creation. God alone is the Creator who freely brings everything into existence *ex nihilo*, preserves its existence and providentially provides and directs its existence. God is sovereign in His right to control and have dominion over all things, and because God infallible knows all, He is able to do all in accordance (not incompatible) with human free will. While no scientific facts are incompatible with creation, some scientific theories are. The Neo–Darwinian theory that calls for the biological development and diversification of all life from a single life form, not only violates the scriptural creation account, but also counters reasoning based on philosophical and scientific principles.

QUESTIONS TO ANSWER

1. How does the account of Genesis 1–2 answer basic questions about creation?
2. What are the source, content, method, time and purpose of creation?
3. Why must the creation account be considered historical?
4. Why is any age of the earth/universe compatible with the Genesis Creation account?
5. What are some biblical and scientific reasons to reject evolution?

| 5 |

Jesus Christ

Have this attitude in yourselves which was also in Christ
Jesus, who, although He existed in the form of God, did not
regard equality with God a thing to be grasped, but emptied
Himself, taking the form of a bond-servant,
and being made in the likeness of men.
Philippians 2:5–7

OUR study of Jesus Christ (Christology) includes Jesus'
Preincarnate state, the anticipation and realization of His virgin
birth, His life of miracles and sinlessness, and the doctrine of His incarnation, His vicarious death and physical resurrection and ascension.

CHRIST'S PREINCARNATE STATE

The title "Son of God" entails that Jesus Christ is of the order of God
(John 3:16–17). Hence Christ is the eternal Son of God which is
clear from both the Old and New Testaments. As Son, He is eternally submissive to the will of the Father to be the Redeemer of humankind (Heb. 10:7–10) and also while on earth (John 15:10) and
in eternity to come (1 Cor. 15:24–28). Both the Old (Ps. 2:6–8, 12)
and New (John 1:1, 17:5; Col. 1:16–17) Testaments affirm Christ's
Eternal Sonship. One of the strongest proofs of Christ's Preincarnate
Sonship and deity in the Old Testament is His appearance as "the
Angel [Messenger] of the Lord." While the term "Yahweh" (Lord) is
used exclusively of God in the Old Testament (Isa. 45:18), "Yahweh"
appeared to the patriarchs" (Ex. 6:2–3). This was done by the

Messenger of the Lord who is Yahweh. Exodus 3:2 says, "The angel of the Lord appeared to him [Moses] in a blazing fire from the midst of a bush." This Messenger of the Lord throughout the Old Testament is called God (Gen. 18:1). It is also clear that the Angel of the Lord is a different Person than the Lord. Zechariah 1:12–13 says, "Then the angel of the Lord said, 'O Lord of hosts, how long will You have no compassion for Jerusalem and the cities of Judah, with which You have been indignant these seventy years?' The Lord answered the angel who was speaking . . ." This same kind of conversation takes place in Psalm 110:1, which Jesus used as an argument for His Messiahship against the Pharisees (Matt. 22:42–45). Hence, it is based on two lines of evidence: 1) The Angel of the Lord in the Old Testament serves the same role as does Christ in the New Testament (Isa. 63:7–10). 2) Once the Son (Christ) came in permanent incarnate form (John 1:1, 14), never again does the Angel of the Lord appear. Angels appear, but no angel that is worshiped or claims to be God ever appears again. The Father and Holy Spirit never appear as a man. Hence, Jesus Christ, as a person, eternally existed and appeared as a man before His virginal conception on earth.

CHRIST'S VIRGIN BIRTH

The Old Testament contains Messianic prophecies that implicitly and explicitly anticipate the virgin birth. Genesis 3:15 says, "And I will put enmity between you and the woman, And between your seed and her seed; He shall bruise you on the head, And you shall bruise him on the heel." The Redeemer coming from the "offspring" or "seed" of the women is important. Descendants are normally traced through their father (Gen. 5) and this is even done for the Messiah (Matt. 1). Hence, by "seed of the women" it is implicit that the Messiah would not have a natural father, and thus be virgin–born. The virgin birth is also implied in the curse, that no offspring of Jeconiah will sit on the throne of David or rule Judah (Jer. 22:30). Jeconiah is in the fatherly line of Jesus (Matt. 1:12). But since Joseph was only Jesus' legal father (by virtue of being engaged to Mary when she became pregnant) and Jesus was the actual son of David through Mary (Luke 3), Jesus did not inherit this curse by virtue of His virgin birth. The virgin birth is predicted in Isaiah 7:14: "Therefore the Lord Himself will give you a sign: Behold, a virgin will be with child and bear a son, and she will call His name Immanuel." Rightfully, this verse is only used of Christ since He will be called "Immanuel" ("Christ with us") which is a clear reference to His deity (Matt. 1:23) and is applied to the entire house of David (Isa. 7:13). Furthermore, the New Testament clearly saw this verse fulfilled in the supernatural birth and deity of Christ (Matt. 1:22, 23).

Matthew 1:18–23 (cf. Luke 1:26–35) contains four factors demonstrating Christ's virgin birth: 1) Mary conceived "before they came together" so it was not a natural conception. 2) Joseph's reaction "he had in mind to divorce her" reveals he had no sexual relations with Mary. 3) The event was supernatural "what is conceived in her is of the Holy Spirit." 4) Mary had no sexual relations with anyone before, during, and immediately after He was conceived–even when He was born. Luke 1:26–35 also demonstrates the supernatural conception of Christ. Mary's reaction of being perplexed and afraid shows she knew she was a virgin. Conception is from "the Power of the most high." Mary's song/meditation on the event shows she knew it was supernatural. Mary knew of Jesus' power to do miracles even though He had not yet done one (John 2:1–5).

CHRIST'S MIRACLES & SINLESS LIFE

The New Testament records about 60 miracles in the life of Jesus. Indeed, John (20:30) says there were "many other signs Jesus also performed in the presence of the disciples, which are not written in this book; but these have been written so that you may believe that Jesus is the Christ, the Son of God; and that believing you may have life in His name." The purpose of Jesus' miracles can be seen in the terms used to describe them. The term "sign" is used of His resurrection as something to be predicted and accomplished (Matt. 12:39–40; John 2:19; Matt. 16:21; 20:19). The term "wonder" and "miraculous sign" is almost always used of a miracle (John 4:48; Acts 2:22) and "power" is a generic term used for humans and angels, but is also used of Christ's power to raise the dead (Phil. 3:10) including the miracle of His virgin birth (Luke 1:35). A miracle is a supernatural event (wonder) that has its source in God (power) and its significance (sign) in confirming a message/messenger from God (Ex. 4:1–5; 1 Kings 18:36). Jesus was known to be from God because of His miracles (John 3:2). Miracles are God's way of accrediting His spokesperson. It confirms the message as true, a sign to substantiate the sermon, an act of God to verify the Word of God (Heb. 2:3–4). Not all believe, even those who witness a miracle (John 12:37). Hence, one result of miracles is the condemnation of the unbeliever (Luke 16:31; John 12:31, 37).

Jesus lived a sinless life. He challenged others to convict Him of sin by saying, "Which one of you convicts Me of sin?" (John 8:46). His opponents and others said He was righteous. Judas who betrayed him said Jesus was "innocent blood" (Matt. 27:4). Pilate who ultimately condemned Jesus called him "innocent" (Luke 23:14, 15, 26) as did a centurion (Luke 23:47). The thief next to Jesus on the cross said He had "done nothing wrong" (Luke 23:41). His supporters and

Apostles who were closest to Him acknowledged He was sinless: John the Baptist called Jesus the "the Lamb of God who takes away the sin of the world" (John 1:29). Only a pure lamb could be sacrificed for sin, and only a perfect man could take away the sin of the world. Peter said Jesus "committed no sin" (1 Peter 2:21, 22). The Apostle Paul said Jesus "knew no sin" (2 Cor. 5:21). He was "righteous" (1 John 2:1). Hence, Jesus actively lived a life perfectly in accordance with the law and passive obedience to willingly submit to the Father's will in giving His life for the sin of the world.

CHRIST'S INCARNATION

Jesus Christ's incarnation (Latin for *in* and *carn*, meaning "flesh") is implicit in His claim to be the promised Jewish Messiah and God. Jesus taught this truth to His disciples and argued for it with His enemies. In Matthew 16:15–17 Jesus posed the question to Peter and the disciples, "But who do you say that I am?" The accepted answer is "you are the Christ, the Son of the living God." And the source of this answer was from God the Father. In Matthew 22:41–46 Jesus poses the question to the Pharisees, "What do you think about the Christ, whose son is He?" The answer was "The Son of David." To prove this, Jesus quoted the Psalm of David (110) putting them in a dilemma: How can He be the son of David and also be David's Lord? The only answer to the question that escapes the dilemma is that Jesus was both God (being David's Lord) and man (being David's son), or God incarnate. A biblical argument for Jesus' deity can be made as follows: 1) God is the only savior. Isaiah 43:11 says "I, even I, am the LORD, and apart from me there is no savior." 2) Jesus is the savior. Luke 2:11 says "Today in the town of David a Savior has been born to you; he is Christ the Lord." 3) Therefore, Jesus is God as Paul calls Jesus, the "Savior . . . the Lord Jesus Christ" (Phil. 3:20).

Jesus is presented in the New Testament as being fully human. He has a human genealogy (Matt. 1:1–17), born of a woman (Matt. 1:18f; Gal. 4:4), He aged (Luke 2:42), increased in knowledge (Matt. 4:12), prayed (Matt. 14:23), grew hungry (Matt. 4:2), tired (John 4:6), had compassion (Matt. 9:36), wept (John 11:35), grew thirsty (John 19:28), and Jesus is referred to as the "Son of Man" and "Son of David" multiple times. Jesus said, "Foxes have holes and birds of the air have nests, but the Son of Man has no place to lay his head" (Matt. 8:20).

Jesus is likewise presented in the New Testament as being fully God. He is the Creator (John 1:1–3) and sustainer of creation (1 Cor. 8:6). He is Eternal (John 8:58) "I tell you the truth," Jesus answered, "Before Abraham was born, I am!" Which is a clear reference to the Yahweh of the Old Testament (Ex. 3:14). In John 17:5 Jesus says,

"And now, Father, glorify me in your presence with the glory I had with you before the world began." Jesus is present everywhere (omnipresence) saying, "Go therefore and make disciples of all the nations . . . Teaching them to obey everything I have commanded you. And surely I am with you always, to the very end of the age" (Matt. 28:20). Jesus is all–knowing (omniscience) "He did not need man's testimony about man, for he knew what was in a man" (John 2:25). But Scripture teaches that only God knows what is in a man's heart (1 Kings 8:39). Jesus is all–powerful (omnipotence) "Then Jesus came to them and said, 'All authority in heaven and on earth has been given to me'" (Matt. 28:18). Jesus is unchangeable (Immutable), "Jesus Christ is the same yesterday and today and forever" (Heb. 13:8). Jesus performs the works of God as Judge (John 5:21–27) and power to do miracles such as raising the dead (John 11:43). But as we have seen only God can be and do all of these (Chapter 3 & 4). Jesus was also worshipped on many occasions (Matt. 28:17; John 9:38; Heb. 1:6), something due to God alone (Matt. 4:10). Hence, Jesus must be fully God.

Theologically the incarnation is described as a hypostatic union. The hypostasis of the second person of the Trinity is said to subsist or cohere in two natures, one divine and one human without mixture, separation, or division. Therefore, Christ can be said to be truly God and truly man: The God–Man. The effecting of this union did not alter the divine nature in any way; both natures retain that which makes them what they are. The human nature being created, limited, and changing is like ours in all respects, except, even though undergoing real temptation, is without sin.

The divine nature being the Second Person of the Trinity (i.e., Divine Logos) took on Himself humanity, but not in a different person or man. Before His conception, He did not possess humanity permanently. He is, since His conception, clothed in humanity forever more. This means that the Second Person of the Trinity, God the Son, while in and united to the human body of Jesus, is not bound by the human nature assumed.

The person of Christ is held to subsist or cohere in two natures, one divine and one human. Explained in the Trinity, this is two "What's" in one "Who"; two objects in one subject, two essences or natures in one person; two sources of objective coherence subsisting in a single subjective center of volitional and intentional activity (Figure 5.1). These natures are united in one person (hypostatic union), not two persons. The two natures of Christ are conjoined within the one person without mixture, separation, or division. The effecting of this union did not alter the divine nature in any way;

Figure 5.1 Person of Christ and the Trinity

both natures retain that which makes them what they are. Therefore, Christ can be said to be truly God and truly man: The God–Man.

Because of the uniqueness of the incarnation, in speaking or answering questions about Jesus it is necessary to ask and answer any question according to each distinct nature. For example, we might ask did Jesus grow tired. We must answer according to each nature, as man (human nature) yes, as God (divine nature) no. Does Jesus know everything? As man no, as God yes. This helps explain why Jesus did know some things that only God knows, such as what was in a man (John 2:25) and did not know other things, that only the Father knows such as the day of His coming (Matt. 24:36). It is the human nature that grows, learns and changes over time. It is the divine nature that is immutable, knows all, and is eternal (Figure 5.2). This distinction also helps answer some questions. While all agree that Jesus did not sin, could Jesus have sinned? The answer is as man, yes, as God no. This enables us to see that His temptation to sin was as real as ours (Heb. 4:15), yet His divine nature ensures that He is sinless, and therefore can be our sinless substitute on the cross (1 Peter 1:24). Also the question as to how many "wills" did Jesus have is answerable. He had two, one human will and the divine will. Hence, He can pray to the Father, "Your will be done" (Matt. 26:42).

Some object that it is contradictory to affirm that Christ is both infinite (fully God) and finite (fully man) in His being at the same time? To be contradictory, one must show that we are affirming "A" and its opposite "non-A" at the same time and in the same sense. The solution is the teaching of the Trinity. The Second Person of the

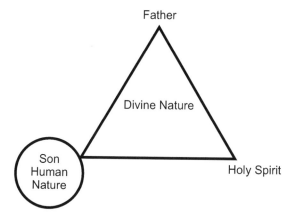

Figure 5.2 Christ's Divine & Human Nature

Trinity or the Divine Logos took on Himself humanity, not another person or already existing man. He did not possess humanity before His conception. He is, since His conception, clothed in humanity forever more. This means that the Second Person of the Trinity, God the Son, while in and united to the human body of Jesus, is not bound by the human nature assumed (see Phil. 2:7–8 ; John 1:14; Rom. 1:3; 8:3; Gal. 4:4; 1 Tim. 3:16; 1 John 4:2, 2 John 7). The person of Christ is held to subsist or cohere in two natures, one divine and one human. That is, there are now two "Whats" in one "Who" two objects in one subject, two essences or natures in one Person (Figure 5.1).

It is true that Christianity affirms that Christ is both infinite and finite at the same time. However, it does not maintain that Christ is both infinite and finite in the same sense (If it did it would be a contradiction). The orthodox position is that Christ is both infinite in one nature and finite in another nature at the same time, but not in the same sense. Infinitude and finitude are predicated of two different natures united in one person without mixture, confusion or division. Hence, no contradiction is involved.

Only the Athanasius view in the early church preserved the orthodox understanding of the Deity and humanity of Jesus Christ. The heretical views that deny or diminish the deity of the Lord are Arianism–denied His deity and held He was created, Adoptionism–Jesus was adopted as a son because of His divine powers, and Subordinationism–the Son is subordinate in nature to the Father. Those that deny or diminish the humanity of the Lord are Docetism–Jesus only appeared to be human and Apollinariansim–diminished His humanity by saying He had no human spirit. Those that sepa-

	DEITY	HUMANITY	RELATION
Athanasian Creed (Orthodxy)	Affirmed	Affirmed	United
Arianism	Denied	Affirmed	United
Adoptionism	Denied	Affirmed	Adopted
Subordinationism	Diminished	Affirmed	United
Docetism	Affirmed	Denied	Merged
Apollinarianism	Affirmed	Diminished	United
Nestorianism	Affirmed	Affirmed	Separated*
Modalism (Sabellianism)	Affirmed	Affirmed	Separated*
Eutychianism (Monophysitism)	Affirmed	Affirmed	Merged

*Nestorians have three persons in the Trinity, but modalists have only one. Nestorians have two separated persons in the Son, one in each nature, while modalists have only one person in God, who is performing three roles.

Table 5.1 Orthodox vs. Heretical Views of Christ

rate the divine and human relations are Nestorianism–held there were two persons in Christ and Modalism (or Sabellianism)–held only one person who appears in different modes. Eutychanism (or Monophysitism) merged or confused the two natures which is contradictory (Table 5.1).

Christ's Vicarious Death

Jesus' death is vicarious or substitutionary because He is a Prophet predicted to come by Moses (Deut. 18:18), confirmed by His miraculous signs and teacher as recorded in the Gospels (Acts 7:37). He is a Priest, who alone is a mediator between man and God and able to lay down His life (John 10:10, 15) as a substitutionary sacrifice for our sins (Isa. 53:4–7; 2 Cor. 5:21). He is also a King who will rule over His people (Matt. 19:28; Rev. 20:4–6), (see Chapter 14).

Christ's Physical Death and Resurrection

Christ's resurrection is predicted in the Old Testament in two central passages. Psalm 2:7 says, "I will surely tell of the decree of the Lord: He said to Me, 'You are My Son, Today I have begotten You.'" This is applied to Jesus' resurrection in Acts 13:33–34 (cf. Heb. 1:5). Psalm 16:10 affirms "For You will not abandon my soul to Sheol; Nor will You allow Your Holy One to undergo decay." Peter argues in Acts 2:29–32 that this must refer to Christ. The concept of the resurrection being in the flesh is also present in the Old Testament. Job 19:25–26 (cf. Acts 2) says, "As for me, I know that my Redeemer lives, and at the last He will take His stand on the earth. Even after my skin is destroyed, yet from my flesh I shall see God."

Jesus predicted His own resurrection early in His ministry (John 2:19–22) and later in His ministry (Matt. 12:39:40). These became more frequent and specific, Matthew 17:22–23 says, "And while they were gathering together in Galilee, Jesus said to them, 'The Son of Man is going to be delivered into the hands of men; and they will kill Him, and He will be raised on the third day.' And they were deeply grieved" (cf. John 10:18).

That Jesus physically died on the cross is well established. Evidence is found in the Bible and outside sources. This is important since only a dead body can be resurrected. Christ's death consisted of passion culminated in the crucifixion to ensure His death. It begins with no sleep the night before He was crucified. He was beaten several times and whipped (shredding His back). He collapsed on His way to the execution site carrying His cross. The nature of the crucifixion assures death. Jesus was on the cross from 9:00 AM to just before sunset (Mark 15:25, 33). He bled from wounded hands and feet and also from a crown of thorns that pierced His head. The loss of blood plus the demand that He constantly pull Himself up in order to breathe, would cause excruciating pain from the nails. Jesus' side was pierced with a spear and "blood and water" (John 19:34) came out which is proof that He had physically died before He was pierced. Just before He died on the cross Jesus declared, "Father, into Your hands I commit My spirit. Having said this, He breathed His last" (Luke 23:46). Roman soldiers, accustomed to crucifixion and death, pronounced Jesus dead. It was common to break the legs of the victim to speed death; however they did not do so with Jesus because He was already dead (John 19:33 cf. Ps. 34:20). Pilate double–checked to make sure Jesus was dead before giving up His corpse to Joseph of Arimathea (Mark 15:44–45). "Nicodemus . . . also came, bringing a mixture of myrrh and aloes, about hundred pounds. So they took the body of Jesus and bound it in linen wrappings with the spices, as is the burial custom of the Jews" (John 19:39–40). Jesus was placed in a sealed tomb for three days. If He was not dead before that (and He clearly was) He would have died from a lack of food, water and medical treatment.

Modern medical authorities have investigated the circumstances and nature of Jesus' death and have published their conclusions in such journals as the *Journal of the American Medical Society* and *Medicine, Science and Law*. They concluded Jesus actually died on the cross. Ancient non–Christian historians and writers from the first and second centuries recorded the death of Christ. These include Flavious Josephus (c. 37–100 A.D.), Cornelius Tacitus (c. 55–

117 A.D.), and the Babylonian Talmud. Early Christian writers, such as Polycarp, Ignatius and Origin, also affirmed Jesus' death and even cited non-Christian writers mentioning Jesus' death.

DIRECT EVIDENCE

Although no human actually saw the moment of the resurrection, there is both direct and indirect evidence for the resurrection of Christ. The direct evidence includes the empty tomb and the resurrection appearances. They must be considered together, since by themselves they do not constitute proof that the body that died had indeed been raised (John 2:19). All the Gospels mention the empty tomb (Matt. 28:1–8; Mark 16:1–8; Luke 24:1–12; John 20:1–8). In each case they see His vacated tomb with an angel to confirm that "He is not here. He is risen" (Matt. 28:6; Mark 16:6; Luke 24:6; John 20:12). John mentions the empty grave clothes with the head cloth folded up in a place by itself. This alone, was evidence enough to convince John that Jesus had risen (John 20:6–8).

In the first century Jewish culture, a woman's testimony was not considered as valuable as a man's. Hence, it is a sign of authenticity that Jesus first appeared to women. He appeared to Mary Magdalene (John 10:20–18) who saw, heard and touched Jesus. She also witnessed the empty tomb and grave cloths. He appeared also to the other women with her (Matt. 28:1–10). They also saw, heard, witnessed the empty tomb, and touched His physical body that came out of the tomb. Jesus appeared to Peter (1 Cor. 15:5; cf. John 20:3–9) and was seen and likely heard him. Peter also previously saw the empty tomb and grave cloths. Jesus appeared to two disciples on the road to Emmaus (Luke 24:13–35; Mark 16:12–13), they saw, heard and ate with Jesus. Jesus appeared to ten disciples (Luke 24:36–49; John 20:19–23), with Thomas being absent, and Jesus was seen, heard and He showed them His wounds also implying that He was touched. He further ate physical food to convince the disciples that He was raised in a literal, physical body. A week later, Jesus appeared to eleven disciples (John 20:24–31) with Thomas being present. There Thomas saw His crucifixion wounds, heard, and likely touched Jesus. Jesus appeared to seven disciples (John 21) who went fishing in Galilee. They saw, heard, and ate breakfast with Jesus further demonstrating His tangible, physical nature of His resurrection body; emphasizing Jesus' real activity in space and time.

Jesus appeared to all the Apostles at the giving of the Great Commission (Matt. 28:16–20; Mark 16:14–18). Here Jesus is seen and heard and Luke records that Jesus ate with the disciples (Acts 1:4). The last appearance of Jesus was to Paul after the Ascension (1 Cor. 15:8; Acts 9:1–9). Paul called this an "appearance" which con-

THE TWELVE APPEARANCES OF CHRIST				
Person	**Saw**	**Hear**	**Touched**	**Comments**
Mary (John 20:10–18)	●	●	●	Empty Tomb
Mary & women (Matt. 28:1–10)	●	●	●	Empty Tomb
Peter & John (1 Cor. 15:5; Jn, 20:1–10)	●	●*		Empty Tomb, grave cloths
Two disciples (Luke 24:13–35)	●	●		Ate food
Ten Apostles (Lk, 24:36–49; John 20:19–23)	●	●	●†	Death wounds, ate food
Eleven Apostles (John 20:24–31)	●	●	●†	Death wounds
Seven Apostles (John 21)	●	●		Ate food
All Apostles (Matt. 28:16–20; Mark 16:14–18)	●	●		
500 Brethren (1Cor, 15:6)	●	●*		
James (1 Cor. 15:7)	●	●*		
All Apostles (Acts 1:4–8)	●	●		Ate food
Paul (Acts 9:1–9; 1 Cor. 15:8)	●	●		

*Implied, †Offered to be touched

Table 5.2 Appearances of Christ

firmed him as an Apostle (Acts 1:22; cf. 1 Cor. 9:1). This reference is important because Paul had "visions" (Acts 26:19), but never referred to Jesus' resurrection as a "vision." Paul saw and heard Jesus which is always indicative of a true physical appearance rather than a mere vision. Those who were with Paul saw and heard the voice which shows the experience was not private. Hence, the evidence for the physical resurrection of Christ is overwhelming (Table 5.2).

Jesus was seen by more than five hundred people during a forty-day period of time and on twelve occasions Jesus was not only seen, but heard. Four times He offered himself to be touched and He was definitely touched twice. Jesus revealed His crucifixion scars on two occasions and ate food on four occasions. Add to this the four times the empty tomb was seen and twice the empty grave clothes were viewed. The sum total of this evidence is tremendous confirmation that Jesus rose and lived in the same visible, material body He possessed before His resurrection.

INDIRECT EVIDENCE

In addition to direct evidence of Jesus' bodily resurrection, there is indirect confirming evidence. These begin with the immediate transformation of the disciples. After Jesus' death His disciples were scared, scattered, and skeptical about reports of Jesus' resurrection (Luke 24:11). Yet within a few weeks these same skeptical disciples (John 20:19) were fearless and openly proclaiming the resurrection of Jesus in the face of death (Acts 4–5). The best explanation for this is the bodily resurrection of Christ. Also, of all the ethical teaching that Jesus taught them, the central focus of apostolic preaching was the resurrection. Acts 4:33 says, "And with great power the Apostles were giving testimony to the resurrection of the Lord Jesus, and abundant grace was upon them all." The best explanation of this is repeated encounters of Jesus alive after His crucifixion. The reaction of those who rejected Christ provides testimony to the resurrection. Since, they did not refute it, rather, they resisted it (Acts 4:2ff). Instead of finding the dead body, they fought the disciples who testified to Him being alive. Another proof of the Resurrection is the very existence of the early church. The fact that Jews believed in only one God (Deut. 6:4) makes it unlikely that they would accept Jesus as God. But they prayed to Jesus (Acts 7:59), exalted him to the right hand of God (Acts 2:33) and called Him Lord and Christ (Acts 2:34–36) which were the very titles that brought the charge of blasphemy from the Jewish high priest. Furthermore, the first Christians were persecuted, beaten, threatened with death and martyred (Acts 7:57–60). Under these conditions, they maintained their belief (which could have been given up, *but was not*) and increased in numbers daily. Add to this the rapid growth (Acts 4:4, 6:1) and the conversion of individuals from very unlikely groups. Such as Jewish Priests (Acts 6:7) and the least likely person Saul of Tarsus, a well-educated Pharisee who persecuted Christians (Acts 9:1). Nothing short of a real encounter with the resurrected Christ can account for all this.

Some have tried to show that Paul's teaching seems to indicate that the resurrection body is spiritual or immaterial. For Paul says, "it is raised a spiritual body. If there is a natural body, there is also a spiritual body" (1 Cor. 15:44) and "that flesh and blood cannot inherit the kingdom of God; . . ." (50–51). However, the use of the term "spiritual" Paul uses can be translated "supernatural" and Paul uses this of a physical "rock" too (1 Cor. 10:4). So Paul is using "spiritual body" to denote the immortal body (not one devoid of matter). It is not used for immaterial and invisible, but immortal and imperishable. It is to designate a body directed by the Spirit of God as opposed to the flesh. When Paul says "flesh and bones" cannot inherit the kingdom of God, it is to designate "perishable" flesh and bones that is mortal. Paul clarifies this by saying, "nor does the perishable inherit the imperishable" (1 Cor. 15:50). We know Jesus' resurrected body was "flesh and bones" (Luke 24:39) and our resurrection bodies will be like His (1 John 3:2).

CHRIST'S BODILY ASSUMPTION AND PRESENT SESSION

The primary text on Jesus' bodily assumption (Acts 1:9–11) into heaven affirms that it was a lateral, visible ascension of His resurrected body. Some have suggested that His body was transformed into being invisible. But the text clearly states, "He was lifted up while they were looking on, and a cloud received Him out of their sight." This does raise the question of where is Jesus presently. Evangelicals have offered two views. One is that He moved literally and physically into another dimension. This seems to be suggested when Jesus appeared and disappeared after His resurrection (Luke 24:31) and modern physics with its many dimensions, makes this a possibility. The other view is that Jesus is still present in the space–time dimension, just hidden from our view. This seems to have support from the text that says He gradually disappeared and was hidden by a cloud, as opposed to immediately disappearing. Whichever view is held, Christ must still exist in the numerically same physical body, now glorified, in which He died, rose, and ascended.

Jesus at present also preforms an important priestly session for believers. Satan is the accuser of God's people (Rev. 12:8–10) but as John says, "My little children, I am writing these things to you so that you may not sin. And if anyone sins, we have an Advocate with the Father, Jesus Christ the righteous" (1 John 2:1–2). Because of Christ's humanity as well as deity, He can sympathize with our human frailties (Heb. 4:14–15; 7:17–26); for Christ is the one that provides a "way out" of our temptation (1 Cor. 10:13).

His ascension (Acts 1:9–11) and session (1 John 2:1–2), also predicted and assured the finished work of redemption and forgiveness (Heb. 1:3; 12:2). It marks the beginning of His invisible reign (1 Peter 3:21, 22) as King someday to be made visible (Second Coming) and the judgments to follow (Rev. 5:6–14; 11:15; 19:11–21; 20:4–15), (Chapter 15).

Summary

The study of Jesus Christ (Christology) shows that He alone is eternally the Son of God who appeared in a Preincarnate state at various times in the Old Testament. His anticipation in the Old shows the importance of His virgin birth which is realized in the New. His miracles and sinless life point to His absolute uniqueness. He is affirmed in the New Testament as having all the attributes of man and all the attributes of God. This is explained as the hypostatic union, that Jesus is the Second person of the Trinity, subsisting without division or mixture in two natures, one human and one divine. Hence, only Jesus' death can be vicarious and His bodily resurrection and ascension provide us with an advocate before the Father that ensures our eternal life.

QUESTIONS TO ANSWER

1. What biblical verses support the Preincarnate Christ?
2. What biblical verses predict and support the virgin birth of Jesus Christ?
3. What does the hypostatic union of Jesus Christ entail?
4. What evidence supports the physical death and bodily resurrection of Jesus Christ?
5. What do the resurrection appearances of Jesus Christ tell us about the nature of the resurrection body?

6. Did you read chapter?

| 6 |

The Holy Spirit

And do not get drunk with wine, for that is dissipation,
but be filled with the Spirit, speaking to one another in psalms
and hymns and spiritual songs, singing and making melody
with your heart to the LORD.
Ephesians 5:18–19

OUR study of the Holy Spirit (Pneumatology) includes His Deity
which is established by His possessing the names of God, the
attributes of God and performing the acts of God. We then turn to
His Personhood and relation to the Trinity. Then we study His work
in creation, redemption, the believer's life, and the gifts of the Holy
Spirit.

DEITY OF THE HOLY SPIRIT

The Holy Spirit is referred to as "God" or "Lord." Acts 5:1–4 says Peter
told, "Ananias, why has Satan filled your heart to lie to the Holy Spirit
. . ." Peter continues and says, "Why is it that you have conceived this
deed in your heart? You have not lied to men but to God." Hence
Peter sees no difference in using the term "Holy Spirit" or "God" to
refer to God. They are synonymous. Other verses in the Bible do the
same thing: "God's Spirit" (1 Cor. 3:16), "Lord" (1 Cor. 12:4–6), and
"eternal Spirit" (Heb. 9:14). Not only are the "names" of God used
but the Holy Spirit has all the attributes of God. These include life
(Rom. 8:2), truth (John 16:13), love (Rom. 15:30), holiness (Eph.
4:30), eternality (Heb. 9:14), omniscience (1 Cor. 2:10–12), omnipotence (Job 33), and omnipresence (Ps. 139:7–10). The Holy Spirit

performs acts that can only be attributed to God. He is involved in the act of creation (Gen. 1:2; Job 33:4; Ps. 104:30) and redemption (Isa. 63:10–11; Eph. 4:30; 1 Cor. 12:13). He performs miracles (Gal. 3:2–5; Heb. 2:4), inspires Holy Scripture (2 Peter 1:21) and bestows supernatural gifts (Acts 2:4; 1 Cor. 12:11).

The Holy Spirit is associated with prayers and benedictions. Jude 1:20 says, "But you, beloved, building yourselves up on your most holy faith, praying in the Holy Spirit." All three members of the Godhead are in the benediction of 2 Corinthians 13:14: "The grace of the Lord Jesus Christ, and the love of God, and the fellowship of the Holy Spirit, be with you all." Even the baptismal formula of Matthew 28:19 contains the Holy Spirit with the members of the Trinity that are all under one "name" (essence): "Go therefore and make disciples of all the nations, baptizing them in the name of the Father and the Son and the Holy Spirit."

THE PERSONHOOD OF THE HOLY SPIRIT

Although the term "spirit" is neuter, the personal pronoun "He" and "His" are always used of the Holy Spirit in Scripture. "But when He, the Spirit of truth, comes, He will guide you into all the truth; for He will not speak on His own initiative, but whatever He hears, He will speak; and He will disclose to you what is to come" (John 16:13, cf. 14:26).

Qualities attributed only to persons are attributed to the Holy Spirit. He has intellect (1 Cor. 2:10), He has a mind (John 14:26), and knowledge (1 Cor. 2:11). He has emotions or feelings (Eph. 4:30) and will (1 Cor. 12:11). The Holy Spirit also does things that only persons can do, such as teach and give commands (Acts 16:6), knowing and searching the mind (1 Cor. 2:11), prayer (Rom. 8:26) and He can be blasphemed (Matt. 12:31–32).

The order in the Trinity emphasizes the specific task each one does. With regard to salvation, the Father plans and sends; the Son is sent and accomplishes redemption; and the Holy Spirit convicts unbelievers and applies salvation to believers. The Holy Spirit was sent by the Father. Jesus said, "I will ask the Father, and He will give you another Helper, that He may be with you forever." He added, "But the Helper, the Holy Spirit, whom the Father will send in My name, He will teach you all things, and bring to your remembrance all that I said to you" (John 14:16, 26).

Although the Eastern and Western churches split long ago on this matter, the Bible indicates that the Holy Spirit also proceeds from the Son. Jesus said clearly, "When the Helper comes, *whom I will send to you* from the Father, that is the Spirit of truth who proceeds from the

Father, He will testify about Me" (John 15:26, emphasis added). So the Holy Spirit is sent "from the Father" as well as from the Son.

WORK OF THE HOLY SPIRIT

The work of the Holy Spirit can be placed into the broad areas of Creation and the believer's life. Similar to the Son (John 1:3; Col 1:16), the Holy Spirit was active in creating the world. He is preset at creation "the Spirit of God was moving over the surface of the waters" (Gen. 1:2). Job said, "The Spirit of God has made me, and the breath of the Almighty gives me life" (Job 33:4 cf. Ps. 104:30).

The work of the Holy Spirit on behalf of the believer is multifaceted. In short, He convicts unbelievers of sin (John 16:8), regenerates believers (Titus 3:5; John 5:21, Eph. 2:1) and seals believers for the day of redemption (Eph. 4:30). He baptizes all believers into the spiritual body of Christ at the moment of salvation (1 Cor. 12:13). He assures us of salvation (Rom. 8:16). He does miracles or signs and wonders (Gal. 3:2–5; Heb. 2:4). He bestows spiritual gifts on believers, (Acts 2:4), reveals (1 Cor. 2:10) and teaches (Luke 12:12, John 14:16, 1 Cor. 2:13, 14). He inspired Scripture (2 Tim. 3:16; 2 Peter 1:20–21), enlightens believers to God's truth (Eph. 1:17–18) and witnesses to God's Word (1 John 5:9–10). He anoints believers for service (1 John 2:20), testifies of Christ and His teachings (John 15:26), guides (John 16:13), intercedes (Rom. 8:26) and commands (Acts 13:2, 4; 8:29, 16:6).

Many other personal acts are attributed to the Holy Spirit. He searches (1 Cor. 2:10); knows (1 Cor. 2:11); speaks (2 Peter 1:20); invites to salvation (Rev. 22:17); testifies (Acts 20:23); commands (Acts 16:6); calls to missions (Acts 13:2); moves (Gen. 1:2); helps (John 14:26); renews (Ps. 104:30); sanctifies (Heb. 9:14); intercedes (Rom. 8:26); unifies (Eph. 4:3); glorifies Christ (John 16:14); orders and directs the Church (1 Cor. 14:30–33); and guides (Acts 8:29).

Regeneration, Titus 3:5 says, "He saved us, not on the basis of deeds which we have done in righteousness, but according to His mercy, by the washing of regeneration and renewing by the Holy Spirit." Hence, the Holy Spirit is the one that imparts eternal life in a human being. He is the agent of regeneration. This occurs at the moment of salvation and is completely and wholly a work of God in a believing or willing human heart that is not opposed to it (Chapter 11).

Baptizing, 1 Corinthians 12:13 says, "For by one Spirit we were all baptized into one body, whether Jews or Greeks, whether slaves or free, and we were all made to drink of one Spirit." This occurs at salvation and is not repeated. It is a work done to the believer, not by the believer. It brings the believer into union in the Body of Christ

(1 Cor. 12:13) and Christ (Rom. 6:3, 5). It is likened to a new birth (John 3:7), the resurrection (John 1:13), and a new creation (Eph. 2:1; 2 Cor. 5:17). It involves a permanent impartation of eternal life that cannot be revoked and cannot be done twice.

Sealing, 2 Corinthians 1:22 says, "Now He who establishes us with you in Christ and anointed us is God, who also sealed us and gave us the Spirit in our hearts as a pledge." This identifies the believer as God's. It is a mark of ownership and security. There is no command or prayer to be sealed. Every believer, even those who were carnal or grieving the Spirit are and remain sealed. It must be permanent, since there are no statements or examples of it ever being undone or lost.

Indwelling, John 14:16 says, "I will ask the Father, and He will give you another Helper, that He may be with you forever." The Helper is the Holy Spirit given at salvation to everyone that believes (Eph. 1:13; Gal. 3:2; Rom. 5:5 cf. 1 Cor. 12:13). It is the permanent indwelling of the Holy Spirit and is a gift (John 7:37–39; 1 Thess. 4:8). Only a believer possesses the Holy Spirit (Rom. 8:9) and He even indwells carnal believers (1 Cor. 6:19; Rom. 8:9; 1 Cor. 5:5). Hence, it is a permanent indwelling (John 14:16; 2 Cor. 1:22; Eph. 4:30; 2 Cor. 5:5). Such indwelling was clearly temporary in the Old Testament (Ps. 51:11). But since Pentecost where the Apostle's waited for the Spirit to "fall" (Acts 8:14–17) the indwelling presence of the Holy Spirit on all believers is a reality. Anointing biblically is the same as Indwelling. First John 2:20 says, "But you have an anointing from the Holy One, and you all know. . . . As for you, the anointing which you received from Him abides in you, . . ."

Filling, Ephesians 5:18 says, "And do not get drunk with wine, for that is dissipation, but be filled with the Spirit." Acts 4:31says, "And when they had prayed, the place where they had gathered together was shaken, and they were all filled with the Holy Spirit and began to speak the word of God with boldness." The indwelling by the Spirit of God is the one that should control or fill our life. This is achieved by filling. The other acts of the Holy Spirit are not commanded, but filling is. Hence it is conditional and repeatable. It is essential for maturity (1 Cor. 3:1–3) and service (Acts 4:31; 9:17–20). We are told not to grieve or quench the Holy Spirit (1 Thess. 5:19). This involves walking by the Spirit which refers to the conduct of our life (Gal. 5:6) and the result of this should be the fruit of the Spirit (Gal. 5:22–24), teaching of the Spirit (1 Cor. 2:9–13; John 16:12–15), joy, thankfulness (Eph. 5:19–20), commitment and conformity to God (Rom. 12:1–2).

John Wesley (1703–1791) developed a teaching called Christian perfectionism. This is deliverance from inward and outward sin. That is, a Christian, he holds, should expect to be saved from all sin before death such that they no longer commit sin in this life. This does not mean that we can never sin again or that all weaknesses, mistakes and infirmities are eliminated. However, some, non–Wesleyans, argue against this view. First, they claim it is unbiblical in that it confuses sanctification (in this life) with glorification (in the next life). Sanctification is not an instantaneous act, but a lifelong process (Rom. 7:13ff). Glorification is not realized in this life, but is instantaneous for the believer after death (1 John 3:2–4), (Chapter 11). Second, they believe that it lacks experiential support since many mature believers say they never completely overcome sin. This is also the case of biblical prophets such as Isaiah (6:1ff) and Apostles such as Paul (Rom. 7:14–18). Some believe perfectionism as a doctrine is also dangerous since they see it as a quick–fix scheme that can lull a person into a false sense of spiritual attainment. Many who claim this do so by redefining or ignoring sin. However, Wesleyanism's quest for true holiness is biblical and commendable. Even non–Wesleyans believe we can get to the place that we are able not to sin, even if we don't get to the point where we are not able to sin.

GIFTS OF THE HOLY SPIRIT

In order for the visible churches to accomplish their mission, they must be gifted. This is done, through gifts given by the Holy Spirit to each member to edify the whole (1 Cor. 12, 14). Some gifts are clearly focused on the internal mission of edifying believers, such as "pastor and teacher" while others are focused on the external mission such as "evangelism."

The Holy Spirit at the moment of salvation, according to His will, gives spiritual (or grace) gifts to every believer for service and work in the body of Christ, the Church. The gifts divide into two categories: 1) sign gifts that involve miracles, which are a sign to unbelievers and 2) abiding gifts that must be developed and used in the Church. While there are lists of gifts (1 Cor. 12, 14; Rom. 12; Eph. 4) none should be considered comprehensive.

SIGN GIFTS

There are divergent views within the church today concerning the existence and function of spiritual gifts. The three views regarding these gifts exist today: 1) Some claim that none of these gifts exist today, believing they were all for apostolic times. 2) Others, e.g., many charismatics, think that all of the gifts exist today and 3) the cessationist's view is that only some of the gifts exist today but all the sign gifts (see below) have passed away.

The debate centers upon the sign gifts that include prophecy, the giving of revelation foretelling the future (2 Peter 1:21), raising the dead (Matt. 10:8; Acts 8:36–42; 20:7–12), healing (Mark 16:17; Acts 4:16; 5:12; 16), exorcism (Mark 16:17; Matt. 10:8; Acts 16:16–18), and tongues and interpretation (1 Cor. 14:22; Mark 16:17). The focus of the debate is specifically on the gifts of tongues and apostleship. In short, the question is: Do believers today possess the power to perform the signs and wonders done by the early–church Apostles?

There are two main reasons put forward by charismatics as to why all the gifts exist today. First, the New Testament is filled with instruction concerning the gift of tongues and nowhere does the New Testament indicate that any gifts have passed away (cf. Rom. 8:26). One verse, 1 Corinthians 13:8–10, says, "if there are tongues, they will cease . . . For we know in part and we prophesy in part; but when the perfect comes, the partial will be done away." This, it is argued, is referring to a change that occurs after death not the end of the apostolic period or completion of the canon of Scripture.

In response, cessationists point out that all of the Bible is *for* us today, but not all of the Bible was written *to* us. Paul recognized that the Old Testament was for our instruction (Rom. 15:4) knowing that some things in it are no longer binding on believers today. Hence, even though tongues are mentioned in the New Testament, it is possible tongues are no longer for today. It may be granted that 1 Corinthians 13:8–10 is not referring to the canon of Scripture that is "the perfect." However, even so, this text (v. 8) indicates that tongues would pass away and the Greek middle voice does indicate that they will cease of their own accord before we get to heaven. The context also suggests that they will last as long as the other revelatory gifts (v. 12) which all Christendom agrees ended with the Apostles.

The second argument is that many persons today possess the gift of tongues. Hence, any interpretation that says they ceased must be wrong since it is contrary to experience. For multitudes of people have experienced speaking in tongues.

In response, experience should never be used to interpret the Bible; the Bible must be used to interpret our experience. Furthermore, there are other ways to interpret the current tongues phenomena than to equate it with biblical tongues. It may be a natural phenomenon or a misinterpretation of spiritual experience. Tongues are experienced among pagan religions and no Christian would take this to mean they must have come from God.

The reason given for the cessationists view is that such gifts were needed only to establish the church, not to continue it. Hence, once they served their foundational purposes, they ceased. Sign gifts, are outward signs (miracles) to establish the new message given by revelation through the Apostles (Heb. 2:3–4).

It can be argued that since the Apostles existed only during the New Testament period (Acts 1:22) and since there are supernatural sign gifts given to Apostles (2 Cor. 12:12), it follows that these sign gifts ceased with the Apostles in the first century. There is no evidence that anyone since the times of the Apostles has had special powers to instantaneously and irrevocably cure incurable diseases, raise the dead, heal a whole city of sick people, and speak in a real but unlearned language.

Several arguments can be given for the cessation of the supernatural sign gifts. First, if Apostles do not exist today, than at least one gift is no longer in operation. To be an Apostle one had to be an eyewitness of the resurrection (Acts 1:22; 1 Cor. 9:1) and possess the signs of an Apostle (2 Cor. 12:12). Hence, Apostles in this sense do not exist today, since only persons living in the first part of the first century could have been eyewitnesses. Second, Paul said there were "signs of a true apostle" (2 Cor. 12:12). These included gifts of healing, evangelism, and raising the dead (Matt. 10:6) as well as tongues and giving the Holy Spirit (Acts 8, 10, 19). If everyone had these gifts it would not have been possible to identify the Apostles. Hence, these "sign" gifts of an Apostle must have passed away with the Apostles. Third, only Apostles received and could give these sign gifts. A close reading of Acts 2 shows that only the Apostles spoke in tongues at Pentecost. Others, such as Stephen, who had the gifts of evangelism and healing, could not receive the gift of the Holy Spirit except by "the laying on of the apostles' hands" (Acts 8:18, cf. 10:44–46, 19:6). Fourth, apostolic tongues were real languages (Acts 2:5–8 cf. 11:15–16) that functioned as a sign to unbelievers (1 Cor. 14:22). The general phenomena of tongue–speaking today are not a literal language but a spiritual gibberish and are similar to what is found among pagan religions. Fifth, the special gift of healing as practiced by the Apostles has ceased. The exercise of this gift resulted in an instantaneous cure (Acts 3:7), that was always successful on all kinds of disease, deformities and even raising the dead. The healing always lasted and glorified God. The Apostles ceased to practice these later in the New Testament period and the later books speak of it as a past event (Heb. 2:3–4, A.D. 68–69). It is clear that no one alive possesses these kinds of powers to performer miracles. Hence, the miraculous *gift* of healing has ceased, which was temporarily given to establish the church's foundation. This does not mean the *fact* of miracles has ceased; God can perform a miracle anytime He chooses.

1 Corinthians 12, 14 (c. A.D. 55–56)	Romans 12 (c. 57)	Ephesians 4 (c. 60–61)
1) Apostles		Apostles
2) Prophets	Prophecy	Prophets
3)		Evangelism
4)		Pastors
5) Teachers	Teaching	Teachers
6)	Exhortation	
7)	Leading	
8)	Serving	
9)	Giving	
10)	Mercy	
11) Miracles		
12) Healings		
13) Helps		
14) Administration		
15) Tongues		
16) Interpretation		
17) Faith		
18) Knowledge		
19) Wisdom		
20) Discernment		

Table 6.1 Spiritual Gifts

ABIDING GIFTS

While the sign gifts that were needed to confirm the apostolic message (Heb. 2:3–4) and laying the church's foundation (Eph. 2:20) have passed away, the gifts needed for the building superstructure have not passed away. Ephesians 4, while not exhaustive (other non-sign gifts may exist see Table 6.1), lists Apostles, prophets, evangelists, and pastor/teachers.

The word *apostle* has two senses. It can refer to the those such as Paul who had the signs of an Apostle which has now passed away, or a broader New Testament sense that included others (like Barnabas—Acts 14:14) who were sent by a church (2 Cor. 8:23). Hence, in this more general sense of "a sent one" (missionary), there could be Apostles today.

The word *prophet* also has two senses: *fore*telling (which foresees what will happen) and *forth* telling (which proclaims the truth already known). The former being a sign gift has passed away, while the latter remains. This could also be understood as someone who brings God's message to the body of Christ for edification (1 Cor. 14:3–4). Only in this sense can there still be prophets in the church today.

While all believers should "do the work of an evangelist" (2 Tim. 4:5) there is a special *gift* of evangelism given only to some (Acts

21:8). These certainly have an ongoing role in spreading the gospel and planting churches.

These two, *pastor* and *teacher* are grammatically connected in such a sense that teachers are listed with pastors signifying that as pastors, one primary role is feeding the flock of God (1 Peter 5:1; cf. 2 Tim. 4:2–3; Eph. 4:12–13).

SUMMARY

The study of the Holy Spirit (Pneumatology) shows that He is called the names of God, has the attributes of God, and performs the acts of God. Hence, the Holy Spirit is the third person of the Trinity who is sent by the Father through the Son to convict the world of sin, regenerate, baptize, seal, indwell, and fill or empower, yielded believers for service. Although sign gifts have passed away with the Apostles, the Holy Spirit still gifts all believers, according to His will, to function in the church.

QUESTIONS TO ANSWER

1. What biblical verses support the Deity of the Holy Spirit?
2. What does the Holy Spirit do on behalf of believers before and after salvation?
3. What is the difference between sign gifts and abiding gifts?
4. Why are sign gifts so important to the foundation of the church?
5. What gifts exist today to help spread the gospel and build up the church?
6. Did you read chapter?

7

Angels

Are they not all ministering spirits sent out to serve for the
sake of those who are to inherit salvation.
Hebrews 1:14

I N addition to the creation of the physical world (Chapter 4) and
humankind (Chapter 9), God created spiritual creatures, many of
whom are called angels (Angelology). Evil angels are called demons
(see Chapter 8). There is a hierarchy of beings that ranges from God
to angels to human beings to animals to inanimate matter. Our study
investigates the biblical origin, names, nature, purpose and organi-
zation of angels. We then develop a biblical doctrine. Satan and demons are studied in the next chapter (8).

ORIGIN OF ANGELS

Although the biblical term "angels" is actually a reference to a certain
kind of spiritual creature (namely, "messengers") that God created,
it is commonly used for all such spiritual creatures. Angels are not
eternal since they were created. Only God is eternal. The psalmist declared, "Praise Him, all His angels; Praise Him, all His hosts! . . . Let
them praise the name of the Lord, For He commanded and they were
created" (Ps. 148:2, 5 cf. Neh. 9:6). Paul says, "For by Him all things
were created, both in the heavens and on earth, visible and invisible,
whether thrones or dominions or rulers or authorities—all things
have been created through Him and for Him" (Col. 1:16). Genesis
indicates that they were created at the beginning by God (Gen. 2:1).
They were probably created when God created the "heavens and the

earth" (Gen. 1:1) and definitely created before the earth, for they sang when its cornerstone was laid (Job 38:6–7).

NAMES OF ANGELS

Angels are given different titles and proper names in the Bible. Some of these titles include "angels ("messengers"– Dan. 4:13), "living creatures" (Rev. 4:6), "angels of God" (John 1:51), "elect angels" (1 Tim. 5:21), "holy angels" (Rev. 14:10), "powerful angels" (2 Thess. 1:7), "chief princes" (Dan. 10:13), "ministers" (Ps. 104:4), "sons of God" (Job 1:6; 2:1), "sons of mighty" (Ps. 89:6; cf. 29:1), "gods" (Heb. 2:7; Ps. 8:5; Gen. 35:7), "holy ones" (Dan. 8:13; Zech. 14:5; Job 15:15), "stars" (Job 38:7; Rev. 12:4), "host" of heaven (Gen. 2:1; Neh. 9:6; Luke 2:13), "chariots" (Ps. 68:17; Zech. 6:5). Some scholars think "elders" in Revelation 4:4 may be angelic beings.

Proper names are given to some angels in the Bible. There is Michael (Dan. 12:1) whose name means "Who is like God?" He is one of the chief princes (Dan. 10:13) and the "archangel" (Jude 9) who disputed with Satan and protects the people of Israel (Dan. 12:1). He is possibly of the cherub class (Ezek. 10:1–13). He is the leader of the heavenly army (Rev. 12:7) and will lead in the final victory over the Devil after the thousand–year reign of Christ (Rev. 12:7). There is Gabriel whose name means "Devoted to God." He "stands in the presence of God" (Luke 1:19). He makes special announcements for God (Luke 1:11–13). He appeared to Mary (Luke 1:26–33) and is a revealer of God's kingdom purposes (Dan. 9:21–22; 8:16). Finally, there is Lucifer (Isa. 14:12) called "son of the morning," who fell and became the Devil. His fallen names are many (see Chapter 8). Presumable, all angels have names. God knows all the stars by number (Isa. 40:26) which are inanimate objects. So God likely has a name for each angel, certainly He knows each one individually since He is all–knowing (Chapter 3).

NATURE OF ANGEL

Similar to God, angels are immaterial beings or pure spirits. Their nature is invisible (Col. 1:16), although they have taken on physical forms and appeared to humans (Gen. 18). Hebrews 1:14 calls them "ministering spirits." In Luke 24:39, Jesus said, "A spirit does not have flesh and bones as you see that I have." Many angels can be present in one place (Luke 8:30). Further, it is only by a miracle that angels can be seen by mortals (2 Kings 6:17).

Since they are created finite spirits without bodies, angels have no gender. Hence, they do not engage in marriage or reproduction (Matt. 22:30). Angels never die, since they are not subject to decay and death. They are immortal (Luke 20:35–36). Angels have free will. Jude 6 says, "And angels who did not keep their own domain, but abandoned their proper abode, He has kept in eternal bonds under darkness for the judgment of the great day" (cf. 2 Peter 2:4; 1 Tim. 3:6). They have great intelligence and wisdom, 2 Samuel 14:20 says, "My lord is wise, like the wisdom of the angel of God, to know all that is in the earth." Such tremendous knowledge is displayed in the Bible (cf. Luke 1:13, Rev. 10:5–6; 17:1). They have great power. They are called "mighty ones" (Ps. 103:20) and "powerful angels" (2 Thess. 1:7). The ones at Jesus' tomb were able to roll back the heavy stone (Matt. 28:2–3). Speaking of false teachers, Peter says, "Whereas angels who are greater in might and power do not bring a reviling judgment against them before the Lord" (2 Peter 2:11). They can also do miracles (Gen. 19:11).

Angels are persons, since they have intellect, will, and emotions, the three characteristics of persons. They choose to communicate their will with God (Job 1:7), humans (Gen. 18:1f) and each other (Rev. 7:1–3). Emotions or feelings are evidenced in their worship of God (Isa. 6:3; cf. Rev. 4:8–9) and they experience joy upon the repentance of just one sinner (Luke 15:10).

Angels are a reflection of God's nature and glory, hence they are lovely beings. Isaiah's vision of them in the temple is one of ineffable beauty (Isa. 6:1–2 cf. Ezek. 1:15–16). Daniel had a similar aesthetic experience when an angel appeared to him (Dan. 10:5–6) and the angel at Jesus' tomb "was like lightning, and his clothing as white as snow" (Matt. 28:2–3). Even fallen angels retain the beauty which enhances their ability to deceive (2 Cor. 11:14).

PURPOSE OF ANGELS

Similar to all of God's rational creatures, angels were created for His glory. They sing (Job 38:7) and praise God (Ps. 148:2). Indeed, some angels continually sing "holy, holy, holy" in His presence (Isa. 6:3). Hence, Angels are created to glorify God, "Worthy are You, our Lord and our God, to receive glory and honor and power; for You created all things, and because of Your will they existed, and were created" (Rev. 4:11). They are to serve God since they were created "for him" (Col. 1:16; cf. Job 1:6; 2:1). Angels reflect God's attributes (Isa. 6:3; Ezek. 1:5, 28). They long for the word and wisdom of God (Eph. 3:10). They minister to God's elect (saved) and are assigned to watch over children (Matt. 18:10) and many can surround a believer (2 Kings 6:17). Specifically, they promote evangelism (Acts 8:26), restrain wickedness (Gen. 18:22), announce and execute judgment (Rev. 8, 14, 16, 19). They can be involved in answering prayer (Acts

12:7) and care for believers at the moment of death eventually escorting them into the presence of the Holy One (Luke 16:22).

NUMBER AND POSITION OF ANGELS

The number of angels is fixed, not increasing or decreasing (Matt. 22:30), and vast, humanly innumerable (Rev. 5:11). They are described as "hosts" (Ps. 46:7; Luke 2:13) and "myriads" (Deut. 33:2). Angels rank under God and above humans. First Peter 3:22, says of Christ "who is at the right hand of God, having gone into heaven, after angels and authorities and powers had been subjected to Him." Psalm 8:4–5 says, "What is man that You take thought of him, And the son of man that You care for him? Yet You have made him a little lower than God, And You crown him with glory and majesty!" This makes it more amazing that God has chosen believers to judge angels (1 Cor. 6:3).

The most common designation of God's spiritual creatures in the Bible is "angel" meaning "messenger" who are sent on errands to earth. There is rank among both good and evil angels or demons (see Chapter 8). For good angels the top is the archangel (Michael–Dan. 12:1). Under the archangel are "other chief princes" (Dan. 10:21). Cherubim (means "knowledge") are glorious creatures who are proclaimers and protectors of God's glory (Gen. 3:24; Ps. 80:1). Other spiritual beings, called "living creatures," worship God and direct His judgments (Rev. 4:7–8). These may be similar to cherubim, but appear different in Ezekiel 1:6. Seraphim (means "burning ones") are proclaimers of God's holiness (Isa. 6:2–3).

THE ABODE AND ABILITIES OF ANGELS

The general sphere of angels is in heaven. Paul speaks of the third heaven or paradise as being the throne of God. The natural abode of angels is the second heaven. However, they have access to the third heaven (Paradise) are active there (1 Kings 22:19; Rev. 4:6) as well as on earth (Gen. 28:12; Heb. 1:14). Angels are called before God's throne (Job 1:6, 2:1). Angels can do superhuman things. This may be due to their nature as spirits not having any spatio–temporal limits. Biblically they are depicted as being able to traverse great distances in a short time (Dan. 10:2, 12). They can perform miracles (Gen. 19:1; Rev. 16:14), the can materialize (assume bodily form) even eating food (Gen. 19:3, 18:2, 8). This may be an ability of only some angels since others only appear in visions (not materializing) and evil angels (demons) seek embodiment or possession in other physical beings, apparently not having any way to materialize. Although angels do not have bodies, they may communicate with God (Job 1:7), humans (Gen. 18:1f) and each other (Rev. 7:1–3). They occupy no space but can relate to beings in space. This is evident in fallen angels (demons) who sometimes possess humans (Luke 8:27–34).

Biblical Doctrine of Angels

Angels are lower than God, but higher than human beings. Hence, angels are greater in knowledge and power than humans. Angels are like God, and unlike humans. They have no matter in their being. They are pure spirits while humans are a unity of spirit (soul) and matter (Chapter 9). Hence, the only way they can be seen by mortal human beings is by a miracle. Either God must perform a miracle so mortal man can see the spirit world, or He must perform a miracle so that an essentially spirit being can materialize and be seen with mortal eyes.

Angels are not temporal beings, nor are they essentially eternal like God. Hence they are aeviternal. That is they are by nature not in time, but can relate to time. They are not eternal as only God is, but they can relate to Him. They are what humans will be when they are beatified (Matt. 18:10; Luke 20:35–36). Angels are immortal, since they have no bodies that can die or parts that can be torn asunder. Hence, as simple spirits they are not subject to death (James 2:26).

Each angel is a species of its own. Since they cannot reproduce with their kind, as humans do, they are simple created beings and have no way to divide or multiply (Matt. 22:30). Each is one of a kind. Angels do not change in nature. Their nature is fixed from the moment of their creation. Unlike humans, they do not grow old, they have no age or undergo any kind of change. Also they have no accidents, that is, characteristics not essential to their nature such as size, color, etc. Hence there is no accidental change. The only kind of change they can undergo is a substantial change such as, creation or annihilation by God.

Since angels cannot change, they are fixed in their nature; hence, once an angel sins, he is doomed forever (2 Peter 2:4; Jude 6). Hence, as the Bible says explicitly Christ did not die to redeem angels (Heb. 2:16). Like all of God's rational and moral creatures, angels were given a choice. And, like humans at death (Heb. 9:27), once they have made their final choice, it is forever too late, and this is something they know (Matt. 8:29).

The difference between God, angels and humans is illustrated in the following chart (Table 7.1).

	GOD	ANGELS	HUMANS
Mode of Being	Uncreated	Created	Created
Limits	Infinite	Finite	Finite
Nature	Spirit	Spirits	Spirit–Body
Simplicity	Absolutely Simple	Relative Simplicity	No Simplicity (A Complex)
Duration	Eternal (Uncreated Eternity)	Aeviternal (Created Everlasting)	Temporal (Created Temporality)
Change	None	None In Nature, Only In Will	Changeable In Nature And Will
Actuality	Pure Actuality	Completed Actuality	Progressively Completed Actuality
Potentiality	None	None Uncompleted	Uncompleted Potentials
Classification (species)	Beyond all classes	Each a class of one	All in one class (a race)
Free will	Unchangeable before and after choice	Changeable before but not after choice	Changeable before and after choice
Redemption	Source Of Redemption	Unredeemable	Redeemable

Table 7.1 God, Angels, Humans Compared

SUMMARY

The study of Angels (Angelology) shows that God created them as spiritual beings. The physical universe is material; angels are immaterial and human beings are composed of both spirit (soul) and matter. Angels are lower than God and humans are a little lower than the angels. Angels were created to glorify God and minister to God's elect. Their abode is heaven and their abilities far exceed that of humans, yet because of their nature they cannot be redeemed once they freely choose their own destiny, their decision is final.

QUESTIONS TO ANSWER

1. What are some important biblical verses on the origin of angels?
2. What are some important biblical verses on the nature of angels?
3. What are some important biblical verses on the purpose of angels?
4. How do angels compare to God and man?

5. Did you read?,

✗ was

Satan and Demons

*Therefore, laying aside falsehood, speak truth each one of you
with his neighbor, for we are members of one another.
Be angry, and yet do not sin do not let the sun go down on
your anger and do not give the devil an opportunity.*
Ephesians 4:25–27

ALTHOUGH fallen and depraved, Satan and demons (Satanology and Demonology) are angels (Chapter 7). Our study covers Satan's reality, names, personality, depravity and activity. Then we turn to the origin, nature, and activity of demons. We conclude with a look at demon possession and spiritual warfare.

SATANOLOGY

Satan is identified as an angelic being (Matt. 25:41; Rev. 12:7) and therefore ✗ created (Col. 1:15) by God with all the powers endowed to angels (Chapter 7). Indeed, according to Ezekiel (28) Satan is the highest of all created beings and a cherub (Ezek. 28:14).

HIS CREATION

Satan was originally a good spiritual being created by God. For "For by Him [Christ] all things were created, in heaven and on earth, visible and invisible . . ." (Col. 1:16). "And without him was not anything made that was made" (John. 1:3). The Psalmist declared, "Praise Him all His angels. . . . For He commanded and they were created" (Ps. 147:2, 5).

HIS REALITY

That Satan is a real being, as opposed to a personification of evil, is affirmed by the Old and New Testaments. Genesis 3:1 says, "Now the serpent was more crafty than any beast of the field which the Lord God had made. And he said to the woman, "Indeed, has God said, 'You shall not eat from any tree of the garden'?" That the serpent was Satan is affirmed by Scripture (Rev. 12:9). Job speaks of Satan having access to the very throng of God "Now there was a day when the sons of God came to present themselves before the Lord, and Satan also came among them" (Job 1:6, cf. 2:1). Every writer of the New Testament recognized the reality of Satan. Jesus was tempted by Satan, Matthew 4:1, says, "Then Jesus was led up by the Spirit into the wilderness to be tempted by the devil." Of twenty–nine references to Satan in the Gospels, Jesus made twenty–five of them. Hence, Jesus teaches the reality of Satan, in Matthew (4:3–4). Jesus speaks directly to Satan and demons (Luke 8:29–30). Jesus also teaches about Satan's Kingdom (Matt. 12:23–25). Hence, Jesus teaches the personal existence of a being called Satan. He is not merely an idea or personification. Furthermore, Jesus never corrected any one for acknowledging the existence and activity of Satan and demons.

Satan is the enemy of God's people. This is seen from the very beginning of Israel's history, since the Messiah will come through the Jews. Genesis 3:15 says, "And I will put enmity between you and the woman, And between your seed and her seed." In the Covenant given to Abram, God assures him and his decedents of His protection: "And I will bless those who bless you, And the one who curses you I will curse" (Gen. 12:1–3; cf. Zech. 3:1). The reality of Satan, also entails the reality of Demons since he is their "prince" (Luke 11:15) and their "king" (Rev. 9:11).

Satan being a real angelic being entails he has all the traits of personhood. He has intellect which is described as crafty (2 Cor. 11:3) and is a tempter (Luke 4:11). He is depicted as having the emotions of desire (1 Tim. 3:6), jealousy (Job 1:8, 9), hate (1 Peter 5:8) and anger (Rev. 12:12). All of these emotions are directed towards thwarting the plan and people of God. He has a will in which he gives commands (Luke 4:3, 9) and leads a rebellion against God and His people (Rev. 20:7–9). He is also held morally responsible for his deception before God. Second Corinthians 11:14–15 says, "Satan disguises himself as an angel of light. Therefore it is not surprising if his servants also disguise themselves as servants of righteousness, whose end will be according to their deeds" (cf. John 16:11).

His Names

Satan has many names in Scripture. He is the "Anointed cherub" (Eze. 28:14) who is perhaps the highest of class of angelic beings. He is the "Prince of this world" (John 12:31; 16:11) and therefore rules this world and opposes God's rule and kingdom. He is the "Prince and power of the air" (Eph. 2:2). Hence he is from above. He is the "god of this age" (2 Cor. 4:4) and his rule and influence is throughout time. He is "The Prince of Demons" (Matt. 12:24; Luke 11:15) and "Beelzebub" (means "lord of the flies") which is an attempt to insult the gods of the Philistines. He is "Lucifer" (means "shining one" Isa. 14:12). He is "Satan" (means "adversary" Zech. 3:1; Rev. 12:9) who is a self–proposed rival of the only true God; he is a counterfeit to the real. He is the "Devil" (means "slanderer" Luke 4:2; Rev. 12:9). He is one who trips up or defames God, Christ and believers. He is the "old serpent" (means "crafty") deceiver (2 Cor. 11:13–15) who leads minds astray (2 Cor. 11:30). He is the "Great dragon" (meaning "terrifying" Rev. 12:3, 7, 9) one who brings total devastation. He is the "Evil one" (John 17:15; 1 John 5:18) that clearly limits him to an individual person. He is the "Destroyer" (Rev. 9:11) of physical and spiritual life. A "Tempter" (Matt. 4:3; 1 Th. 3:5) who tries to entices men to evil. The "Accuser" (Job 1:9; Zech. 3:1; Rev. 12:10) who has access to God's presence and the "Deceiver" (Rev. 12:10, cf. Eph. 6:11) of the whole world.

Personality & Depravity

The nature of Satan is that of a created spirit (Col. 1:16) who is under judgment (John 12:31; Eph. 2:2). He is very powerful, but not omnipotent (see Table 8.1). He is very beautiful and uses this beauty to disguise his deception (2 Cor. 11:14). He is totally and permanently evil in a moral sense (John 17:50).

GOD	SATAN
Infinite	Finite
Uncreated	Created
All Good	Evil
All Knowing	Limited in Knowledge
All Present (everywhere)	Local Presence (here)
All Power	Limited Power
Create Life	Cannot Create Life
Miracles	Cannot do Miracles
Supernatural	Supernormal
Raise the Dead	Cannot Raise the Dead

Table 8.1 God Compared to Satan

His Fall and Depravity

The depravity of Satan is pictured in the demise of the prince of Tyre. It begins with recognizing that he is originally created perfect (Ezek. 28:12, 13). He had a heavenly estate (Jude 6), the Garden of God or paradise. He was the guardian of God's glory (Ezek. 28:14; 2 Cor. 12:4). The occasion of his sin is his power and beauty. Ezekiel 28:16, 17 says, "By the abundance of your trade you were internally filled with violence, And you sinned; Therefore I have cast you as profane from the mountain of God. And I have destroyed you, O covering cherub, "Your heart was lifted up because of your beauty; you corrupted your wisdom by reason of your splendor. I cast you to the ground." The nature of his sin is pride. Isaiah 14:13–14 says, "I will make myself like the Most High." (cf. 1 Tim. 3:6). The cause of his sin is personal free choice. God cannot cause sin (Hab. 1:13; Jas 1:13), therefore there was no one else to temp him. The result was expulsion from heaven (Rev. 12:9; cf. Isa. 14:12), the corruption of his character (1 John 5:18; cf. Ezek. 28:15), perversion of his power (Eph. 2:2, cf. Isa. 14:12) which led to the defection of other angels (Rev. 12:4). This all leads to his final destruction (Rev. 20:10).

The time of Satan's sin is definitely before Adam (Gen. 3:1) and probably after the creation of the heavens (Gen. 1:10, cf. Job 38:7). Some have suggested it was on the second "day" of creation since this is the only day of which it is not said, "It was good."

In considering these things, we must not forget the overriding providence of God (see Chapter 4) that reminds us that God created only good things (Gen. 3:1). Yet, God permitted evil and Satan (cf. Acts 17:30; 2 Peter 3:9) in order that He could produce a greater good. This is accomplished through Christ by defeating sin. Paul says in 1 Corinthians 15:25, "For He must reign until He has put all His enemies under His feet." Christ is able to destroy Satan. First John 3:8 says, "The one who practices sin is of the devil; for the devil has sinned from the beginning. The Son of God appeared for this purpose, to destroy the works of the devil." And Christ is able to redeeming His servants. Paul says "but where sin increased, grace abounded all the more" (Rom. 5:20).

His Activity

Satan opposes God directly and indirectly. He directly opposes God by his original sin (Isa. 14) and slander (Job 1:9). He indirectly opposes God by attacking God's image in man (Gen. 3) and attacking God's word (Gen. 3:1). He attacks God's Son (Matt. 4:1) and God's program. Satan opposes God's program in heaven (Ezek. 28) and on earth. On earth he does this through false philosophies (Col. 2:8), false religions, specifically false "gospels" (Gal. 1:6, 8) and idolatry (1 Cor. 10:19, 20), false ministers (2 Cor. 11:14, 15), false doctrine (1 Tim. 4:1; 2 Peter 2:1), promoting schisms (2 Cor. 2:10, 11) and planting doubt (Gen. 3:1, 20).

Satan provokes us to sin through *pride*, 1 Timothy 3:6 says, "And not a new convert, so that he will not become conceited and fall into the condemnation incurred by the devil." We are provoked through *worry*, Matthew 13:22 says, "And the one on whom seed was sown among the thorns, this is the man who hears the word, and the worry of the world and the deceitfulness of wealth choke the word, and it becomes unfruitful." Through *self–reliance*, 1 Chronicles 21:1 says, "Now Satan stood up against Israel, and moved David to number Israel." Through *discouragement*, 1 Peter 5:6, 7 says "Therefore humble yourselves under the mighty hand of God, that He may exalt you at the proper time. Casting all your anxiety on Him, because He cares for you." Through *worldliness*, 1 John 2:16 says, "For all that is in the world, the lust of the flesh and the lust of the eyes and the boastful pride of life, is not from the Father, but is from the world" (cf. 5:19); and through *sexual sin*, 1 Corinthians 7:5 says "Stop depriving one another, except by agreement for a time, so that you may devote yourselves to prayer, and come together again so that Satan will not tempt you because of your lack of self–control."

DEMONOLOGY

The Old Testament acknowledges the reality of demons. Deuteronomy 32:17 says, "They sacrificed to demons who were not God, . . ." Their activity as evil spirits is also acknowledged (1 Sam. 16:14–16). The New Testament mentions demons in every book, except Hebrews, and Christ affirmed their existence and gave authority to His disciples to cast them out (Matt. 10:1). Paul mentions that believers will judge them (1 Cor. 6:3). James says demons believe God is one and shudder (James 2:19).

THEIR ORIGIN AND FALL

There are several false views concerning the origin of demons who are sometimes called unclean spirits (Matt. 17:18; Mark 9:25; Luke 10:17–20; Matt. 8:16). Some have supposed they are the spirits of deceased wicked people. This was an ancient Greek belief. However, both the Old and New Testament firmly assert that the deceased unsaved are confined in a place of torment (Chapter 14). Psalm 9:17 says, "The wicked will return to Sheol, Even all the nations who forget God." Jesus teaches about the Rich man and Lazarus, in Luke 16:23 (cf. Rev. 20:13–14) saying, "In Hades he lifted up his eyes, being in torment, and saw Abraham far away and Lazarus in his bosom." Hence, nowhere in Scripture is their support for demons being the spirits of deceased wicked people. Others have suggested that demons are the disembodied spirits of a pre–Adamic race. That is, there was a race of humans before Adam. However, there is no biblical support for this assertion. Jesus taught in Matthew 19:4 saying, "Have you not read that He who created them from the beginning made them male and female." Hence there is no possibility of humans existing before their creation as recorded in Genesis. The final false view is taken from Genesis 6:1–4. Some have argued that angels were the "sons of God" (which are angels in Job 1:6) married the daughters of men. The offspring of this unholy union, upon their judgment and death, became demons that exist today. However, there are other interpretations such as "sons of God" being believers or great ones on the earth. Even if it is a reference to angels, it is pointing to already fallen angels who possess human beings, who intermarry. Hence, it could not be the origin of demons.

According to Scripture, demons are angels who rebelled with Satan. The book of Revelation says, one third of all the angels fell with Satan (Rev. 12:4). There are two groups of rebellious demons. There are loose and active demons (Eph. 6:11–12) who have Satan as their prince (Matt. 12:24) even a ranking of demons that is similar to good angels (Eph. 3:10; 6:12). The second group is confined demons. Some fear this confinement (Luke 8:31). For some demons it is permanent as is mentioned in 2 Peter 2:4: "For if God did not spare angels when they sinned, but cast them into hell and committed them to pits of darkness, reserved for judgment." And some may be only temporarily confined (Rev. 9:1–15).

THEIR NATURE

The New Testament depicts demons with personal pronouns (Luke 8:27–30), having intellect (1 Tim. 4:1–3), will (Luke 8:32) and emotions (Luke 8:28). Hence they have the full angelic capabilities (Chapter 7) but with a bent towards evil. They are further described as: "unclean spirits" (Matt. 10:1), "evil spirits" (Luke 7:21), "spirit of an unclean demon" (Luke 4:33), and "spiritual forces of wickedness" (Eph. 6:12). Although an appropriate description, they are never referred to in Scripture as "fallen angels."

As with all angels, bodies (flesh and blood) are not intrinsic to the nature of demons and their power is localized. They can appear or make their presence known by various means (Acts 19:15; Rev. 9:1–12; 16:13). However, the lack of appearance of demons materially may suggest that they are unable or prevented from doing so. Demons seem to seek embodiment in physical beings through possession (Matt. 8:28–32) and this may be because of their inability to materialize.

THEIR ACTIVITIES

The powers of demons include super–human or supernormal displays especially in possessed humans (Mark 5:3; Acts 19:16). Their intellect can pretend to predict the future (Acts 16:16). They can enter or possess human and animal bodies (Luke 8:30). They are limited, not infinite, even in their collective influence. They have supernormal power to do false signs and wonders (2 Thess. 2:9).

The overall goal of demons is to follow Satan in promoting everything and anything opposed to the plan and goodness of God. This is achieved through specific activities identified in Scripture. They extend Satan's activities (Eph. 6:11–12), oppose the plan of God (Dan. 10:10–14; Rev. 16:13–16) and promote idolatry (Lev. 17:7; Deut. 32:17; 1 Cor. 10:20). They instigate false religions, teach against the incarnation and resurrection (1 John 4:1–4; 1 Tim. 3:16–4:3) and against salvation by faith alone (1 Tim. 4:3–4). They are against what is morally right and promote acts of immorality (Rev. 2:20–24). They are also used by God (Judg. 9:23; 1 Sam. 16:14; 1 Kings 22:22; 2 Cor. 12:7) to achieve His good ends.

In relation to people in general they can cause affliction through physical disease (Matt. 9:33; 12:22; 17:15–18), mental disorder (Mark 5:4–5; 9:22; Luke 8:27–29; 9:37–42) and death (Rev. 9:14–19). However, it is important to note that not all illness is demonic (Matt. 4:24; Mark 1:32; Luke 7:21; 9:1). They can cause perversion through promoting immoral life styles (1 Tim. 4:1–3), through individual evil activities (Deut. 32:17; Ps. 106:37–39) and even through the nations (Lev. 18:6–30; Deut. 18:9–14).

In relation to believers and the church they can tempt us to sin and rely on our flesh (1 Cor. 5:1–5; Eph. 2:2–3; 1 Thess. 4:3–5; 1 Tim. 3:6; 1 John 2:16), inflict maladies (e.g., Paul's "thorn in the flesh" – 2 Cor. 12:7–9 cf. Job 2:7–9), hinder ministry travel (1 Thess. 2:18), and create division (Eph. 4:3) including doctrinal division (1 John 4:1–4; 1 Tim. 4:3–4, 8; 2 Tim. 3:5; 2 Peter 2:1–2), promote jealousy, self–ambitions (1 Cor. 3:1–4; 2 Cor. 2:5–11), counter and pervert the gospel (2 Cor. 4:3–4; 14–15) and even be the cause of persecution (Rev. 2:8–10).

DEMON POSSESSION

Demonic possession or control is when a demon, or more than one, is exercising their will or power, in control of a human being. A scriptural distinction is made when an illness is demonic as opposed to a natural illness that is a cause of physical disease, mental disorders and death. Acts 5:16 says, "the people from the cities in the vicinity of Jerusalem were coming together, bringing people who were sick and afflicted with unclean spirits, and they were all being healed" (emphasis added). No believer, who is indwelt by the Spirit of God (1 Cor. 6:19 cf. 2 Cor. 6:14–18), can have a demon at the same time. Demons can produce muteness, blindness, and convulsions (Matt. 9:32; 12:22; Luke 9:36), tendencies to self–destruction (Mark 5:5; Luke 9:42), insanity (John 10:20), supernormal strength (Mark 5:3–4), and occultic power (Acts 16:16–18).

Demonic possession of a believer does not seem to be well supported in Scripture. This is especially true given what is done on the behalf of the believer by the Holy Spirit at the moment of salvation (Chapter 6). The believer becomes the possession of God through sealing (2 Cor. 1:22; Eph. 1:13–14) and the permanent indwelling (John 14:16) of the third person of the Trinity. The believer has the present and permanent possession of eternal life (John 5:24 – see Chapter 12). Given this, demonic possession seems limited to unbelievers. However, demonic oppression, attack from without, is a possible reality for a believer and can be quite sever (Job 1:11; 2:5, 9; Luke 22:31–32).

Believers may experience *oppression* or be influenced by demons, but there is no clear example of a believer being possessed or demonized. Possession is the direct willful control of a person's body by a demon. In oppression, demons attack from the outside, not the inside.

Spiritual Warfare

Some Scripture seems to suggest that God is the cause of evil spirits or demons (1 Sam. 16:15) and may even use occult divination (1 Sam. 28:7f) as in the story of Saul who consulted the medium of Endor. However, God is the efficient causation of all things (Chapter 1) and God uses even evil for achieving His good ends through Providence (Chapter 4). Saul was rebuked for what he did and the occultic means is consistently condemned in Scripture. Consider the following explicit prohibitions that involve the demonic: false predictions (Deut. 18:21–22), contacting departed spirits (Deut. 18:11), using instruments of divination (Deut. 18:11a), advocating idolatry of images (Ex. 20:3–4; Deut. 13:1–3), denial of Christ's humanity or deity (Col. 2:9; 1 John 4:1–2), advocating abstinence from certain foods for religious reasons (1 Tim. 4:3–4), depreciating or denying marriage (1Tim. 4:3), promoting immorality (Eph. 2:2–3; Jude 7), encouraging legalistic self–denial (Col. 2:16–23), denying death

(Gen. 3:4), encouraging self–deification (Gen. 3:5; 2 Thess. 2:9), promoting lying (John 8:44), and advocating astrology (Deut. 4:19; Isa. 47:13–15).

Ephesians 6:10–20, provides a reminder of the weapons that Christian's must daily use to combat spiritual warfare. The warfare is not physical, but just as real. The spiritual enemy is the devil, his schemes, spiritual forces of the world and wickedness. The believer's protection and fight, begins by living in the Spirit (Eph. 4–6). Then we may stand firm and put on the armor of God that includes: truth, righteousness, good news of peace, faith, salvation and prayer. Persevering in these will protect us from the evil one and his daily attacks. Satan's attacks come from the world and the lust of our flesh (1 John 2:15–17). The Devil is defeated and if we submit ourselves to God and resist him, he will flee from us (James 4:7).

Summary

The study of Satan and demons (Satanology and Demonology) shows they are spiritual creatures that have freely rebelled against God and are therefore morally evil. They are active in our world promoting everything and anything opposed to the plan and goodness of God. They are providentially used by God to achieve His good ends. They have been judged and defeated by the work of Christ on the cross. However, they can afflict and oppress believers and therefore, we must be on our guard equipped to engage in spiritual warfare.

Questions to Answer

1. What biblical verses support the existence, depravity, personality, and activity of Satan?
2. What biblical verses support the origin, nature, and activity of Demons?
3. What can Satan and demons do and not do to believers?
4. What must believers do to fight spiritual warfare?

9

The Nature of Man

Then the LORD God formed man of dust from the ground, and
breathed into his nostrils the breath of life;
and man became a living being.
Genesis 2:7

GOD created human beings (Anthropology) who are ranked below the angels (Chapter 7–8) but above non–rational animals
and inanimate matter (Chapter 4) since man bares the image of God.
Our study investigates the biblical origin and nature of humankind.
The fall and depravity of man is covered in the next chapter (10).

THE ORIGIN OF HUMAN BEINGS

God is absolutely perfect (Chapter 3). Only perfection can come
from an absolutely perfect being. Deuteronomy 32:4 says, "His
[God] work is perfect." Second Samuel 22:31 says, "As for God, his
way is blameless [perfect]" and Matthew 5:48: "Your heavenly Father
is perfect."

STATE OF INNOCENCE AND PERFECTION

Man was originally created in a virtuous state (Eccl. 7:29). This
entails that his nature was morally perfect, with no knowledge of evil
(Gen. 3:5). Such a state was supernaturally or naturally caused by
God. Since God is absolutely perfect, the environment He created
for human existence was "very good" (Gen. 1:31). This entails that

it was materially and morally perfect. Creation was not subject to corruption as it was after the fall, Romans 8:22 says, "For we know that the whole creation groans and suffers the pains of childbirth together until now." There was no human death. Romans 5:12 says, "Therefore, just as through one man sin entered into the world, and death through sin, and so death spread to all men, because all sinned." The first humans were created with no evil in their natures, they were complete and innocent of any sin; they "did not know good and evil" (Gen. 1, 2). They were morally perfect; this is not simply the lack of vice, but the reality of virtue since "God made men upright." (Eccl. 7:29).

In their original state humankind was not a servant of nature, but a master over it. Genesis 1:28 says, "Fill the earth and subdue it. Rule over the fish of the sea and the birds of the air and over every living creature that moves on the ground." They were morally accountability to God: "the Lord God commanded the man, 'You are free to eat from any tree in the garden; but you must not eat from the tree of the knowledge of good and evil, for when you eat of it you will surely die'" (Gen. 2:16–17).

Adam was free in the sense of his moral actions were self–determined. No one else, including Satan (the Serpent), made Adam and Eve commit sin. These perfect persons in a perfect paradise were not without in imperfect intruder. Satan, a fallen angel of God (Rev. 12:4, see Chapter 8) led Eve, and through her Adam into disobedience against God (Rom. 5:19; 1 Tim. 2:14). Adam and Eve were not enticed to lie, cheat, steal or curse. They were not vulnerable to these temptations since they were morally perfect. The command God gave them was not a command to stay away from intrinsic evil. Instead, their only vulnerability or test they could undergo was to whether or not they would obey God, because He said it.

Their moral responsibility to God was with regard to an object that was morally neutral. God could have said, for instance, "Don't pick the daisies." The issue was not that the sin was inherent in the substance in which they partook; the temptation to sin was in the enticement to defy God, and subsequently to be conscious of the evil of choosing against Him. *No evil from within or from without drew them to their transgression.* Only a raw act of freedom, wrongly exercised, carried out their disobedience and sealed their doom. Most likely, only disobedience to God's specific command would precipitate the Fall and plunge the whole creation into death and disaster (Rom. 5:12; 1 Tim. 2:14).

ORIGIN OF THE HUMAN SOUL

There are three views of the origin of the human soul: 1) Preexistence, 2) Creation and 3) the Traducian view. The Preexistence view says the soul existed before creation. The Creation view says the soul is specially created by God when the person comes to be. The Traducian view says the soul is instrumentally caused to exist through the parents when the person comes to be.

The non–Christian understanding of the Preexistence view sees the soul as never being created; instead it exists eternally as a form. This was the Platonic view, from the Greek philosopher Plato. Some early Christians adopted this view but added that it was created from eternity by God. Origen (c. 185–254 A.D.) and the early writings of Augustine (354–430 A.D.) hold this view. However, neither view finds support in Scripture, which clearly teaches the creation, hence the beginning of a soul/body. Human beings have a beginning (Gen. 1:27) and the Bible declares the soul and body are created (Gen. 2:7). Human life begins at conception (Ps. 22:9–10) and no human (temporal) being can be eternal (uncreated).

The creationist view says God directly creates a new individual soul for everyone born into this world and leaves just the body to be generated by the parents. Some biblical texts are cited for this: Psalm 51:5 says, "Behold, I was brought forth in iniquity, And in sin my mother conceived me." And Matthew 1:20 says, "For the Child who has been conceived in her is of the Holy Spirit." This view also acknowledges that all genetic information is present at conception. Not all creationists agree on when God implants the newly created soul. Some say it is at the moment of conception, others at implantation and others hold it is after implantation. Thomas Aquinas (1224/5–1274) held that an animal soul was generated by the parents, and then God created a rational human soul at animation (movement in mother's womb). Other more extreme views have said creation is at birth or even at first breath.

One serious problem with the creationist view, no matter when it takes place, is that it must attribute the direct creation of each sin nature to God (Ps. 51:5) to account for inherited sin (Chapter 10). Yet this is impossible since God cannot create sin or any sinful substance. Scripture says God has ceased creating after the sixth day of creation (Gen. 2:3). Aquinas' view suffers from an outdated view of biology and science. Aquinas himself held that the body exists for the sake of the soul, and if the body has distinct human only features, such as a complete genetic code at conception that forms the basis of developing human organs, a human rational soul must be present to direct all these human only features. Furthermore, developmental changes

	Pre–Existence View	Creationism	Traducianism
TIME OF CREATION	From Eternity (Plato) Before World (Origen)	1) At Conception, 2) Or Implantation 3) At Animation, or 4) At Birth	Originally in Adam Instrumentally through parents
GOD'S ROLE	Created all souls	Creates each soul	Creates body and soul through parents
PARENT'S ROLE	Soul: none Body: efficient cause	Soul: occasional cause Body: efficient cause	Body and Soul: Instrumental Cause
NATURE OF MAN	Man *is* a soul (Man *has* a body)	Man *is* a soul (Man *has* a body)	Man is soul–body unity
IMAGE OF GOD	In soul only	In soul only	In soul and body*
IMMORTALITY	Soul only	Soul only	Soul and body

*Some Traducianists do not see that this is a logical entailment of their view.

Table 9.1 Views on the Human Soul Compared

in the soul do not make it a different entity or nature, only more mature. The creation of a soul at birth or breath is only the observing of life, not the beginning of life (Gen. 5:1ff). Animals have breath, but are not human and human life exists even when there is no breathing (Phil. 1:23). Hence, Scripture speaks of full human life in the womb at conception (Ps. 51:5; Matt. 1:20). In short, the creationist view does not explain the inheritance of original sin.

The term "Traducian" comes from the Latin *tradux* which means "branch of a vine." This view says each new human being is a branch of the parents. Both soul and body are naturally generated together by the father and mother. This must be the case because God's creation was completed on the sixth day (Gen. 2:2) and He is now resting (Heb. 4:4). Scientifically it says once the sperm and ovum of the parents are conceived in the womb a full individual human person exists. There is a good deal of biblical support for this view.

The biblical basis for the Traducian view is found throughout Scripture. The creation of Adam's soul by God is a special case since he was the first human and was perfect. But Eve was made from Adam, and not separately (Gen. 2:21–22). This shows the unity of male and female since the female is made from the male (1 Cor. 11:8). Eve is called the "mother of all the living" (Gen. 3:20) and Adam had children in his image (Gen. 5:3). This only makes sense if full human life is transmitted by natural generation. The term "flesh" as used in Scripture can mean the "whole person with body" rather than just their physical body (John 3:6; Rom. 1:3; 3:20). Furthermore God's offspring, who bare His image are "one blood" and this was accomplished by natural processes (Acts 17:26). Levi was in Abraham's loins which implies physical transmission (Heb. 7:10). The human body in the womb is a full human person (Ps. 22:9–10; Jer. 1:5). This also accounts for how all sinned through one man (Rom. 5:12) which implies sin can be transmitted by natural processes. We are born with a sinful nature (Eph. 2:3) which makes no sense if it is just the body without the soul since bodies without souls cannot sin. We are conceived in sin (Ps. 51:5) which is something not possible unless a soul is present. Finally, Jesus, is from the "loins" of David indicating a ge- ~~about~~ netic connection (1 Kings 8:19). All this indicates ~~that~~ the biblical view is that the personal substance is more than physical and, since God has rested from creating (Gen. 2:1–3; Heb. 4:4), was made instrumentally in the womb by natural process.

In addition to the biblical support, there are other reasons to favor the Traducian view. This view accounts for the imputation of sin from Adam to the entire posterity which must be by natural processes. Romans 5:18 says, "So then as through one transgression there resulted condemnation to all men, even so through one act of righteousness there resulted justification of life to all men." Life or the soul begins at conception. This helps explain the universal natural inclination to sin (Eph. 2:3; John 3:6) that favors the Traducian view. Also the soul/body unity view, which is defended below, favors the Traducian view, since both are transmitted from parent to child. Scientifically human DNA is naturally passed on from parent to child. Hence, biologically everything is present at conception to constitute a human person. This is also supported by analogy with the animal world; non–rational animal souls likewise are passed on from parents to offspring. Hence, humans are a psychosomatic, soul/body unity. The physical body is not the whole person and neither is the immaterial soul, but together they constitute a complete human being.

Some have objected to this view saying Hebrews 12:9 calls God the "Father of our spirits." However, it does not say He created our spirit at conception. Even if fathering is creation, it does not say how it was done. Fathering may be indicative of care related to His disciplining us. Others have objected that Isaiah 57:16 says, "The breath of man [soul] that I have created." Here it should be noted that the

Traducian view acknowledges that God is the efficient cause of the human soul, but not the secondary instrumental cause. Also "soul" in Scripture is often used of the whole person, body and soul. And the term "created" could be understood as "made" that does not usually entail "creation from nothing." Furthermore, this text does not indicate how or when. Hence, with these considerations in mind, a Traducian understanding is still possible.

In short, the Traducian view correctly acknowledges that all creation depends upon God's necessity. It does not deny the efficient cause of God, only the instrumental cause. The parents cause the becoming of their child, only God can cause their being (existence) and the parents do pass on the soul–body unity, which only God did and can create and sustain.

The Nature of Human Beings

Man is created in the image of God. Genesis 1:27 says, "And God created man in His own image, in the image of God He created him; male and female He created them" (cf. Gen. 5:1). First Corinthians 11:7 says, "For a man. . . is the image and glory of God" and Colossians 3:10 says of believers that we "have put on the new self who is being renewed to a true knowledge according to the image of the One who created him."

The Image of God in Man

The meaning of this image and likeness entails that man resembles God in several ways. It includes an intellectual likeness to God. God alone is all knowing, but humans have intelligence and will (Col. 3:10; Jude 10). It includes a moral likeness to God. God is love, but humans can love (1 John 4:16). God can create, but human beings can reproduce and make (Gen. 1:28). Humans represent God on earth (Gen. 1:28) and humans are morally responsible to God; able to choose right from wrong (Gen. 2:16–17). Also, the image of God is evident in the reasons humans should not be harmed or cursed, since it is wrong to murder or curse humans. Genesis 9:6 says, "Whoever sheds man's blood, by man his blood shall be shed, for in the image of God He made man." And James 3:9 says, "With it [tongue] we bless our Lord and Father; and with it we curse men, who have been made in the likeness of God."

Furthermore, the image of God not only applies to the immaterial aspect of humans, the soul, but also includes the body which emphasizes the soul/body unity that constitutes the whole person. This understanding is strongly supported in Scripture. God created matter good which constitutes the body (Gen. 1:31). He created humans male and female which entails their bodies in the image of God (Gen. 1:27). The basis for murder being wrong is that it includes God's image in the body which humans can kill not the soul alone which cannot be killed (Gen. 9:6). Christ incarnate, in bodily form is the image of God according to Hebrews 1:3 that says, "And He [Jesus Christ] is the radiance of His glory and the exact representation of His nature." Also, the fact that there is a resurrection of the body shows it is part of the whole person that is in God's image.

But man in the image of God; does not entail God in the image of man. This teaching does not imply God has a body; any more than the "word" I write with material ink on material paper means the thought in my mind must also be material, as it is on the ink and paper. Furthermore, angels are like God since they are immaterial, but God is not like them in the sense of being created and finite.

Also of importance is that fallen man is still in God's image (Gen. 9:6; 1 Cor. 11:7; James 3:9). Even the most vile of human beings retain God's likeness, be it oh so vitiated by sin. And redeemed humans are being renewed after God's image. Ephesians 4:24 says, "And put on the new self, which in the likeness of God has been created in righteousness and holiness of the truth." And 1 John 3:2 says, "Beloved, now we are children of God, and it has not appeared as yet what we shall be. We know that, when He appears, we shall be like Him, because we shall see Him just as He is" (cf. Rom. 8:29; 2 Cor. 3:18; Col. 3:10).

The image of God in humans entails several areas of moral responsibility. Man is responsible for himself (Eph. 5:28, 29), for the world (Gen. 1:28), to fellow man (Gen. 4:9; 9:6; Acts 17:26) and ultimately to God (Gen. 2:16, 17). Such responsibility entails and should point us towards our intended ultimate end which is to see God, our creator, face to face. (1 John 3:2; Rev. 22:4).

HUMAN FREE WILL

An important aspect of the image of God (Gen. 1:27) in man is his free will. Man was created with free will. This is implied in the commands of God toward man (Gen. 1:28; 2:16, 17). Such responsibility implies that man has the ability to freely respond. This is also clearly entailed in the command to love (Matt. 22:37). Love can be commanded but not demanded. Forced love is a contradiction. Man exercised his own free will to sin and fallen man is willfully rebellious to God (Rom. 1:18; Eph. 2:2). It is true that fallen man cannot of his own sinful will be saved (John 1:13). But man is free with respect to so-called "horizontal" matters and even some "vertical" matters. With respect to horizontal matters he is free to choosing a mate (1

Cor. 7:39), make family decisions (1 Cor. 7:37), decisions within the church (1 Peter 5:2), the giving of money (2 Cor. 9:7) and making requests to friends (Philemon 14).

While humans are not free to initiate or attain their own salvation, they are free to accept God's free gift of salvation (Matt. 23:37; 2 Peter 3:9). We can accept God's revelation of salvation: since it is the "gift" of salvation that must be "received." John 1:12 says, "But as many as received Him, to them He gave the right to become children of God, even to those who believe in His name" (cf. Rom. 6:23). Even the Old Testament recognized that a new heart from God is "given" (Ezek. 11:19). God expects us to "choose" Him (Deut. 30:15; Josh. 24:14; 1 Kings 18:21).

Human free will is the God given power of moral and spiritual self–determinism. That is the ability to do otherwise. Freedom is doing what one decides, not what one desires. One can decide contrary to their desires. This is entailed by God holding us responsible for our decisions. Responsibility implies the ability to respond. Determinism is ultimately self–defeating since according to determinism non–determinists should accept their view; "ought" implies free to change but according to the determinists view they are determined not to hold it. Since such a view takes away free choose from a person, they are no longer persons. It reduces a person to an object: turns an "I" into an "it." Furthermore, praise and blame become meaningless if we are not free and even God's commands would be meaningless. Nonsense or humor also is only possible if someone can willfully violate the rules of language. For the compatibility of God's sovereignty and human free will see Chapter 3. For objections to free will that come from man's sinful condition see Chapter 10.

Body/Soul Relationship

The Bible uses several terms to designate the immaterial or spiritual dimension of humans. The term *soul* sometimes actually includes the body. This is evident in Genesis 2:7 which says, "Then the LORD God formed man of dust from the ground, and breathed into his nostrils the breath of life; and man became a living being." And Psalm 16:10 says, "For You will not abandon my *soul* to Sheol (Grave); nor will you allow Your Holy One to undergo decay." Sometimes it is used to distinguish the soul from the body (Gen. 35:18). *Spirit* is almost always used for the immaterial dimension of humans and is sometimes used interchangeable with *soul* (Luke 1:46, 24:38–39; James 2:26; John 19:30, 4:24). The term *heart* is used for the whole inner person and includes the mind (Rom. 10:9; Deut. 6:5; Matt. 12:34). The term *mind* is used for the inner dimension that thinks and imagines (Mark 12:30; 12:2; Rom. 8:6–7, 12:2; 2 Cor. 10:5).

Likewise, there are terms used for the material dimension of humans. *Body* is used for the material aspect of humans (Matt. 10:28; James 2:26; 1 Cor. 15:42–44, 53) and *flesh* is used for the physical dimension (Luke 24:39; Acts 2:31). Some phrases are also used, "flesh and blood" (Matt. 16:17; 1 Cor. 15:50) emphasizes the mortal aspect of humans. Analogies are also found in Scripture, especially by Paul who uses "earthen vessel" (2 Cor. 4:7), "earthly tent" (2 Cor. 5:1; John 1:14) and "outward man" (2 Cor. 4:16).

Philosophically there are six views of the soul–body relationship. 1) Materialism says only the body exists; there is no soul (Thomas Hobbes 1588–1679). 2) Idealism says only the soul exists; there is no body (George Berkeley 1685–1753). 3) Monism says the soul and body are two sides, inner and outer, of one substance or the same thing (Benedict Spinoza 1632–1677). 4) Dualism (Dichotomy) says the soul and body are two separate substances or parallel entities that never intersect (attributed to Plato c. 427–347 B.C.). 5) Trichotomy says there is body, soul, and spirit (origins in Plato, Plotinus 205–270 B.C. and Tertullian c. 155–225 A.D. adopted it). And finally 6) Hylomorphism says humans are a soul/body unity. The roots of Hylomorphism are in the Old Testament, found philosophically in Aristotle (384–322 B.C.) and corroborated by Thomas Aquinas.

Materialism cannot be supported by Scripture since the body and soul exist and are distinguishable. The body will perish, not the soul (2 Cor. 4:16; 5:1; Gen. 35:18). This view is self–defeating since the materialistic view or concept is not made up of matter. There must be a transcendent "I" to even account for the existence of the view. Also, the universe has a non–material origin "out of nothing" (Chapter 4). Hence, Mind produced matter, not the reverse, matter producing mind. Furthermore, there are other immaterial things; for example, the moral law is not material, since it is prescriptive (not descriptive), and there must be a principle of life that distinguishes living things from nonliving things. Hence, materialism that there is only a body or matter cannot be true.

Idealism also is not supported in Scripture since God created a material universe (Gen. 1) and God is Spirit (John 4:26). Matter is finite and destructible (1 Cor. 15:42), yet God is not (1 Tim. 6:16). The soul and body are different since they are separated at death (Luke 24:30; John 2:26) and Scripture argues for the resurrection of the "body." Yet, if there is no material body, why should there need to be a resurrection to constitute the person? This view begs the question, since it assumes only minds exist. It assumes ideas are the only formal objects of knowing. Yet this is contrary to experience since we know that there is a difference between eating real food verses thinking (an idea) about eating food. Finally, this view charges God with deception. God may be all powerful to create a world of just ideas, but He is also all good and cannot deceive us making us think it is other than what it is. Hence idealism, that there is only a soul and no body or matter, cannot be true.

Monism, that soul and body are one substance, is not supported either since it denies the two dimensions (soul/body) that the Bible affirms. Such a view cannot explain how the soul survives death which the Bible affirms. Further, it cannot explain how Jesus is alive between death and resurrection (Luke 24:46; John 19:30). Such a view must entail annihilationism or immediate resurrection at death. Yet the Bible denies both of these (Chapter 14). This view also assumes an identical understanding of the body and soul. Such a position is contrary to consciousness and thoughts that are clearly different from and not dependent upon the body or matter. Hence Monism, that there is only one substance to constitute a human, cannot be true.

Dualism says the soul and body are two separate substances or parallel entities that never intersect. However this view denies the biblical teaching of unity (see Hylomorphism below). It also suffers from the problem of having no way for the immaterial soul to know the material world. Actually, it has no way for the soul to even know its own body. Some have postulated a third medium to connect the soul to a body so it can know the world and itself. However, this just complicates matters. What is that third medium made out of, soul or matter? It also entails humans are essentially immaterial. That is a soul using a body as a sailor uses a ship. But this leads to asceticism since human essence is then just spiritual. That is, a human person is a soul and has a body. Hence, this view cannot be true either.

Trichotomy says that humans are body, soul, and spirit. Usually the body is identified with world–consciousness, the soul is identified with self–conscious, and the spirit with God conscious. This has been argued for from Scripture, for example, Hebrews 4:12 says soul and spirit are divided. However, this is a figure of speech describing the power of the Word of God that is able to divide the indivisible and not a reference to the nature of humans. They point to 1 Thessalonians 5:23 that list all three, "spirit and soul and body" separately. But this could also be a way of stressing wholeness and lists both "soul and spirit" to emphasize completeness. They point to Romans 8:16 that speaks of spirit being connected with God; but there are counter examples of the soul being connected to God (Matt. 22:37; Luke 1:46). Some have also pointed to Mark 10:45 saying that Jesus gives his life

[soul], not spirit. But if so, then John 19:30 says He gave up His spirit. So if the Trichotomist view is true, Jesus would not be fully human.

Ultimately the problem with this view is that it is trying to force a Platonic view, that the soul alone is the person which just has a body, into Scripture. Some Christians have adopted this view seeing that it portrays a Trinity in man. However, it is inconsistent, since the same linguistic use applies to "heart" and "mind" which would make man not three parts but five parts. And of most importance is that it follows an incorrect view of language in its interpretation of Scripture. That is, it thinks meaning is absolute because words must correspondence to things in the world in a fixed one–to–one relationship. However, as we have shown (Chapter 1), words have a one–to–many relationship. That is, the same word can describe multiply things and still show meaning is absolute.

The preceding views are unable to support the biblical data and correct understanding since they do not acknowledge the immaterial dimension (Materialism), the material dimension (Idealism), the possibility of separation (Monism) or material/immaterial interaction (Dualism), or the correct biblical grammatical use of terms (Trichotomy). Only the view of anthropological Hylomorphism, which finds its roots in the Old Testament, expresses humanity as a soul/body unity (not an identity) which can explain the biblical data and correct understanding. The difference between the Platonic and Christian view of human nature is clearly seen in Table 9.2 which is adapted from George Ladd, *The Pattern of New Testament Truth*, Eerdmans, 1977.

Creation involves a unity of dust (matter) and breath (soul) as described in Genesis 2:7. Also, as we have shown soul can mean person and includes the body (Ps. 16:10 cf. Acts 2:30–31) and the soul can be used of a dead body (Lev. 19:28; 21:1). Also, if humans are not a unity, then murder of a body would not be wrong. But Genesis 9:6 clearly indicates it is wrong because it is an attack on the image of God that includes the body. Paul says in 2 Corinthians 5:1–4 that the soul without a body is naked. This imagery is not possible without a unity. Furthermore, the resurrection is supernatural and makes no sense if we are complete without a body.

Such a view also allows for a knowing intellect since they function as a unit. This is easily seen through psychological interaction since together they constitute one substance. The soul influences the body and vice versa. Upon hearing sad news the emotion of grief affects not only the soul, but also the body when it cries. Likewise pain experienced in the body affects the immaterial soul or mind.

Platonic view of Human Nature	Christian View of Human Nature
Dualistic	Unity
Is a Soul (Soul is complete without body)	Is a Soul/Body (Soul is not complete without body)
Matter is not good	Matter is good
Reincarnation into another body	Resurrection in the same body
Body is prison/tomb	Body is expression of the soul
Body is the enemy of soul	Body is the friend of soul
Soul is simple	Soul is composed
Soul is indestructible	Soul is destructible
Salvation from the body	Salvation in the body
Salvation is by knowledge	Salvation is by faith
Soul is divine	Soul is human
Soul is eternal	Soul had a beginning
Soul preexisted	Soul was created
Earth is an alien place	Earth is a friendly place
Humans have three parts (body, soul, and spirit)	Humans have two dimensions (inner and outer)
Sin results from body burdening soul	Sin results from rebellion of will
Redemption of soul	Redemption of whole person
God is known by fleeing the world	God is known in and through the world
Salvation is by human effort	Salvation is by divine visitation
Reality is in the invisible realm	Reality includes the visible realm

Table 9.2 Platonic vs. Christian View of Human Nature

One objection raised is how can the soul separate from the body, if both are one? However, we have argued that soul/body is a unity, not an identity. This is not the Monistic understanding. The soul is to the body as thought is to words on paper. Words are a physical expression of thought; but thought remains even when the paper perishes. Unity does not entail that they are inseparable.

SUMMARY

The study of human beings (Anthropology) shows that the first human couple was created by God in a perfect state in the image of God. Hence, we resemble God in terms of an intellectual and moral likeness. This image also entails human free will which is still operative after the fall. While God is the efficient cause of the human soul, it is instrumentally generated through the parents. This best accounts for the transmission of sin. It is also in agreement with the understanding of humans as a soul/body unity that constitutes the whole person.

QUESTIONS TO ANSWER

1. What are the three main views regarding the origin of the soul?
2. What biblical verses support the Traducian view of the soul?
3. What is the significance and meaning of humans being made in the "image of God?"
4. What biblical support is there for the presence of human free will after the fall?
5. What biblical support is there for the understanding of the soul/body unity?

6. Read chapter?

10

Sin

*There is none righteous, not even one; there is none who
understands, there is none who seeks for God; all have turned
aside, together they have become useless; there is none who
does good, there is not even one.*
Romans 3:10–12

A LTHOUGH God created the first human couple perfect and set
them in a perfect environment (Chapter 9), they disobeyed the
word of God and fell into sin. Our study of sin (Hamartiology) covers
the origin, the nature and the effects of sin.

THE ORIGIN OF SIN

Because of God's perfect nature (Matt. 5:48), He cannot sin or produce sin (Gen. 1:31). He cannot do evil (Heb. 6:18; Titus 1:2). He
cannot tempt anyone (James 1:13), and He cannot approve of sin
(Hab. 1:13). While God cannot produce or approve of sin, He can
and does permit sin.

PERMISSION OF SIN (BY GOD)

God is the standard of all perfection. Matthew 5:48 says, "Your
heavenly Father is perfect." As we have studied (Chapter 3), a flawless Being cannot act in a flawed way. Genesis 1:31 says, "God saw all
that He had made, and behold, it was very good." God did not create
evil (Gen. 3:1f.; 1 Tim. 3:6). Instead, human and angelic creatures
introduced sin into God's creation and therefore fell into condemnation.

It is also true that God cannot do evil (Heb. 6:18). Titus 1:2 says, "God, who cannot lie, . . ." and God cannot tempt any one to do evil. James 1:13 says, "God cannot be tempted by evil, and He Himself does not tempt any." God also cannot look on sin with approval. Habakkuk 1:13 says, "Your eyes are too pure to approve evil, And You can not look on wickedness with favor."

However, God can permit sin. Permitting sin is not necessarily a sin. The Government permits sin by allowing cars to be driven on the roads. Allowing cars is not evil, even though they can produce evil. God by creating the good of free choice, permitted sin (but freedom is good). Genesis 50:20 says, "As for you, you meant evil against me, but God meant it for good in order to bring about this present result, to preserve many people alive." And Hebrews 12:11 says, "All discipline for the moment seems not to be joyful, but sorrowful; yet to those who have been trained by it, afterwards it yields the peaceful fruit of righteousness." It is also true that God can produce a greater good out of sin. Romans 5:20 says, "Where sin abounded, grace abounded much more" (cf. Rom. 5:3f). Also James 1:2–4 says, "Consider it all joy, my brethren, when you encounter various trials, knowing that the testing of your faith produces endurance. And let endurance have its perfect result, so that you may be perfect and complete, lacking in nothing."

ORIGIN OF SIN (BY CREATURES)

As we have seen, God created only good creatures (Gen. 1:31; 1 Tim. 4:4; Ps. 148:2, 5) and sin began in heaven. Satan and one–third of the angels sinned or rebelled against God (1 Tim. 3:6; 2 Peter 2:4; Jude 6; Rev. 12:3-4). Sin began with the first human couple on earth (Gen. 3). After they sinned their eyes were opened . . . naked . . . covered themselves (Gen. 3:7) and hid from God (8). They blamed each other (12) and the serpent (13). As a result God pronounced a curse on the serpent, the women and Adam. Creation is cursed because of the man's sin: "Cursed is the ground because of you [man]" (17) and death resulted: now he (man) will return to dust (17). The origin of earthly evil is through human free will.

What is the cause of human sin on earth? To properly answer this question, we must take into account the different kinds of causes (Chapter 1). The efficient cause of sin is the person (that *by which* sin came to be). The final cause is pride (that *for which* sin came to be). The formal cause is disobedience (that *of which* sin came to be). The material cause is eating forbidden fruit (that *out of which* sin came to be). The exemplar cause does not exist or is none; since it was the first human sin (that *after which* sin came to be). And the instrumental cause is the human power of free choice (that *through which* sin came to be).

Was Adam determined to sin? There are only three logically possible answers. The first possibility is called Determinism that says all human actions are caused by another (not by one–self). This has two versions, hard and soft. The Hard Determinism says there is no free choice at all. The Soft Determinism posits free choice, but sees it as controlled by God. The second possibility is Indeterminism that says human actions are not caused by anything. The final possibility is Self–determinism that says human free actions are self–caused (caused by one's self). Either Adam's sin was caused by another (determined), uncaused (indetermined), or caused by himself (self–determined). However, it was not determined by God, because God cannot and did not cause Adam to sin. And neither did the tempter (Satan) force him to sin. It also was not Indeterminism, since there is no lack of wholeness in Adam that would give rise to sin (he was perfect–see Chapter 9) and there are no such things as uncaused actions. Therefore, Adam's sin is self–determined, that is, determined by himself. Adam must have caused it himself. Adam was free in the sense that his act was self–determined (Gen. 2:16). His evil choice was not inevitable (Gen. 2:17). He had the power to obey or disobey and he was held responsible, which implies the ability to respond.

THE NATURE OF SIN

What is a moral wrong? There are many names for moral wrong in the Bible. Some of these include *sin* that means "to miss," "to forfeit," or "to lack" (Ps. 51:4), "to miss the mark," "to err," "to sin" (Rom. 3:23). *Trespass* means "to cover up," "to act covertly, treacherously, grievously" (Num. 31:16), "to slip," "to stumble aside," "to offend," or "to sin" (Gal. 6:1). *Iniquity* means "perversity," "fault," "iniquity" (Isa. 53:11), "morally wrong," "unjust," "unrighteous" (James 3:6). *Evil* means "bad," "harmful," "wrong," "calamity" (Isa. 7:15), "evil in effect" (Matt. 7:11), "evil in character" (Rom. 7:21). *Wickedness* means "morally bad" or "ungodly" (Ps. 1:1), (Matt. 23:28; 24:12; Rom. 6:19; 2 Cor. 6:14). *Desire* is also used for evil "strong desire," "passion" or "lust" (Rom. 7:8; Col. 3:5; 1 Thess. 4:5).

There are two basic kinds or categories of sin in the Bible. The first includes sins of commission which is doing what we should not do. First John 3:4 says, "Everyone who sins breaks the law; in fact, sin is lawlessness." The second are sins of omission that is not doing what we should do. James 4:17 says, "Anyone, then, who knows the good he ought to do and doesn't do it, sins." Both kinds of sins, commission and omission, are blame worthiness (Isa. 53:6, cf. Lev. 16:21).

While all sin is offensive to God, not all sins are considered by God to be equal. There are degrees of sin and severity. Jesus said there are "weightier matters of the law" (Matt. 23:23), we have a higher duty in the "first and greatest commandment" (Matt. 22:38) and some are "guilty of a greater sin" (John 19:11). Some sin can even lead to God taking the person's life (1 John 5:16; 1 Cor. 11:29–30). There is also the greatest sin, blasphemy of the Holy Spirit (Matt. 12:32). There are even degrees of eternal punishment for the heaviness or severity of the sins committed (Rev. 20:12).

Sin always has an offender, someone who is offended by the sinner. Proverbs 8:36 says, "But he who sins against me injures himself; All those who hate me love death." Hence, the sinner first offends himself by his own sin. Proverbs 6:32 says, "The one who commits adultery with a woman is lacking sense; He who would destroy himself does it." It is also offence against others and society. First Corinthians 15:33, says "Do not be deceived: 'Bad company corrupts good morals.'"

Humans are so sinful that no comparison exists between them and God (Rom. 3:10–18). Hence, sin is most importantly offence against heaven or the eternal God (Luke 15:18). Sin is unbelief (Rom. 14:23; John 3:18; Heb. 11:6), sin is rebellion (1 Sam. 15:23; Prov. 17:11; Neh. 9:17), sin is transgression (Rom. 5:14; 1 John 3:4; Ps. 51:4), and sin is pride (1 Tim. 3:6; Ezek. 28:17; 1 John 2:16). In short, sin is being the opposite of God (Table 10.1).

God is Holy	Sin is Being Unholy
God is Righteousness	Sin is Unrighteousness
God is Perfect	Sin is Moral Imperfection
God is Love	Sin is Being Unloving
God is Truth	Sin is Being Untruthful

Table 10.1 God Compared to Sin

The process of sin is explicitly identified in James 1:13–15: "Let no one say when he is tempted, 'I am being tempted by God'; for God cannot be tempted by evil, and He Himself does not tempt anyone. But each one is tempted when he is *carried away* and *enticed* by *his own lust*. Then when lust has *conceived*, it gives *birth to sin*; and when *sin is accomplished*, it brings forth *death*" (emphasis added).

Some have argued that God must have created sin, saying that
1) God created everything.
2) Sin is a real thing.
3) Therefore, God created sin.

It would seem we must either reject (1) or (2) in order to deny (3). It is true that God did create everything that is every substance; however sin is not a substance. It is a privation or lack in a good substance. Sin exists only in something good, as a corruption of its goodness. Evil or sin is not a thing or substance; hence God did not create it. Instead, it is a privation, lack or corruption of essentially good things. We must also keep in mind the sovereignty of God and His providence (see Chapter 4). God is the one that is "upholding all things by the word of His power" (Heb. 1:3). God prevents some sins from happening (Gen. 20:6; 31:24; Ps. 19:13; 1 Cor. 11:30; 1 John 5:16) and God permits some sin to fulfill His own plan and good purposes (Ps. 81:12; Isa. 53:10).

Some have objected that God's absolute standard of perfection makes it irrational to demand mortal humans to comply. However, it must be kept in mind that Adam was created with the ability to adhere to the standard and was not tempted on moral matters, but on obedience to God. God cannot lower or diminish His ultimate standard (Heb. 6:18; 2 Tim. 2:13). The ultimate answer to the problem is God's enabling grace. It is impossible for us to please God in our sinful flesh (Isa. 64:6; Titus 3:5; Rom. 7:18; John 15:5). We cannot do it in our own strength, but with His grace it is possible (Phil. 2:13; Phil. 4:13; 1 Cor. 10:13). Ought implies can, and we can only by His grace.

THE EFFECTS OF SIN

The effects of Adam and Eve's sin resulted in three kinds of death for the human race. The first is spiritual death. The moment Adam sinned he experienced spiritual isolation, that is separation from God (Gen. 3:7–8; John 3:3, 5–7). The second is physical death. The moment Adam partook of the forbidden fruit he began to die physically (Gen. 2:16–17; Rom. 5:12–14). The third is eternal death. This is the "second death" or eternal separation from God (Rev. 20:14–15). As a result those who are born only once (physically) will die twice (physically and eternally); however, those who are born twice (physically and spiritually) will die only once (physically). As Jesus says in John 11:26, "Everyone who lives and believes in Me will never die. Do you believe this?"

Effects of Sin on Adam's Descendants

Adam's sin affected his offspring in that all have sinned "through one man" (Rom. 5:12). All of humanity was present and represented in Adam's sin. All were present potentially since every human is derived from the first human in terms of the same human nature passed on according to the Traducian view. All are present seminally (Heb.

7:9–10) since all biologically are fully derived from the first humans. And all are legally (judicially–legal) represented in Adam as the appointed head of the human race.

The transmissional effects of Adam's sin include imputation and inheritance. Imputed sin is that fallenness and depravity were imputed or attributed to his descendants directly and immediately. Inherited sin is the original sin nature that is transmitted indirectly and mediately to everyone generated naturally from Adam. Ephesians 2:1–3 says, "And you were dead in your trespasses and sins, in which you formerly walked according to the course of this world, according to the prince of the power of the air, of the spirit that is now working in the sons of disobedience." Hence we are sinners by nature because we are born in it and because we inevitably do what is natural: we sin.

How is this sin nature transmitted? It is transmitted according to the Traducian view (Chapter 9). The judicial or legal effects of Adam's sin indicate that Adam has the God given power of attorney for the whole human race. As Paul says in Romans 5:18–19: "So then as through one transgression there resulted condemnation to all men, even so through one act of righteousness there resulted justification of life to all men. For as through the one man's disobedience the many were made sinners, even so through the obedience of the One the many will be made righteous." All were not made sinners actually at the moment Adam sinned, since they did not actually exist at the time. However, they were potentially and legally present in Adam, and, as such, received the imputation of the consequences of his sin.

The effects of sin on our relationship with God was immediate spiritual separation from God. This entails our total inability to achieve/obtain the solution to our sin by ourselves. It does not entail the total inability to accept it from God. This resulted in guilt and shame coming from the reality of his failure (Rom. 5) and shame coming from the recognition of the failure (Gen. 3:7). It also resulted in the loss of fellowship. Adam no longer wanted to talk with his Creator, but hid from Him (cf. 1 John 1:6–7).

There are effects of sin on the image of God in humans (Chapter 9). This image of God in humans is effaced but not erased. Sin effaces this image, but does not erase the image of God; it is marred but not eliminated. The fallen state includes the image of God (Gen. 9:6; James 3:9–10).

Sin is extensive, but it is not intensive. Sin is pervasive, extending to every dimension of our being (body, soul, will). But it does not mean humans are as sinful as they could be, apart from Christ we are not as good as we should be. Sin does penetrate and permeates our whole being. No element of human nature is unaffected by inherited evil, even though no aspect is completely destroyed by it. Total depravity taken too far eliminates the ability for one to be depraved. Taken too far one's ability to ever know and choose good over evil is destroyed.

The noetic (relating to the mind) effects of sin on humans entail that depravity brings spiritual darkness and blindness (Rom. 1:28). Second Corinthians 4:4 says, "In whose case the god of this world has blinded the minds of the unbelieving so that they might not see the light of the gospel of the glory of Christ, who is the image of God." John 12:46 says, "I [Jesus] have come as Light into the world, so that everyone who believes in Me will not remain in darkness" (cf. Eph. 5:8; Acts 26:18).

The volitional (relating to the will) entail that humans cannot, unmoved by divine grace, seek God. Romans 3:11 says, "There is none who understands. There is none who seeks for God." Hence, we cannot initiate salvation (John 1:13) and we cannot attain salvation (Rom. 9:16). We are free in things below in social and moral choices and we are free to receive or reject the gift of salvation. John 1:12 says, "But as many as received Him, to them He gave the right to become children of God, even to those who believe in His name." Romans 9:16 says, "So then it does not depend on the man who wills or the man who runs, but on God who has mercy."

The act of faith is prompted and aided by God but He does not perform it or choose for us. First Corinthians 2:4–6 says, "And my message and my preaching were not in persuasive words of wisdom, but in demonstration of the Spirit and of power so that your faith would not rest on the wisdom of men, but on the power of God. Yet we do speak wisdom among those who are mature; a wisdom, however, not of this age nor of the rulers of this age, who are passing away" (cf. 2 Cor. 3:5).

So what does it mean to have a fallen human nature? It means we are born this way (Ps. 51:5; 58:3). It means we are born with the propensity to sin and the necessity to die. It is our nature for us to sin, an inclination; it does not have to be taught. Sin is inevitable, given an opportunity to manifest itself and we are incapable of saving ourselves; because we sin by nature and practice; thus making it impossible to enter God's perfect heaven.

What does it *not* mean to have a fallen human nature? It does not mean that everyone is as sinful as they could be. It does not mean sin is excusable since we are responsible. It does not mean that we are unable to avoid sin since we are accountable (Rom. 14:12; Rev. 20:12). It does not mean that any particular sin is inescapable for believers (1 Cor. 10:13) and unbelievers (Titus 2:11–13). And it does not mean that we have no choice in our salvation.

God not only wants all to be saved (1 Tim. 2:4; 2 Peter 3:9), He provides the ability for all who desire it (Phil. 2:13). Our free choice does not *initiate* (1 John 3:19) and cannot *attain* (John 1:13) the unmerited gift of salvation, but by God's grace (Eph. 2:8–9) our will can receive it (John 1:12; 3:16–18).

THE EXTENT OF SIN (DEPRAVITY)

There are four views of depravity. The first view is that of Pelagius, a British monk (c. 354–c. 420 A.D.). His view was condemned at the Council of Carthage (416–418 A.D.) because he held that human beings are born innocent, just as Adam was created innocent. This view says humans inherit no sin from Adam, so they are able to obey God. The only thing Adam bequeathed to humanity is a bad example. Only our own sins are imputed to us as opposed to ours and Adams. Even physical death is not the result of Adam's sin, we are just created mortal. The image of God in this view is untarnished, and grace is not needed for salvation.

Jacob (James) Arminius (1560–1609) said that imputed sin entails that all are born with a weakened nature since they are potentially or seminally in Adam and bent toward sin. He taught that all are deprived but can by God's grace obey God. Some who follow this view do add grace. The image of God is effaced. Death entails all are spiritual separated from God from birth, which does not entail the loss of the human ability to respond. God's grace does not work irresistibly on all, but only on the elect. It works sufficiently on all awaiting their free cooperation before it becomes saving.

John Calvin (1509–1564) from which Calvinism comes has two forms: strong and moderate. The two views are contrasted in Table 10.2.

Position	Strong (Extreme) Calvinism	Moderate Calvinism
Grace	Operative	Cooperative
Actions	Monergistic	Synergistic
Recipient	Passive object	Active agent
Free act	No	Yes
Resistibility	Irresistible on the unwilling	Irresistible on the willing.

Table 10.2 Strong vs. Moderate Calvinism

The strong view, following Theodore Beza (1519-1605) and the Synod of Dort (1618-1619), was adopted by Reformed theology. It asserts that imputed sin entails that all human beings sinned in Adam (legally or naturally) and inherit a sinful nature. Depravity is total in the sense of extent and intensity. The image of God in humans is for all intents and purposes destroyed. Fallen humans are "dead" in sin (Eph. 2:1). Death entails that all cannot understand or respond to the gospel since they are dead (from birth) in the sense of being unable to respond. And the grace of God must be irresistible grace and regenerate the sinner (even against his will) to be saved. Only the elect have irresistible grace, that involves no choice to understand and believe. It is often understood under the acrostic TULIP: T-otal Depravity; U-nconditional Election; L-imited Atonement; I-rresistable Grace, and P-erseverence of the Saints (that all the regenerate will persevereve to the end and be saved).

The moderate view, which is presented above and in the Chapters on salvation (11-12), sees imputed sin as all human beings sinned in Adam legally or naturally and therefore inherit a sinful nature. Depravity entails that all are depraved totally in extent, but not in intensity. Hence, we can understand and obey by God's saving grace. The image of God is effaced but not erased. Death entails that all are spiritual separated from God (from birth) but does not involve the loss of human reason and free will, although these can be influenced by sin. Guilt can only be overcome by God's saving grace. Grace is not merely sufficient for all; it is efficient for the elect. Irresistible grace is only on the willing, not the unwilling.

In summary, Pelagianism is contrary to orthodoxy since it sees humans as innocent at birth and able to respond to God. Arminianism (or Semi-Pelagianism) sees humans as depraved but able to cooperate with God. Calvinism has two forms: 1) Strong Calvinism sees humans as totally depraved, to the extent that the image of God in humans is destroyed and humans cannot cooperate with God. 2) Moderate Calvinism sees humans as totally depraved with the image of God in humans effaced, and humans can cooperate with God. The views are contrasted in Table 10.3.

Can everyone believe? Salvation is a gift for all men, and all are responsible to believe. By God's grace, they are able to believe. John 3:16-18 says, "For God so loved the world that He gave His only begotten Son, that whoever believes in Him shall not perish, but have eternal life. For God did not send the Son into the world to judge the world, but that the world might be saved through Him. He who believes in Him is not judged; he who does not believe has been judged already, because he has not believed in the name of the only begotten Son of God." But as stated in John 12:37-40, some will not believe:

	Pelagianism	Arminianism	Moderate Calvinism	Strong Calvinism
State at birth	Innocent	Depraved	Total Depraved (extensively)	Totally Depraved (intensively)
Ability	Can obey God	Can cooperate with God	Can cooperate with God	Can't cooperate with God
Guilt	None	Potential	Judicial (and/or actual)	Actual (and/or judicial)
"In Adam" (Rom. 5:12)	Not at all (rather, we sinned like Adam)	Potentially (or seminally)	Legally (and/or naturally)	Naturally (and/or legally)
What is inherited from Adam	Bad example	Propensity to sin; necessity to die.	Propensity to sin; necessity to die.	Necessity to sin; necessity to die
Deaths incurred	Spiritual and eternal	Physical and spiritual	Physical, spiritual, and eternal	Physical, spiritual, and eternal
What is imputed	One's own sin	One's own sin (we ratify Adam's sin)	One's own sin and Adam's sin	One's own sin and Adam's sin.
Spiritual image of God	Retained	Effaced	Effaced	Erased*
Effect of grace	None	Sufficient for all	Irresistible on the willing	Irresistible on the unwilling

*Logical outworking of the view.

Table 10.3 Theological Views on Sin Compared

> But though He had performed so many signs before them, yet they were not believing in Him. This was to fulfill the word of Isaiah the prophet which he spoke: "Lord, who has believed our report? And to whom has the arm of the Lord been revealed?" For this reason they could not believe, for Isaiah said again, "He has blinded their eyes and He hardened their heart, so that they would not see with their eyes and perceive with their heart, and be converted and I heal them.

The context of this passage is hardhearted Jews who witnessed Jesus' miracles and were called upon repeatedly to believe (John 8:24–36). The responsibility is still to believe since God held them responsible for not believing. Their own stubborn unbelief caused their blindness (John 8:24). We also know that the work of Satan shows men can believe (2 Cor. 4:3–4). Faith is not a gift offered only to the elect. As Ephesians 2:8–9 "For by grace you have been saved through faith; and that not of yourselves, it is the gift of God."

Can anyone believe without God's special grace? The answer is no! Faith is possible for the unsaved, but no one can have saving faith without the aid of God's grace. John. 6:44 says, "No one can come to Me unless the Father who sent Me draws him; and I will raise him up on the last day." Gracious action of salvation is not monergistic-or an act of God alone–it is synergistic or an act of God and our free choice. Grace is exercised on an active agent, not a passive object.

SUMMARY

Our study of sin (Hamartiology) shows that God cannot cause sin, but He can permit sin. By Adam's self–determined act of disobedience he plunged the entire human race into sin, such that through Adam sin is imputed and inherited. As a result, humans are born separated spiritually from God and will suffer physical death, and unless born again will suffer eternal death. Such depravity effaced the image of God in man, but did not erase it. Sin is extensive, but not intensive. Everyone can believe and cooperate with God's grace, but not everyone will.

QUESTIONS TO ANSWER

1. What can God do and not do regarding sin?
2. How can humans be held to the perfect standard of God?
3. What are the effects of sin on Adam's descendants?
4. What does it mean and not mean to have a fallen human nature?
5. What are the differences between the different views of depravity?

11

The Salvation of Man ~ Part 1

*But now apart from the Law the righteousness of God has
been manifested, being witnessed by the Law and the
Prophets, even the righteousness of God through faith in Jesus
Christ for all those who believe; for there is no distinction;
for all have sinned and fall short of the glory of God, being
justified as a gift by His grace through the redemption which is
in Christ Jesus.*
Romans 3:21–24

HUMANS, because of their fallen sinful nature (Chapter 10), are
doomed to a death that entails eternal separation from his Holy
Creator. Our only hope of salvation (Soteriology) must be provided
by God through the work of the one and only savior, the Son of God.
Here we study the origin and nature of salvation, followed by the evidence and assurance of salvation. In the next chapter (12) we cover
the extent, results, conditions and contents of salvation.

ORIGIN OF SALVATION

The origin of salvation is in the will of God (Jonah 2:9; 1 Tim. 2:4;
Rom. 9:16). God in electing or predestination (Eph. 1:5) must act according to His nature which is Love (1 John 4:16) and Justice (Gen.
18:25). Hence, the elect are chosen according to the foreknowledge
of God (1 Peter 1:2) and is unconditional from the standpoint of
the Giver (God) but conditional from the standpoint of the receiver
since we must believe in order to be saved (Acts 16:31; Rom. 4:5;
Eph. 2:8–9).

The nature of God's salvation is Grace. Grace and works are mutually exclusive; in other words working for Grace is a contradiction. As Romans 11:6; 4:4–5 says, "But if it is by grace, it is no longer on the basis of works, otherwise grace is no longer grace . . ." "Now to the one who works, his wage is not credited as a favor, but as what is due. But to the one who does not work, but believes in Him who justifies the ungodly, his faith is credited as righteousness." The nature of Grace is the unmerited favor of God in brining or turning man to Himself. The object of Grace is the repentant or willing sinners.

The result of salvation is provided for all. John 3:16 says, "For God so loved the world, . . ." Romans 5:18 says, "condemnation to all men, even so through one act of righteousness there resulted justification of life to all men." Second Corinthians 5:14 says, "that one died for all, therefore all died . . ." (cf. 2 Cor. 5:19; 1 Tim. 2:4; 4:10; Titus 2:11; 1 John 2:2).

SALVIFIC DECREES

Debate exists regarding the origin of salvation and the decrees of God. There are four basic views; *Supralapsarian* is the view that orders the election or predestination of God logically prior to the decree to permit the Fall; *Infralapsarian* is the view that orders the decree of election logically after the decree to permit the Fall. *Sublapsarian* is the view that orders God's provision of salvation before His order to elect. *Wesleyan Infralapsarianism* is the view that orders God's election, after permission of the fall, but based on His foreknowledge and makes it conditional or able to be lost (Table 11.1).

Supralapsarianism	Infralapsarianism	Sublapsarianism	Wesleyanism
(1) Elect some and reprobate others	(1) Create all	(1) Create all	(1) Create all
(2) Create both the elect and non–elect	(2) Permit the Fall	(2) Permit the Fall	(2) Permit the Fall
(3) Permit the Fall	(3) Elect some and pass others by	(3) Provide salvation for all	(3) Provide salvation for all
(4) Provide salvation only for the elect	(4) Provides salvation only for the elect	(4) Elect those who believe and pass by those who do not	(4) Elect based on the foreseen faith of believers
(5) Apply salvation only to the elect	(5) Apply salvation only to the elect	(5) Apply salvation only to believers (who cannot lose it)	(5) Apply salvation only to believers (who can lose it)

Table 11.1 Views on the Decrees of God

However, all the above views implicitly deny the simplicity of God and limit atonement to the elect denying God's omnibenevolence (Chapter 3). Since God is simple, there is no chronology or order in God's decrees. God does not think in a temporal sequence because He is eternal. All His thoughts are simultaneous. Hence, God's decrees are not chronological. Also, there is no logical order. God does not think sequentially or discursively or syllogistically. He knows all things immediately and intuitively, since He is simple, eternal, and immutable in His being. Sequence and order is only proper for temporal beings, and God is not a temporal being.

As a simple Being, God therefore knows all things simply, which is why the Bible speaks of election as being "in accordance with" His will (Eph. 1:5; cf. 1 Peter 1:2) and not based on or independent of other attributes. All of God's attributes, thoughts, and decisions are eternal in accord with one another, and none is logically dependent on or independent of another. If it were, there would be contradictory logical sequences in a God who has no multiplicity, not even in His thoughts.

To be sure there is an operational order. That is, God wills from eternity all things to happen in a certain temporal sequence, such as one thing happening after another. Hence, God willed to create before the Fall, and then to provide salvation after the Fall. This is similar to a Doctor's prescription. The patent is not cured immediately at the moment the cure is issued, but only over time when the medicine has its effect.

Salvation is applied to believers. The Strong Calvinists say: "If it was intended for all, then all would be saved, since God's sovereign intentions must come to pass, and if it was not intended for all, then it was intended only for some and that is the elect." But this is a false dilemma. The atonement was intended to provide (offer) salvation for all, as well as to procure (apply) salvation for those who believe. The Strong Calvinists wrongly assumes: 1) that there is only one intention for the Atonement and 2) that the one purpose of the Atonement was to procure salvation for the elect. This view, limited atonement, leads to a denial that God truly wants all persons to be saved, which of course is contrary to God's omnibenevolence.

The origin of salvation is found in the nature of God. A simple Being who eternally wills good or love for all (omnibenevolence). Likewise the basis for God's will (1 Tim. 2:4) to save sinful humans is found in His omnibenevolence which wills to save all men. However, in His omniscience, God wills this in accordance with His knowledge of human free choices.

Monergism which is the view of Strong Calvinists hold that regeneration or conversion is totally the result of God's operation with no human cooperation. Synergism which is the view of Moderate Calvinists hold that God's action of regeneration or conversion is done in agreement or cooperation with human will.

Monergism is based on irresistible grace on the unwilling which violates God–given human free choice. Such a view is not supported in Scripture. As Jesus said in Matthew 23:37: "Jerusalem, Jerusalem, who kills the prophets and stones those who are sent to her! How often I wanted to gather your children together, the way a hen gathers her chicks under her wings, and you were unwilling." Furthermore, it is not supported by faith alone (*sola fidea*), since it makes faith prior to salvation. It is not supported by omnibenevolence, since God is not all–loving in a redemptive sense (John 3:16). And it is not supported by the fact of free will, since God cannot force anyone to love Him.

Synergism preserves God's sovereignty and human free will without sacrificing either the purpose of salvation or sanctification. Such is also reflected in Scripture (John 1:12, 1 Peter 1:2) and this agrees with God's omnibenevolence (John 3:16).

THEORIES OF THE ATONEMENT (SALVATION)

There are various theories of the atonement. There is some aspect of truth in all of them, but one is superior to the others, namely the substitutionary theory of atonement, because it is able to account for most of the data and it is basic to the other ones.

The atonement theories are as follows: the *Recapitulation* sees Christ's perfect human life that rose from the dead as a victor over the Devil (Rom. 5:15–21). The *Ransom* sees Christ paying the price to God to purchase us from the clutches of Satan (Mark 10:45). The *Moral-Example* sees Christ's death providing an example of faith and obedience (Rom. 5:8; 5:17–19). The *Necessary-Satisfaction* sees it was necessary for God's offended justice to be satisfied by the penalty only Jesus could pay (1 John 2:1). The *Moral-Influence* sees the self–sacrificing love at the cross to have a moral influence on us (Rom. 5:8; 5:17–19). The *Optional-Satisfaction* sees the atonement as necessary (best means), but not absolutely required for God to forgive sinners (Luke 19:10). The *Substitutionary* sees the atonement as a necessary substitution for the sins of all human beings (2 Cor. 5:21; Rom. 3:21–25). The *Government* sees it as necessary to forgiveness and to retain moral structure in the world (Isa. 42:21). The *Mystical* sees it achieving a mysterious spiritual union with Christ (Eph. 4:3–4; 5:30–32).

Theories	God's Attribute	Basic Goal	Object	Key Verses	Proponent
Recapitulation	Omnipotence	Reverse the Fall	Satan	Romans 5:15–21	Irenaeus
Ransom	Wisdom	Defeat Satan	Satan	Mark 10:45	Origen
Moral–Example/ Influence	Love	Show God's love to us	Humanity	Romans 5:8; 5:17–19	Pelagius & Abelard
Necessary Satisfaction	Majesty	Pay the debt of sin	God	1 John 2:1	Anselm
Optional Satisfaction	Mercy	Restore the sinner	Humanity	Luke 19:10	Aquinas
Substitution	Justice	Appease wrath, release mercy	God	2 Corinthians 5:21; Romans 3:21–25	Calvin
Government	Sovereignty	Keep moral order	God and humanity	Isaiah 42:21	Grotius
Mystical	Oneness	Unite us with God	Humanity	Ephesians 4:34; 5:30–32	Schleiermacher

Table 11.2 Theories on the Atonement

All the theories explain some aspects of the atonement, that is true (Table 11.2), but only the substitutionary theory incorporates correct elements of the other theories while emphasizing what is most important.

Nature of Salvation

The nature of salvation is described in terms of pre–salvific acts and salvation because of the substitutionary atonement of Jesus Christ. Pre–salvific descriptions use the word *Election* of believers (2 Tim. 2:10; 1 Peter 1:21). The word *chosen* is used of disciples (Acts 1:2), even Judas (John 6:70), and believers (Eph. 1:11). The word *predestined* indicates who would be saved (Rom. 8:29; Eph. 1:4–5). The word *foreknowledge* is used of those who eternally would be saved (Rom. 8:29; Eph. 1:4–5). Also used is the term *calling* to salvation (Rom. 8:28–30) and *conviction* of sin (John 16:8). The term *prevenient Grace* also concerns a pre–salvation act in time that entails God's unmerited work in the human heart prior to salvation (Titus 2:11; 2 Cor. 8:9).

The word *salvation* is used of physical deliverance (Luke 1:68) and spiritual (Acts 4:12; Rom. 1:16). It is the process by which God, through the work of Christ, delivers sinners from their sin in three stages of justification, sanctification, and glorification. The term *effectual grace* (efficacious) refers to the producing of salvation in the elect that He has foreordained (Phil. 1:6; 2:13). The word *sealing* is a salvific act that guarantees our ultimate salvation (Eph. 1:4, 4:30; Rom. 8:9).

The word *redemption* can be physical deliverance (Heb. 11:35) and spiritual (Rom. 3:24), forgiveness of sin (Eph. 1:7; Col. 1:14) and also being ultimate (Luke 21:28). The word *mediation* (1 Tim. 2:5) in reference to Christ has three aspects: 1) Prophet (Heb. 1:2) as He represents God to man; 2) Priest (Heb. 9:15) since He represents man to God; and 3) King (Ps. 2) since He reigns over man for God. The word *regeneration* (Matt. 19:28; Titus 3:5 cf. Ezek. 37:1–10) is the impartation of spiritual life, by God, to the souls of those who were "dead in trespasses and sins" (Eph. 2:1) and made alive through faith in Jesus Christ (Eph. 2:8). Its source is God that results in Sonship and it is by the Holy Spirit and is therefore eternal in duration (John 1:12–13).

The word *adoption* is spiritually being placed as a child in God's family (Rom. 8:15; Gal. 4:5; Eph. 1:5). The word *reconciliation* is to bring together (Matt. 5:23–24; Rom. 5:11; Heb. 2:7; 2 Cor. 5:18–20). It consists of two sides: the first is the objective or potential to save all given what Christ accomplished for all human kind (v. 19) and the second is subjective, for those who actually become reconciled to God (v. 20). The word *forgiveness* is to remit sins (Acts 13:38). It does not erase the sin in the sense that it did not happen, but it does remove the record of it (Eph. 1:17).

The word *justification* is used of humans (Matt. 1:19) in a practical sense (Matt. 3:15) or positional sense (Rom. 1:17). The justification is to God (Luke 7:29); to Christ (1 Tim. 3:16), as Romans 4:2–5 says, "To declare righteous" (not make righteous). It is done apart from works (Rom. 1:17; 2:20; 4:2–5), done on sinners (Rom. 3:21–23), and it is a judicial act (Rom. 4:4–6; 5:18). Justification is the act of God by which we who are unrighteous in ourselves are declared righteous before God. It is judicial or a forensic act of pronouncing one right in God's sight. The word *propitiation* or expiation is "to satisfy God on behalf of the sinner" (1 John 2:2; 1 John 4:10 cf. Heb. 9:5; Rom. 3:25; Luke 18:13; Heb. 2:17). The word *atonement* means "to cover," "expiation," "wiping away" and it involves forgiveness that looks forward to the cross (John 8:56; Gen. 15:6) and a blood sacrifice (Heb. 9:22).

SUBSTITUTIONARY ATONEMENT

The necessity of a substitutionary atonement is grounded in God's absolute justice that demands a perfect substitute for our sins because they cannot be overlooked. It is seen in total depravity in that it demands a perfect substitute for sins, since we cannot measure up to God's holiness. The Old Testament foresaw this and pictured it in the animal sacrifices which imply a substitutionary atonement when hands were laid on an animal to symbolize the transfer of guilt (Lev. 1:3–4). Isaiah 53:5–6 is explicit about substitutionary atonement:

> But He was pierced through for our transgressions,
> He was crushed for our iniquities;
> The chastening for our well–being fell upon Him,
> And by His scourging we are healed.
> All of us like sheep have gone astray,
> Each of us has turned to his own way;
> But the Lord has caused the iniquity of us all
> To fall on Him.

Jesus was presented as the Passover lamb (John 1:29; 1 Cor. 5:7) and claimed to be the fulfillment of Isaiah 53. He presented His death as a ransom, payment or offering of substitute (Mark 10:45), and presented himself as a consecrated Priest and sacrifice (John 17:19). His death was "for" another which implies substitution (Luke 22:19–20; John 10:15; Rom. 5:8; Gal. 3:13), and His death was "for" an explicit substitution (Matt. 20:28). Expiation is used of Christ's death that implies substitutionary sacrifice (1 John 2:2), and appeasing God's wrath by Christ's death also implies substitutionary death (Rom. 3:25).

THREE STAGES OF SALVATION

There are three stages to salvation: 1) Justification, 2) Sanctification and 3) Glorification.

1) Justification is salvation from the *penalty* of sin. It is an act of God, as Judge, that declares the sinner not guilty (Rom. 8:1). Corruption is present at the center of human beings and depravity extends to every aspect of humanity. Depravity prevents humans from pleasing God, unless enabled by grace. Our corruption extends to every corner and culture of the human race. This does *not* mean that humans are destitute of all natural goodness, since the image of God is effaced, not erased (Ps. 32:1–2; 2 Cor. 5:19), (Chapter 10). Also of historical importance is to note that this understanding of justification, also called forensic justification, was largely lost in Christian history, and regained by the Reformers.

2) Sanctification is salvation from the *power* of sin. It is a continual process by which God is making us righteous through our struggles (Rom. 6) in three areas of victory: the world (1 John 5:4); the flesh (Rom. 7:24–25) and the Devil (James 4:7). Romans chapter six provides the steps to victory; it can be outlined as follows:

I. Knowing we are dead to sin through Christ (v. 6);

II. Reckoning this to be a fact (v. 11);

III. Yielding ourselves to God's righteous demands (v. 13).

3) Glorification is salvation from the *presence* of sin. It is a future act of God that removes or saves us from the presence of sin (Rom. 8:18–23). Thus because sin is abolished and we see God face to face (Rev. 22:4; Matt. 5:8) freedom is perfected in that the ability to sin is removed. When we behold absolute Goodness, we will no longer be able to sin. First John 3:2 says, "Beloved, now we are children of God, and it has not appeared as yet what we will be. We know that when He appears, we will be like Him, because we will see Him just as He is."

JUSTIFICATION	SANCTIFICATION	GLORIFICATION
Penalty of Sin is removed Romans 4–5	Power of Sin is removed Romans 6–7	Presence of Sin is removed Romans 8

Table 11.3 Three Stages of Salvation

Some object that the preceding view of salvation entails universalism, that all will be saved. However, this fails to see there is a difference between *procurement* of salvation for all and *application* to those who believe.

Some object that it was unfair for God to punish Jesus Christ for our sins (John 10:17–18). But Christ is God (Chapter 5); so the One who demanded the penalty (God) was the One who willingly paid it. God's justice demands that all sin be punished, but not necessarily that all sinners be punished for their sin. Furthermore, mercy triumphs justice. God's justice demands punishment of the sinner, but the Cross (His love) wins out. The obligation to what is always wrong, not to punish the guilty, is suspended in view of the higher obligation to what is always right, to save the repentant sinner.

Some object saying righteousness cannot be transferred to another. However, it is possible for it to be imputed legally or judiciously to those who believe because they are united to Christ. We are righteous in Christ, not ourselves (2 Cor. 5:17).

Finally, some object saying the sacrifice of Christ was not necessary, that God could forgive sins without it. However, our ability to forgive is based on Christ's forgiveness. No mortal has the inherent ability to forgive (Mark 2:7). God is absolutely just by nature and cannot overlook sin (Hab. 1:13). He cannot overlook or accept sin since it causes a debt that can no more be overlooked than He can change His nature. And since God made a covenant (Heb. 9:16, 22) that demands the shedding of blood for the forgiveness of sins, then the sacrifice of Christ is necessary for the forgiveness for salvation.

Evidence & Assurance of Salvation

The evidence and assurance of salvation primarily concerns the relationship between faith and works, the terms and views on the assurance of salvation, and the eternal security of the believer.

Faith and Works

All of Christendom agrees that believers need to manifest good works (Matt. 5:16; 2 Cor. 9:8; Eph. 2:10; Phil. 1:6; Col. 1:10; 1 Tim. 2:9–10; 5:99–10; 25; Titus 3:8) but they do not all agree on how they relate to faith.

Works do not flow *automatically* from saving faith as the Strong Calvinist holds. Sanctification is a process involving obedience, which is an act of the will—grace works cooperatively, hence is synergistic (Rom. 6:16). Sanctification is a manifestation of our love for God, and love is not automatic, but a free act. We are rewarded and suffer loss for good works (or failure), which is meaningless if they come automatically (1 Cor. 3:11; Rev. 22:12).

Works do flow *naturally* from saving faith. True believers are "born again" (John 3:3, 7) and will grow naturally. This is illustrated in Scripture in that saving faith is likened to a seed that grows naturally in good soil (Luke 8:11–18; 1 Peter 1:23). It involves trust which leads naturally to good actions toward the one trusted. It involves true repentance that leads naturally to good works. It involves love that leads naturally to good works for the one who is loved. Saving faith is not mere mental, that is, intellectual or mind–based assent, but involves the will. Finally, sanctification is conditioned upon obedience, which leads to righteousness (Rom. 6:16).

Some object that if works are natural, then there is no need for grace or teaching. But this confuses natural with automatic. It is not *automatic*, some *additional* fruit may only come with arduous work, and *teaching* helps produce better fruit (John 15:2).

That works naturally flow from faith also accounts for the fact that true believers can fall into sin. Scripture indicates that it is possible to "backslide" (Jer. 3:14), be "overtaken in any trespass" (Gal. 6:1) and commit "sin" (1 John 1:8–9). Even in the Old Testament David (2 Sam. 11); Lot (2 Peter 2:7) and Noah (Gen. 9) all fell into sin. In the New Testament, John the Baptist had doubts (Luke 7:19); Peter denied the Lord (John 21:15–19); Paul spoke of "carnal" believers (1 Cor. 3:1, 3); and not all will receive rewards in heaven (1 Cor. 3:12–14).

True believers are disciplined when they sin. That salvation is by grace alone (*sola gratia*) is sometimes charged with licentious living. Paul identifies and answers this charge in Romans 6:1–2, "What shall we say then? Are we to continue in sin so that grace may increase? May it never be! How shall we who died to sin still live in it?" Titus 2:11–12 says, "For the grace of God has appeared, bringing salvation to all men, instructing us to deny ungodliness and worldly desires and to live sensibly, righteously and godly in the present age." Believers are disciplined who do not avail themselves of God's grace (Heb. 12:6). There is even a sin that leads to death (1 John 5:16 cf. James 5:20); even abuse of the Lord's Table (1 Cor. 11:30). Sin will affect our judgment before Christ (2 Cor. 5:10; 1 Cor. 3:13–15).

Can believers lose their faith? Continued faith is not a condition of obtaining justification. An act of faith is. There are no conditions on eternal security (Rom. 11:29). Continued faith and fruit is a manifestation of true faith, it is not a condition of it. Continued faith is a natural manifestation of one's true salvation. True faith may be dormant for a time, but eternity is unquestionably secure. Faith is not a work, but true faith continues to work (Luke 8:13, 15). True faith preserves us to the end (1 Peter 1:5; Phil. 1:6). Believers who faltered did not lose eternal hope and no one born of God will continually practice sin (1 John 3:9). Scripture indicates that those who depart from the faith, were not truly within it (1 John 2:19).

True believers are not always faithful. Continuing in faith and continuing in faithfulness are not the same. One can continue to believe in Christ, and manifest a few good works without being a faithful and fruitful Christian. True believers are not always faithful (2 Tim. 2:13). Some in the Bible were unfaithful at times to God's commandments, but not without faith in the God of the commandments. There are no undisputed scriptural examples of anyone known to be saved who completely gave up his faith in God.

Good works are a result of and an evidence of (not condition for) salvation. They are the fruit of salvation, not the root of salvation. Believers should have love for the brethren (1 John 2:3; 3:14, 19, 24; 4:2, 13; 5:2, 13, 18–20), keep God's commandments (1 John 2), and display the fruit of the Spirit (Gal. 5:22–23).

TERMS AND VIEWS ON THE ASSURANCE OF SALVATION

There are four views on the assurance or security of salvation. Moderate Calvinism holds that believers are eternally secure in heaven and can be presently (temporally) sure of it on earth. Strong

Calvinism holds there is security for the elect, but no assurance one is elect until there is perseverance to the end. Hence if so, no one can have true assurance of salvation until death. Classical Arminianism holds that a saved person can lose salvation but only by apostasy, which is a complete denial of Christ. Once salvation is lost it can never be regained. Wesleyanism holds that a saved person can be lost by any serious intentional sin, but salvation can be regained by repentance of sin.

But having true assurance of eternal salvation is *exhorted* in the Bible. Second Corinthians 13:5 says, "Test yourselves to see if you are in the faith; examine yourselves! Or do you not recognize this about yourselves, that Jesus Christ is in you--unless indeed you fail the test?" Jude 21 says, "Keep yourselves in the love of God, waiting anxiously for the mercy of our Lord Jesus Christ to eternal life." Romans 14:4 says, "Who are you to judge the servant of another? To his own master he stands or falls; and he will stand, for the Lord is able to make him stand." And 1 John 5:13 says, "These things I have written to you who believe in the name of the Son of God, so that you may know that you have eternal life." If it is not possible to have such assurance, why is it so strongly exhorted in Scripture for us to have it?

Eternal security is explicitly taught in both the Old and New Testament.

From the Old Testament

> Job 19:25: As for me, *I know that my Redeemer lives,* And at the last He will take His stand on the earth. "Even after my skin is destroyed, Yet from my flesh I shall see God." (emphasis added)

> Ecclesiastes 3:14: I know that *everything God does will remain forever*; there is *nothing to add to it and there is nothing to take from it,* for God has so worked that men should fear Him. (emphasis added)

From the New Testament

> The Gospel of John: 3:18 *He who believes in Him is not judged [condemned]*; he who does not believe has been judged already, because he has not believed in the name of the only begotten Son of God.

> 5:24 Truly, truly, I say to you, he who hears My word, and *believes* Him who sent Me, *has eternal life,* and does not come into judgment, *but has passed* out of death into life.

6:39 This is the will of Him who sent Me, *that of all that He has given Me I lose nothing*, but raise it up on the last day. For this is the *will of My Father*, that everyone who beholds the Son and believes in Him will have eternal life, and I Myself will raise him up on the last day.

17:9–24 I ask on their behalf; I do not ask on behalf of the world, but of those whom You have given Me; for they are Yours; . . . Holy Father, keep them in Your name, the name which You have given Me, that they may be one even as We are. . . . I do not ask on behalf of these alone, *but for those also who will believe in Me* . . . Father, *I desire that they also, whom You have given Me, be with Me where I am, so that they may see My glory* which You have given Me, for You loved Me before the foundation of the world. (emphasis added)

Romans: 4:5–6: But to the one who does not work, but believes in Him who justifies the ungodly, his faith is credited as righteousness, just as David also speaks of the blessing on the man to whom God credits righteousness apart from works.

8:29–30: For *those* whom He foreknew, He also predestined to become conformed to the image of His Son, so that He would be the firstborn among many brethren; and *these* whom He predestined, He also called; and *these* whom He called, He also justified; and *these* whom He justified, He also glorified.

8:33: Who will bring a charge against God's elect? God is the one who justifies;

8:35; 37–39: Who will separate us from the love of Christ? Will tribulation, or distress, or persecution, or famine, or nakedness, or peril, or sword? But in all these things we overwhelmingly conquer through Him who loved us. For I am convinced that neither death, nor life, nor angels, nor principalities, nor things present, nor things to come, nor powers, nor height, nor depth, nor any other created thing, will be able to separate us from the love of God, which is in Christ Jesus our Lord. (emphasis added)

The conditions of having such assurance are stated in First John:
- if we keep His commandments (2:3)
- if we keep His word (2:4)
- if we walk as He did (2:5)
- If we love the brethren (3:14)
- if we love in deed, not only in word (3:19)
- if we have the Holy Spirit within us (3:24)
- if we love one another (4:13)
- if we do not continue in sin (5:18)

Eternal security is supported by Scripture. Jonah declared that "Salvation is of the Lord" (Jonah 2:9) and Paul said "God cannot deny Himself" (2 Tim. 2:13). Election is from Eternity for Eternity (Eph. 1:4; Rev. 13:8; 2 Tim. 1:9) and God has infallible foreknowledge (omniscience). Salvation was completed by Christ (John 17:4; Heb. 10:14) and is an irrevocable gift (Rom. 11:29; Rom. 6:23; Eph. 2:9; 2 Tim. 2:13). Salvation is an unconditional promise (Heb. 6:17–18) and cannot be gained or lost by our good works (Eph. 2:8–9). Bad behavior can no more cause one to lose salvation, than good behavior can cause one to obtain it (Eph. 2:8–9; Titus 3:5). Since it is a free choice to receive, it cannot be relinquished by our free choice. Salvation is an unconditional gift (Rom. 11:29). Hence, it is similar to physical life. God's character guarantees that He will never renege on His promise. Just as some tangible acts of freedom are one–way acts (e.g., suicide), so too is true faith. The fact that it is received by faith does not mean it can be lost by lack of faith. It is not dependent on continual faith; since it is a present possession (John 5:24) and cannot be retracted (Rom. 11:29).

The Arminian and Wesleyan positions present an implicit denial of salvation by grace alone (*sola gratia*). If believers can lose salvation by bad actions, then this is a tacit form of salvation by works. Since it entails that one must do good works to keep his salvation.

While there are some verses that seem at first to be against eternal security, they are all able to be reconciled with it. Either the verse is referring to those who say they are believers but are in fact not; *professing* but not *possessing* believers, or the verse is referring to true believers losing rewards in heaven, not their eternal salvation. For example, Matthew 7:22–23 speaks of professing believers when it says,

> Many will say to Me on that day, 'Lord, Lord, did we not prophesy in Your name, and in Your name cast out demons, and in Your name perform many miracles?' "And then I will declare to them, 'I never knew you; DEPART FROM ME, YOU WHO PRACTICE LAWLESSNESS.'

The following references are examples of verses that concern the danger of true believers losing rewards in heaven: Galatians 5:4; 1 Corinthians 9:27; Hebrews 6:4–6, 10:26–29.

SUMMARY

This part of the study of Salvation (Soteriology) shows it is from the Lord. God provides for our salvation through the substitutionary death of Jesus Christ for the forgiveness of sins. This enables salvation to be procured for all, but is only applied to those who believe. God saves us in accordance with our free will, and good works nat-

justification

urally flow from saving faith. Salvation results in our justified from the penalty of sin, and we can presently have power over sin and we await our future deliverance from the presence of sin. Because salvation is not dependent on us but on God, it is eternally secure and such assurance can be experienced in this life.

QUESTIONS TO ANSWER

1. What are the different views on the order and meaning of the decrees of God concerning salvation?
2. Why can't there be any logical or chronological order to the decrees of God?
3. Why is the substitutionary atonement the best explanation of atonement?
4. What is the relationship between faith and works in salvation?
5. What is entailed in each stage of salvation?
6. How can we have assurance of our salvation?
7. Did you read?

12

The Salvation of Man ~ Part 2

It is done I am the Alpha and the Omega, the beginning and
the end I will give to the one who thirsts from the spring of the
water of life without cost. He who overcomes will inherit these
things, and I will be his God and he will be My son.
Revelation 21:6–7

H AVING studied the origin, nature and assurance of salvation
(Soteriology) in Part 1 (Chapter 11) we now turn to the extent,
results, condition and contents of Salvation.

EXTENT OF SALVATION

Limited atonement asserts that Christ died only for the elect.
Unlimited atonement asserts that Christ died for all humanity. Unlimited atonement finds supported in Scripture in the Old
Testament: Isaiah 53:6 says, "All of us like sheep have gone astray,
Each of us has turned to his own way; But the LORD has caused the
iniquity of us all To fall on Him." The New Testament also affirms the
unlimited nature of the atonement:

> John 1:29: The next day he sees Jesus coming to him and
> says, "Behold, the Lamb of God who takes away *the sin of the*
> *world!* (Emphasis added)

> John 3:16–17: For God so loved the world that He gave His
> only begotten Son, that whoever believes in Him shall not
> perish, but have eternal life. For God did not send the Son

into the world to judge the world, but that the world might be saved through Him.

Romans 5:18–19: So then as through one transgression there resulted condemnation to *all men*, even so through one act of righteousness there resulted justification of life to *all men*. For as through the one man's disobedience *the many* were made sinners, even so through the obedience of the One *the many* will be made righteous. (Emphasis added)

1 Timothy 2:3–4: This is good and acceptable in the sight of God our Savior, who desires all men to be saved and to come to the knowledge of the truth.

Hebrews 2:9: But we do see Him who was made for a little while lower than the angels, namely, Jesus, because of the suffering of death crowned with glory and honor, so that by the grace of God *He might taste death for everyone*. (Emphasis added)

2 Peter 2:1: "But *false prophets* also arose among the people, just as there will also be *false teachers* among you, who will secretly introduce destructive heresies, even denying the *Master who bought them*, bringing swift destruction upon themselves. (Emphasis added)

1 John 2:2: and He Himself is the propitiation for our sins; and not for ours only, but also for those *of the whole world*. (Emphasis added).

The doctrine of limited atonement claims that all for whom Christ died will be saved. However, the above passages and many others reveal, in contrast to limited atonement, that Christ did die for all and not all will be saved. Therefore, it obviously follows that not all for whom Christ died will be saved, and the doctrine of limited atonement is apparently contradictory to the teaching of Scripture.

God is omnibenevolent. Limited atonement claims that God loves only the elect salvifically and double–predestination maintains that He hates the non–elect. If so, this is an implicit denial of God's omnibenevolence which entails a denial of His simplicity, since He is not all of the attributes attributed to Him (Chapter 3). A denial of simplicity is a denial of God's pure actuality (Chapter 1). Hence, such a view is inconsistent and should be rejected.

Some have objected saying there are verses that seem to teach atonement is limited. For example, John 5:21 says, "For just as the Father raises the dead and gives them life, even so the Son also gives life to whom He wishes." And John 6:37 says, "All that the Father gives Me will come to Me, and the one who comes to Me I will certainly not cast out."

However, these passages and others like them that are put forth as teaching limited atonement, make reference to those to whom salvation is *applied*. Invoking the vocabulary of predestination, "chosen us" does not entail that Jesus did not die for everyone. Since we have established the compatibility of God's omniscience and free will (Chapter 3), terms such as "we, our, and us" must be speaking of those whom the atonement is *applied*, not of all those for whom it was *provided*.

Those who adhere to substitutionary atonement but reject limited atonement believe that Christ's sacrifice for sins on all humanity did not automatically save anyone but rather made them savable. It did not release God's saving grace into anyone's life but satisfied or propitiated God on their behalf, awaiting their faith to receive the unconditional gift of salvation made possible by Christ's atoning work. In short, Christ paid the debt for all sins. The money is in the bank on their account. All they have to do is draw on it by faith. And all the elect do.

Universalism teaches that God desires and does save all. This was condemned at the 5th Ecumenical Council of Constantinople in A.D. 553. Such a view is contrary to God's love (omnibenevolence). Love cannot be forced and justice must punish those who do not believe. Hence, it is contrary to the image of God in man, his free will, and the doctrine of hell (Chapter 14). As C. S. Lewis wrote,

> When one says, "All will be saved," my reason retorts, "without their will, or with it?" If I say, "Without their will," I at once perceive a contradiction; how can the supreme voluntary act of self-surrender be involuntary? If I say, "with their will," my reason replies, "How, if they will not give in?" (*Problem of Pain*, 106–77).

RESULTS OF SALVATION

The results of Christ's work of salvation are all–encompassing. It affects not only the saved in a positive way, since they accept its benefits, but also the lost in a negative way, since they reject it. Here we concern our study with the question of salvation related to infants, or those who cannot believe, and the salvation of the heathen, those who never hear to believe.

SALVATION ON INFANTS

Infants are conceived in sin (Ps. 51:5) and are "by nature children of wrath" (Eph. 2:3). The Bible proclaims that faith is a condition for receiving God's gift of salvation (John 3:16–18) and infants cannot believe. Five views have been put forward to answer this difficulty.

1. Baptized Infant View
2. The Elect–Infant View
3. Foreknown–Infant View
4. Evangelized After Death View
5. All–Infant Salvation View

The Baptized Infant view says baptism is efficacious and necessary for their salvation. Roman Catholics, Lutherans, and Anglicans hold this position. However, baptism is a work of "righteousness" (Matt. 3:15), and as is clear from Scripture we are not saved by righteous works (Rom. 4:5), therefore baptism, including infant baptism does not save. Further, this view portrays God as cruel and harsh, but He is actually infinite in mercy, grace, and love. How can a child who is innocent of actual fault be banned from heaven and cast into hell (Ezek. 18:20)?

The Elect–Infant view says that only deceased babies who go to heaven are elect which implies that all non–elect infants go to hell. Some Presbyterian and Strong Calvinist hold this position. This view reasons that since God chose the elect before the foundation of the world, it is reasonable to infer He chose some infants to be saved and not others. However, this denies universally accessible salvation (1 John 2:2; 2 Peter 2:1). If God desires all to be saved (1 Tim. 2:4) and it is possible to save some apart from personal faith, why not elect all of them. This position excludes God's love from some. It does not distinguish the inherited sin nature from personal rebellion against God. And from the practice of ministry dealing with parents who have lost infants, there is no comfort in this.

The Foreknown–Infant view says God foreknows what infants would have believed if they had lived long enough to choose. Some Presbyterian and Strong Calvinist hold this position. Such a position does preserve God's omnibenevolence and avoids the declaration that God saves some apart from their willingness. However, this view usually presents foreknowledge as based on freedom at the compromise of sovereignty. It could be revised to say potential free choice is in accordance with free will (1 Peter 1:2). But how can someone be saved by potential faith? Depending on how that question is answered this view may reduce to another view. This position lacks explicit biblical support and condemns non–foreknown infants to hell who never actually sinned. It could be revised to say all who died

View	Description	Reason/Scripture	Groups/Positions
Baptized Infant	Infant baptism is efficacious and necessary for Salvation.	Baptism (Sacramentalism) is necessary for salvation.	Roman Catholics Greek Orthodox Lutherans Anglicans
The Elect–Infant	Only deceased babies who go to heaven are elect	God regenerates the soul with or without their knowledge/will (Rom. 8:29).	Some Presbyterian/ Strong Calvinist
Foreknown–Infant	God foreknows what infants would have believed if they had lived long enough to choose	Preserves Omnibenevolency of God.	Some Presbyterian/ Strong Calvinist
Evangelized After Death	Infants will mature after death and then be given an opportunity to believe.	Act of faith is necessary for salvation.	Some Roman Catholic Theologians
All–Infant Salvation	God saves all infants because they cannot believe.	Mark 10:14; 2 Sam. 12:23; Ps. 139:13–16; Rom. 5:18–19	Some Strong and Moderate Calvinists

Table 12.1 Views on Infant Salvation

would have believed, but then it becomes the same as the all infant saved view (see below).

The Evangelized After Death view says all infants will mature after death (immediately) and will then be given an opportunity to believe. Some Roman Catholics hold this view. Those that do not believe, if there are any, will be lost. Salvation taking place before death could be normative as opposed to absolute (Matt. 28:18–20). But there are biblical texts that teach there is no hope for salvation beyond the grave (Heb. 9:27; Luke 16:26–31; John 8:24). However, these texts may apply only to those who live to the age of account-ability. Such a view does make the act of faith necessary for salva-tion and preserves unlimited atonement. The difficulty, however, is that there is no explicit biblical support for evangelism after death for those who cannot believe. It also ignores verses that support univer-sal salvation for those that cannot believe.

The All–Infant Salvation view says that God saves all infants be-cause they *cannot* believe. Of course, He does not save those who *will not* believe. Some strong and moderate Calvinists hold this view. This does find support from the fact that inherited depravity, because of Christ, in and of itself is not sufficient for eternal condemnation and that faith in this life is, while normative, not absolutely essential for eternal salvation. Romans 5:18–19 says,

> So then as through one transgression there resulted condemnation to all men, even so through one act of righteousness there resulted justification of life to all men. For as through the one man's disobedience the many [i.e., all] were made sinners, even so through the obedience of the One the many [i.e., all] will be made righteous.

The question is how are *all* somehow "made righteous" by Christ's obedient death? It cannot mean universal salvation or forensic justification that comes with faith (Rom. 1:17; 3:21–26). But it could mean that original sin brought by Adam's choice is canceled by the work of Christ. If so, humans are not hell–bound as the result of inherited depravity. They must commit personal sins to eventuate such a condemnation. Hence, those not yet able to believe could all be saved.

There does seem to be further support in Scripture that all children will be in heaven. Mark 10:14 implies that every little child will be in the Kingdom of God. Second Samuel 12:23, records David affirming that he will see his lost child in heaven (Ps. 16:10–11; Heb. 11:32). Scripture does affirm that there is a point at which the child develops moral awareness (Isa. 7:15; Deut. 1:39; John 9:41). The main criticism of this view is that it may tend some towards universalism and eliminate faith as a salvific condition. Also, it is possible to interpret Romans 5 in other ways.

If faith is not absolutely essential but normatively necessary, then all that cannot believe can be saved. There is a difference between the innocence of infants and conscious rejection of salvation by adults. If faith is absolutely essential, then those that cannot believe may mature after death and make their decision.

SALVATION ON HEATHEN

The question is if God is all–loving, how can He send to an eternal hell people who have never heard the gospel? Most of the world's population, by some estimates, has never heard the gospel. Two responses have been offered to this question.

1. The General Revelation View
2. The Special Revelation View

The general revelation view says what an individual understands and accepts from general revelation is sufficient for eternal life. That is, the heathen are saved by the work of Christ, even though they are not aware of it.

The special revelation view, which is the orthodox position, says that general revelation is sufficient only for condemnation, not for salvation. Salvation is not possible apart from *knowledge of and belief in* the death and resurrection of Christ. There are several biblical passages pointing in this direction (John 3:36, 18, 8:24, 10:1, 9, 11, 14; Acts 4:12; Rom. 10:9; 10:13–14; 1 John 5:10–13).

Are all the heathen lost? Yes, apart from Christ the heathen are lost (Rom. 1:20; 2:12; 5:12). Can the heathen be saved apart from the work of Christ? The biblical answer is no. John 14:6 says, "Jesus said to him, 'I am the way, and the truth, and the life; no one comes to the Father but through Me.'"

Can the heathen be saved apart from accepting Christ? The answer is no. Acts 4:12 says, "And there is salvation in no one else; for there is no other name under heaven that has been given among men by which we must be saved."

Is it just to condemn those who have never heard the gospel? Yes, since they have been given the light of general revelation concerning God's existence (Rom. 1:20) and their moral condition (Rom. 1:18; John 3:19). Furthermore, based on the nature of God and specific Scripture it is reasonable to conclude that He would provide special revelation, if they seek Him through general revelation. Hebrews 11:6 declares that "whoever would draw near to God must believe that he rewards those who seek him." And Acts 10:35 asserts that "in every nation anyone who fears God and does what is right is acceptable to him."

Is there a second chance after death? There is no biblical support for this. Hebrews 9:27 says, "It is appointed for men to die once and after this comes judgment." Upon death people go immediately to their final destiny (Luke 16:19f.; 2 Cor. 5:8; Rev. 20). Such a belief undermines the Great Commission (Matt. 28:18–20). Some cite 1 Peter 3:18–20; 4:6 as evidence of a second chance. However, it does not say He evangelized them, but proclaimed His victorious resurrection, and it was not to all people. Likewise, 1 Peter 4:6 is a reference to those alive in the past that are now dead.

Condition of Salvation

There are five views concerning the condition of Salvation.
1. Roman Catholic View
2. Strong Calvinism View
3. Church of Christ View
4. Lordship Salvation View
5. Free Grace View

Roman Catholic

The Roman Catholic view of the condition of salvation says,

If anyone shall say that the good works of the man justified are in such a way the gift of God that they are not also the good merits of him who is justified, or that the one justified by the good works . . . does not truly merit increase of grace, eternal life, and the attainment of eternal life (if he should die in grace), and also an increase of glory; let him be anathema" (Denzinger, *Sacred Catholic Doctrine*, 809.257, 842.261).

A comprehensive analysis of Roman Catholic doctrine that incorporates church tradition reveals that they do allow for an initial justification that is similar to Protestant forensic justification. However, after that they clearly part, and Roman Catholicism affirms that works are necessary to maintain salvation through progressive and final justification (what Protestants call sanctification and glorification) which Protestants rightly deny.

	Initial Justification	Progressive Justification	Final Justification
Grace Needed	Both Affirm	Both Affirm	Both Affirm
Works Needed	Both Deny	**R.C. Affirm Protestant Deny**	**R.C. Affirm Protestant Deny**

Table 12.2 Roman Catholic and Protestant View of Faith and Works

In response, Church tradition as understood by the Magisterium (the authority and power of the church to teach religious truth) is not on equal footing with Scripture (Chapter 2). Given that, there are clear verses that show salvation is based on faith alone (Eph. 2:8–9; Titus 3:5; Rom. 4:4). Other verses used to support progressive justification (what Protestants call sanctification Matt. 5:12; 25:34; Rom. 2:6–7; 1 Cor. 3:8) show that works are necessary for receiving rewards in heaven, but not for salvation. Roman Catholicism is committing a similar error to that of Galatianism (Gal. 3:2–3, 5). Some in this church were adding Jewish requirements of the law to the Gospel and requiring Christians to adherence to that law in order to be saved. But Paul clearly condemned this saying, "This is the only thing I want to find out from you: did you receive the Spirit by the works of the Law, or by hearing with faith? Are you so foolish? *Having begun by the Spirit, are you now being perfected by the flesh?*" (emphasis added). Hence, we are saved and sanctified by faith alone, but sanctification is naturally accompanied by good works. Only the kind of faith that manifests itself in good works can save us (James 2:24; 2:17 cf. Rom. 2:6–7). Further, Roman Catholicism confuses merited reward (payment) with unmerited reward (gift), salvation is unmerited (Heb. 11:6). It is faith alone that does the sanctifying, even as the faith that sanctifies is accompanied by good works. This is because true faith naturally produces good works.

STRONG CALVINISM

The Strong Calvinism view of the condition of salvation affirms an understanding of humanity that is so totally depraved to the extent that we cannot understand or receive the gospel. Election is unconditional. The atonement is limited to the elect. The grace by which we are regenerated is irresistible which all comes before faith and is itself a gift. As such they are guaranteed to persevere in their salvation. In short: we do not believe in order to be saved; we are saved in order to believe.

In response, total depravity does not entail the inability to respond to God (Chapter 10). Election is in accordance with free will (Chapters 3, 9). The atonement is unlimited (Chapter 11) and justification is not prior to faith (John 1:12; 3:16; 3:18; 3:36; 5:24; 5:40; Acts 13:39; Acts 16:31; Rom. 3:22; 3:26; 4:3; 4:5; 5:1). Faith is not a gift since it is through faith (Eph. 2:8). But even if this point is granted, then "faith" still must be received or rejected by the person. Saving faith and repentance can be exercised by anyone (Luke 13:3; John 3:16; 6:29; 11:40; 12:36; 20:31; Acts 16:31; 17:30; 20:21; Heb. 11:6). Exercising faith is not a meritorious work (Rom. 4:4). The act of receiving a gift is no more meritorious than a beggar receiving a handout (James 1:17). No one can receive the gift of salvation without the aid of grace: salvation is actualized in our lives by our cooperation. C. S. Lewis pointedly asserts, "The Irresistible and the Indisputable are the two weapons which the very nature of [God's] scheme forbids Him to use. Merely to override a human will . . . would be for Him useless. He cannot ravish. He can only woo" (*Screwtape Letters*, 128).

CHURCH OF CHRIST

The Church of Christ view asserts that there are four conditions for salvation: faith, repentance, confession, and water baptism.

In response, faith and repentance are not separate acts. Mark 1:15 and Acts 20:21 say "repent and believe" or "have faith" which are used for clarification as to what is involved, not to represent two separate conditions. Just as I cannot "go there" without "leaving here," so too one cannot have faith without repentance or have repentance without faith. As we have seen, the New Testament teaches that faith alone is the means of salvation (Eph. 2:8–9).

Confession as a condition is taken from Matthew 10:32–33 that says, "Therefore everyone who confesses Me before men, I will also confess him before My Father who is in heaven. But whoever denies Me before men, I will also deny him before My Father who is in heaven." However, "confession" is not a condition to becoming a believer, as those hearing this were already disciples. It is a condition for receiving a reward, and being honored by Christ. The Bible speaks of believers who did not openly confess him (John 19:38); such clearly jeopardizes one's reward, not their salvation. Romans 10:9 says, "That if you confess with your mouth Jesus *as* Lord, and believe in your heart that God raised Him from the dead, you will be saved." This does concern salvation, but the order given is to match the order given in Deuteronomy 30:14. The next verse (Rom. 10:10) conveys the order of belief that starts in the heart (v. 10) and is then manifested in confession. Hence, these are not two separate steps to salvation. Confession before others is a manifestation, not a condition, of salvation.

Baptism in water is not a condition for salvation, but a symbol of our identification with Christ (Chapter 13). As we have shown, salvation is by faith alone (Eph. 2:8–9). John's Gospel says faith is the only condition for receiving eternal life (John 20:31). Jesus called water baptism a work of righteousness (Matt. 3:15), and Paul said water baptism is not part of the gospel (1 Cor. 1:17). Hence, water baptism is a directive to those who are saved, not a condition for being saved (Matt. 28:18–20).

LORDSHIP SALVATION

The Lordship Salvation view claims it is not sufficient to accept Christ as savior only, it is also necessary to accept Him as Lord to be saved? This view understands Lordship as being an explicit condition of Salvation. It says one must accept Christ as Lord meaning master of their lives as well as savior in order to be saved. He must not only be our savior from sin, but there must also be an explicit commitment to Him as Lord of one's life.

In response, this view explicitly makes Lordship, the promise of doing good works, a condition of salvation. But this fails to distinguish what is implicit in faith, namely obedience, with what is explicitly necessary to be saved, namely faith. It also overstates the important connection between faith and works by claiming there is an "inevitable connection" between them. That is, one flows automatically from the other, rather than naturally (Chapter 11). It makes a dichotomy, rather than a distinction between justification and sanctification. Having Strong Calvinistic influence, it makes faithfulness or perseverance to the end a condition of knowing for sure one is saved. And it inconsistently admits a true believer can be a "secret" believer and even "backslidden" for a long time.

FREE GRACE

The Free Grace view makes intellectual assent alone equal to faith as the condition for salvation. It strips away repentance of sin as not part of saving faith, and says saving faith cannot be distinguished from non-saving faith by its fruits or works.

In response, this view fails to acknowledge the difference between faith *that* (which does not save) and faith *in* (which does save); thus it reduces faith to a mere cognitive, not a life-changing decision. It denies the biblical truth that repentance is a condition of salvation. This view denies the natural and vital connection between faith and works by undermining the biblical connection between faith and implicit obedience. It further denies that works are an evidence of saving faith, thus making the unsubstantiated claim that one can totally deny Christ and still be saved.

Lordship Salvation	Free Grace
Faith and Repentance are Necessary	Only Faith is Necessary
Must Accept Christ as Lord and Savior	Only Need to Accept Christ as Savior, not as Lord
Faith Involves Obedience	Faith Does not Involve Obedience
True Faith Brings Change in One's Life	True Faith Does not Necessarily Bring Change in One's Life
Works Flow Inevitably from Saving Faith	Works Do not Flow Inevitably From True Faith
Real Believers Will Never Deny Christ	Real Believers Can Deny Christ

Table 12.3 Lordship Compared to Free Grace

BIBLICAL CONDITION OF SALVATION

The meaning of the term *faith* is to believe *in* something, to be convinced of something, to be dependent on or give credence to something or someone, or to put one's trust in someone. Hence faith and belief (a synonym) implies trust in, commitment to, obedience to, and hope (i.e., confidence) in its object. As applied to faith in Jesus, the implications for saving faith are clear: it is the kind of belief that has trust and confidence in Jesus Christ for salvation and thereby implies a commitment to follow and obey Him.

The meaning of the term *repent* is "to change" one's mind, to feel remorse and to be converted. Saving faith involves repentance. Some biblical texts do refer to repentance of sins after salvation. But some seem clearly directed towards unbelievers (Luke 24:47; Acts 17:30; 20:21). Acts 20:21 says, "I solemnly testifying to both Jews and Greeks of repentance toward God and faith in our Lord Jesus Christ." Hence, faith and repentance are not two acts, but two facets of the same action. Two sides of the same coin or two results of the same act: Just as I cannot "go there" without "leaving here."

Thus, there is more to saving faith than repentance about Christ and obedience to the gospel. It also has an implicit willingness to obey Christ's commands and an implicit willingness to repent of our sin. While no overt obedience and willingness is soteriologically necessary, nonetheless, the very nature of saving faith and true repentance is such that it naturally tends to lead people to become willing and obedient. We are saved by faith alone, but the kind of faith that saves us is not alone; it is the kind that is accompanied by good works.

Saving faith involves several things. It involves trust and receiving Him. Faith and trust are interweaved in the New Testament (John 1:12). It involves commitment: that we fully commit ourselves to Him as the means of delivering us to our destiny (2 Tim. 1:12). It involves obedience to the gospel, and leads to an obedient life. However, there is no evidence that one must express obedience to the lordship of Christ as a condition for receiving salvation or justification (Rom. 15:18). Saving faith involves love (Gal. 5:6; Matt. 22:37; 1 John 3:18–20). Unbelievers "perish because they refused to love the truth and so be saved" (2 Thess. 2:10). Saving faith involves humility: "Truly I say to you, unless you are converted and become like children, you will not enter the kingdom of heaven" (Matt. 18:3–4).

Hence the above view moderates between the extreme views of Lordship and Free Grace (Table 12.4).

Lordship View	Moderate View	Free Grace View
Faith and repentance of Sin are necessary	Faith and repentance about the Savior are necessary	Only faith is necessary, not repentance
Must be willing to obey all Christ's commands	Must be willing to obey Christ's command to believe	Faith itself does not involve obedience
True faith brings change in one's life	True faith brings change in one's life	True faith does not necessarily bring change in one's life.
Works flow inevitable from saving faith	Works flow naturally (not inevitable) from saving faith	Works do not flow inevitable or naturally from saving faith.

Table 12.4 Moderate View Compared to Lordship and Free Grace

Contents of Salvation

The contents of salvation center on some important questions. However, to understand the answers to these questions it is important to know the definitions of the following terms: *absolutely necessary* means there are no exceptions. *Normatively necessary* means there are possible exceptions. *Explicitly* means fully and clearly expressed or demonstrated. *Implicitly* means implied, rather than expressly stated. The questions that need to be answered to appreciate the contents of salvation include the following.

First, what is necessary to be so in order for one to be saved? There seems to be at least eleven truths necessary for salvation, even though there may be more or sub-points to these, they include:

1) Monotheism (one God exists).
2) Trinitarianism (God is three co-equal, eternal persons).
3) Full Deity of Christ.
4) Full Humanity of Christ.
5) Hypostatic Union of Christ's two natures.
6) Virgin Birth of Christ.
7) Sinlessness of Christ.
8) Substitutionary Atonement of Christ.
9) Physical Resurrection of Christ.
10) Physical Ascension of Christ.
11) Present Session of Christ.

Second, there are truths absolutely necessary to believe in all ages to be saved. These are explicitly necessary to believe to be saved in all ages:

1) That God exists (Rom. 1:19–20; Acts 14:15–17).
2) That God is gracious to save all who call on Him (Gen. 4:26; Gen. 15:6; Heb. 11:6; Jonah 3:3; 4:2; Rev. 14:6).

What is implicitly necessary to believe to be saved in all ages?

1) That we are sinful (Rom. 1:18f; 2:12–15).
2) That we cannot save ourselves (we need God's help/grace Eph. 2:8–9).

Third, there are truths normatively necessary for this age to be saved. Namely, what is explicitly necessary normatively to believe for this age to be saved?

1) One God (John 14:1; 1 Tim. 2:5).
2) Jesus is Lord, the Son of God (Acts 16:31).
3) Death and resurrection of Jesus Christ (1 Cor. 15:1–8).

What is implicitly and necessary normatively to believe for this age to be saved?

1) Trinity
2) Virgin Birth
3) Deity of Christ
4) Christ's Atonement for our sins.

Fourth, there are also truths that cannot be denied consistently and one still be saved. That is, one could be ignorant of them, inconsistent with them or not see the logical connection between them and still be saved. But one could not have a clear understanding of these, deny them, and be truly saved. These include:

1) Monotheism (That one God exists).
2) Trinitarianism (That God is in three co-equal eternal persons)
3) Full Deity of Christ.
4) Full Humanity of Christ.
5) Hypostatic Union of Christ's two natures.
6) Virgin Birth of Christ
7) Sinlessness of Christ
8) Substitutionary Atonement of Christ
9) Physical Resurrection of Christ
10) Physical Ascension of Christ
11) Present Session of Christ

Finally, can a heretic be saved? The answer is yes, (1) if he is heretical on non-salvific doctrines (such as inspiration of the Bible or Second Coming); (2) if he believes what is absolutely necessary for salvation in all ages, and (3) if he believes what is normatively necessary to believe in this age to be saved. For example, can one be saved and not believe in the virgin birth? No, if they consistently deny it knowing what it is and its logical connection they cannot be saved. However, if they are inconsistent in the sense of not knowing about it, or if he does know about it but does not see the logical connection of it with salvation, then yes they can be saved. Likewise, can one be saved and deny the Deity of Christ? If they consistently deny it knowing what it is and its logical connection, then they cannot be saved. However, if they are ignorant of the doctrine of Christ's full deity or if he does not deny Christ's full deity (2 Tim. 2:19), then, yes, he can be saved.

Revelation 21:6-8 says,

> Then He said to me, "It is done I am the Alpha and the Omega, the beginning and the end I will give to the one who thirsts from the spring of the water of life without cost. He who overcomes will inherit these things, and I will be his God and he will be My son. But for the cowardly and unbelieving and abominable and murderers and immoral persons and sorcerers and idolaters and all liars, their part will be in the

lake that burns with fire and brimstone, which is the second death

SUMMARY

This part of the study of Salvation (Soteriology) shows the extent of the atonement is not limited, but unlimited. Christ died for all humanity, but salvation is only applied to those who believe. Thus, universalism (which claims all will be saved) clearly violates Scripture and God's love that cannot be forced. The results of salvation have extension to those that cannot believe (infants) and if willing, those that have not heard to believe (heathen). The explicit condition of salvation is faith alone, and works flow naturally from saving faith. The content of salvation involves things that must *be true* for us to be saved and things that must *be believed* in order for us to be saved.

QUESTIONS TO ANSWER

1. What are some biblical verses that indicate that Christ's atonement is unlimited in extent but limited in application?
2. What are some reasons against universalism?
3. What are the different views on infant salvation?
4. What does the special revelation view say and not say regarding the heathen?
5. What are the explicit and implicit conditions of salvation?
6. What must be *true* in order to be saved and what must be *believed* in order to be saved?

7. Did you read?

| 13 |

The Church

*I also say to you that you are Peter, and upon this rock I will
build My church; and the gates of Hades will not
overpower it.*
Matthew 16:18

OUR study of the Church (Ecclesiology) concerns its origin, its
nature of both the universal Church and visible churches, including its government and ordinances.

ORIGIN OF THE CHURCH

The word *church* means "assembly" and is used in the New Testament
to refer to an assembly of believers who have been placed in the spiritual Body of Christ by the Holy Spirit (1 Cor. 12:13) at the moment of
regeneration (Titus 3:3–6) when they placed their faith in the Lord
Jesus Christ as their savior (Acts 16:31).

They meet regularly (Heb. 10:25) for edification (Eph. 4:12),
worship (John 4:24), and practice the ordinances of baptism and
the last supper. The term in the New Testament is never used of a
physical, structure: most early churches met in homes. There is a
scriptural distinction between the universal church which is the invisible body of all believers, and local churches. Contrary to Roman
Catholicism, there is no one visible Church. Local churches are the
only visible manifestations of the universal church (1 Cor. 1:2; Gal.
1:2; Rev. 1:11). Other terms include the church visible or militant,
living on earth, and the Church invisible or at rest, in heaven.

Although the Church is not mentioned in the Old Testament, preparation for it was made through Abraham's spiritual seed (Gen. 12:1–3, cf. Rom. 4:13–16, Gal. 3:7–14), the prediction of a New Covenant (Jer. 31:31–33 cf. Heb. 8:13), and the coming Messiah (Isa. 49:6).

The mystery in the Old Testament is not that Gentiles would be brought into redemption, but *how* Jew and Gentile would unite into one body in Christ known as the Church.

The Church did not exist in the Old Testament. Ephesians 3:1–6 says,

> For this reason I, Paul, the prisoner of Christ Jesus or the sake of you Gentiles—if indeed you have heard of the stewardship of God's grace which was given to me for you; that by revelation there was made known to me the mystery, as I wrote before in brief. By referring to this, when you read you can understand my insight into *the mystery of Christ, which in other generations was not made known to the sons of men,* as it has now been revealed to His holy *apostles and prophets* in the Spirit; *to be specific,* that the Gentiles are fellow heirs and fellow members of the body, and fellow partakers of the promise in Christ Jesus through the gospel. (emphasis added)

Paul says in Colossians 1:26–27: "the mystery which has been hidden from the *past* ages and generations, but has now been manifested to His saints, to whom God willed to make known what is the riches of the glory of this mystery among the Gentiles, which is Christ in you, the hope of glory" (emphasis added).

Christ predicted the Church (Matt. 16:17–18) saying, "I will build My church; and the gates of Hades will not overpower it (v. 18). The foundation only existed after Christ's death and resurrection (Eph. 2:19–20). The Church began at Pentecost. One is placed in the body of Christ only by baptism in the Holy Spirit as 1 Corinthians 12:13 says, "For by one Spirit we were all baptized into one body, whether Jews or Greeks." And Romans 12:5 says, "We, who are many, are one body in Christ, and individually members one of another." John 7:39 says, "But this He spoke of the Spirit, whom those who believed in Him were to receive; for the Spirit was not yet given, because Jesus was not yet glorified." This kind of baptism only started to take place on the Day of Pentecost. Acts 1:5 says, "For John baptized with water, but you will be baptized with the Holy Spirit not many days from now." Pentecost is the only Spirit–activated event that initiated all of these. Later references to the church imply Pentecost was its origin (Acts 2:47, 5:14). Peter speaks of the Spirit's work being the same as the "beginning" (Acts 11:15). The body or church cannot exist without the gifts of the Holy Spirit and these were not in operation until

Christ was lifted on high or ascended (Eph. 4:8) and the Spirit came (Eph. 4:8, 11–12).

Covenant Theology denies that the church began at Pentecost. It asserts that the Church begin with the people of God, the children of Israel. Hence, the Church is "spiritual Israel." In response, as indicated above, the Church was a mystery not known in the Old Testament; it could not exist until Christ died and ascended, and it could not be actual until believers were spirit–baptized into His body. There have always been believers before the church, just as there were before the theocratic nation of Israel. The Kingdom of God is broader than the church. All who are in the church are in the kingdom of God, but not all in the kingdom of God are in the church—again such as Old Testament saints, John the Baptist, and other believers who died before the message of Pentecost came to them. The Spiritual Kingdom would also include those Gentiles from other nations who believed in the God of Israel and the coming Messiah. The Church is part of a broader spiritual community, it is a narrower group made up of all believers since Pentecost who have been baptized by the Spirit into Christ's body (Figure 13.1)

Some (viz., Ultra Dispensationalists) say that the Church did not begin until after the Day of Pentecost either Acts 9 or Acts 28. In response, as shown above the Church (body of Christ) did begin on the Day of Pentecost. The Church is the Body of Christ (Acts 1:22–23). One is placed in this body by baptism of the Holy Spirit (1 Cor.

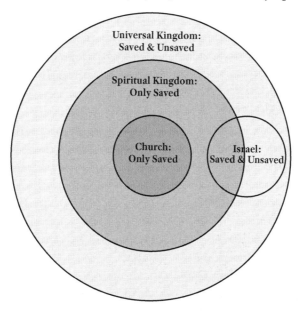

Figure 13.1 Relationship between the Church and Israel

12:13) and this first took place in Acts 1. Therefore, the church began on the Day of Pentecost. Acts 2 includes Gentiles in the Body of Christ (Acts 2:5, 10, 38) and clearly the Church existed before Acts 9. Acts 2:47 says, "Praising God and having favor with all the people. And the Lord was adding to their number day by day those who were being saved" (cf. 5:14). Acts 11:15 speaks of the "beginning" of which the only answer could be the beginning of the Church in Acts 1.

The church was chosen before the foundation of the world (Eph. 1:4). All of God's decisions including the Church are eternal. And Jesus Christ is the foundation of the Church (Rev. 13:8). God knew and ordained not only the church in general but also each person in particular who would be in it. His foreknowledge is infallible, and His providence is specific and minute.

Since God's will or decisions are unchangeable, the Church is assured that it will not be discarded. Hebrews 6:13–15; 17–18 says,

> For when God made the promise to Abraham, since He could swear by no one greater, He swore by Himself, saying, "I will surely bless you and I will surely multiply you." And so, having patiently waited, he obtained the promise . . . In the same way God, desiring even more to show to the heirs of the promise the unchangeableness of His purpose, interposed with an oath, so that by two unchangeable things in which it is impossible for God to lie, we who have taken refuge would have strong encouragement to take hold of the hope set before us.

God not only *cannot* change, it is *impossible* for Him to change. God not only knows all things (omniscience), but knows the best means to an end (omnisapience) in sending His Son to sacrifice His life (omnibenevolence). Hence, the Church is dependent upon God's infinite wisdom to conceal it as a great mystery (Eph. 3:10–11). That is, the omnisapient God conceived a plan in which Satan bit on the bait of Christ's humanity and got caught on the hook of His deity; the serpent struck the heel of the women's Seed, who used that very heel to crush the serpent's head (Gen. 3:15). And in His plan, Israel was permitted blindness, to shine the gospel to the Gentiles (Rom. 11:25).

Nature of the Universal Church

The word *church* occurs about 115 times in the New Testament. Three times it is used in a non–religious sense (Acts 19:32, 39, 41). It is used twice for the assembly of Jews (Acts 7:38; Heb. 2:12). All the rest of occurrences are to the universal Church, local churches, or both. For example, Acts 20:28 uses the term for the universal Church, "Therefore take heed to yourselves and to all the flock, among which the Holy Spirit has made you overseers, to shepherd the church of God . . ." First Corinthians 1:2 uses it for a local church, "To the church of God which is at Corinth . . ." And 1 Corinthians 10:32 uses it for both, "Give no offense either to Jews or to Greeks or to the church of God . . ." Phrases for the church include "body of Christ" (1 Cor. 12:12–27), "bride of Christ" (Eph. 5:24–25), "building of Christ" (Eph. 2:20), "spiritual house" (1 Peter 2:5), "holy priesthood" (1 Peter 2:5), "chosen people" (1 Peter 2:9), and "flock" (John 10).

The universal Church was chosen from eternity (Eph. 1:4); it is invisible (Heb. 12:22–23), it is increasable (Col. 2:19; Eph. 4:15–16), it is indivisible (Eph. 4:3; 1 Cor. 12:13) and invincible (Matt. 16:18; cf. Eph. 3:9–11). The universal Church is doxological, that is, chosen to glorify God (Eph. 1:6, 12; 3:20–21), apostolic being founded (Eph. 2:20) by special "signs of an apostle," on their teaching (Acts 2:42) and in government (Acts 5:1ff).

It is also ethnically neutral (Gal. 3:28), spiritually equal (Col. 1:27; Eph. 3:6) and consists only of regenerate saved members (Matt. 25). It does not contain, as do local churches, wolves (Acts 20:28–29), false brethren (Gal. 2:4) or unbelievers (1 Cor. 14:23; Jude 4).

The universal Church never denotes a visible ecclesiastical union on earth as is with visible *churches* which are multiple self–governing, independent churches (Rom. 16:4). The universal Church is not spiritual Israel but a mystery not known in the Old Testament (Eph. 3:3–6). It is spoken of in the future (Matt. 16:16–18) whose foundation was complete after Christ (Eph. 2:20) and began after the death and resurrection of Christ (Acts 20:28; Eph. 4:8–11). The Church was gifted to operate after Christ ascended (Eph. 4:11–12; 1 Cor. 12:4) on the Day of Pentecost (Acts 11:15).

Universal Church	Local Church
Invisible	Visible
One Church	Many churches
An Organism	An organization
Only saved members	Saved and lost members
Dead and living members	Only living members
Whole Body of Christ	Only part of Body of Christ
Christ is Visible head	Christ is Invisible head
No Elders or Deacons	Elders and Deacons
No ordinances	Two ordinances
No denominations	Many denominations
Indestructible	Destructible

Table 13.1 Universal and Local Church Compared

Nature of the Visible Churches

Contrary to the claim of Roman Catholicism, there is no one visible Church. Of 155 references to the church, about 100 are to local churches. John wrote to seven churches (Rev. 1–3) and all of Paul's letters were to local churches. The authority of a local church is *sola Scriptura,* rather than apostolic succession. Protestants agree that there is no infallible head of the visible church(es). All concur that Christ (the Word) is the invisible Head of the visible church and that the visible church's only infallible authority is Holy Scripture (the Word).

The Protestant principle of *Sola Scripture* (the Bible alone) does not mean the Bible is the only source of truth. Paul acknowledges truth outside the Scriptures in General Revelation (Romans 1, 2). *Sola Scripture* entails that the Bible is the only *written* source of *infallible* truth from God. Further, *Sola Scripture* does not claim that everything in Scripture is clear. It only affirms that Scripture's central teachings are clear: "the main things are the plain things, and the plain things are the main things." The main things are things stated in simple, easy to understand language. For example, 1 John 5:12 says, "He who has the Son has the life; he who does not have the Son of God does not have the life." And John 14:6 records "Jesus said to him, 'I am the way, and the truth, and the life; no one comes to the Father but through Me.'"

There is no apostolic succession. The Apostles lived only in the first century. They were needed for the foundation of the church (Eph. 2:20). The special gifts of an Apostle (2 Cor. 12:12) ceased in the first century (Chapter 6). Jesus gave kingdom authority to His Apostles (Matt. 16:19), not their successors, and the Apostles never appointed Apostles to succeed them. This is evident in the claim by some second century writings that claimed apostolic authorship to gain acceptance (Chapter 2).

This kind of autonomy preserves Christ as the invisible head of the Church. It also helps the Church to be less vulnerable to doctrinal and moral corruption. It allows for accountability with local deacons and elders. It further allows for the exercise of discipline and gives the congregation a vital voice.

The purposes of the local church are at least five. (1) They are to glorify God, Ephesians 3:21 says, "To Him be the glory in the church and in Christ Jesus to all generations forever and ever. Amen." (2) They are a visible manifestation of the universal Church. Ephesians 4:3–6 says, "Being diligent to preserve the unity of the Spirit in the bond of peace. There is one body and one Spirit. . ." (3) They are to edify the Body of Christ. Ephesians 4:14–15 says, "But speaking the truth in love, we are to grow up in all aspects into Him who is the head, even Christ." (4) They are to do evangelism and discipleship. The Great Commission, Matthew 28:18-20 says, "Go therefore and make disciples of all the nations, baptizing them." (5) They are to exhibit wisdom and the grace of God. Ephesians 3:9-11 says, "so that the manifold wisdom of God might now be made known through the church."

The destiny of the Church is to be completed (Acts 15:13-16), then raptured (1 Thess. 4:16-18) and then be part of the marriage supper of the Lamb where she (the universal Church) will be united with the Bridegroom (Christ) forevermore (Chapter 15).

GOVERNMENT OF THE VISIBLE CHURCHES

The names of the three views of local church government are derived from the biblical terms for *bishop, elder,* and *church*. 1) Episcopal (bishop) sees the final authority with a bishop over local elder/congregational rule. Roman Catholics, Eastern Orthodox, some Lutheran, Anglican, Episcopal, and Methodist follow this view. 2) Presbyterian (elder) sees final authority with a board of elders. Presbyterian, Reformed churches, Plymouth Brethren, some Baptist and independent churches follow this view. 3) Congregational (church-assembly) sees the final authority with the congregation. Baptist and independent churches follow this view.

All of the New Testament is *for* us, but not all of it was written *to* us. Hence, in interpretation it is important to distinguish at times what is descriptive, the way the Church was in its founding (Acts), and what is prescriptive (Epistles) for the Church today.

The founding of the Church established a new way of God dealing with humans, and this involved God doing special things that are not normative for all of God's people after that period. For example today, Scripture from the Apostles and prophets is the rule now for the Church, as opposed to living Apostles and prophets as it was in the first century; Apostles and prophets (Eph. 2:20; 2 Thess. 2:2) were the foundation for the universal Church. Their gifts ensured the revelation of the New Testament. Also, pastors, elders, and evangelists are gifts to the local churches (Eph. 4:10-11; 1 Cor. 12:4-11, 27, 28; Rom. 12:3-8), while elders and deacons (1 Tim. 3:1-12; Titus 1:5-9) are the only two offices recognized in the New Testament. The church can determine who the officers are, but they cannot determine who receives what gift, that is the role of the Holy Spirit (Chapter 6). Paul sets out the overall principle of government in 1 Corinthians 14:40, "But all things must be done properly and in an orderly manner." This was given in the context of a church with multiple problems such as people speaking at the same time (v. 27), out of place (vv. 28, 34), and abusing gifts (v. 19). The need for such order was expressed in the context of orderly elections (Acts 6:1–6), keeping rolls of membership (Acts 1:15; 2:41; 4:4), keeping track of those that need to receive help (1 Tim. 5:9), setting rules for orderly procedures (1 Cor. 11:1–34; 14:1–40) and keeping track of finances (1 Cor. 16:2).

ELDERS & DEACONS

The term *elders* (Hebrew) is used interchangeable with *bishop* (Greek). They were appointed by Apostles to oversee doctrinal and spiritual matters (Acts 6:2–4) in every church (Acts 14:23 cf. Phil. 1:1), town (Titus 1:5) and local church (Acts 14:23; Phil. 1:1) as a position of authority (Acts 25:15). The function of Elders are to be overseer (1 Peter 2:25), teacher (1 Tim. 3:2; 1 Tim. 2:24), apologist (Phil. 1:17; Titus 1:9), arbiter of disputes (Acts 15; 1 Cor. 6:1–4), and watchman of souls (Heb. 13:17; Gal. 6:1). The gender of an Elder is male since they must be "a husband" (1 Tim. 3:2; 2:11–15). Women differ only in function with respect to men. Women are not naturally inferior to men, any more than Jesus is naturally inferior to God the Father (1 Cor. 11:3; 15:28) because He was submissive to Him. In the New Testament they are equal in redemptive status (Gal. 3:28), equal in spiritual gifting (Acts 21:29; 18:26), but different in function (1 Tim. 2:15).

Should every church have Elders? Paul exhorts Titus to appoint elders (plural) in every city (1:5). The church at Philippi had a plurality of elders (1:1) and every church had a plurality of elders (Acts 14:23).

How should Elders be treated? Elders should not be rebuked, only entreated (1 Tim. 5:1–2), they should be honored (1 Tim. 5:17), not unfairly accused (1 Tim. 5:19), receive submission (1 Peter 5:1, 5), be obeyed (Heb. 13:17), be prayed for (Heb. 13:18), be remembered (Heb. 13:7), greeted (Rom. 13:7, 24), and be called for when prayer is needed (James 5:14).

The origin of Deacons (Acts 6:1–6) shows they are subordinate to Elders, and their duties and their concern is for physical and social matters (1 Tim. 5:9). Paul sets the qualifications (1 Tim. 3:8–13) as men worthy of respect, sincere, not indulging in much wine, hold deep truths of the faith, tested, have a wife worthy of respect, not malicious talkers, temperate, trustworthy, husband of one wife, and manage his children and household well.

There are important distinctions between Apostles, Elders, Deacons and the Congregation. Deacons are subordinate to the

Elders (Acts 6:1–6). Elders are over doctrinal and spiritual matters (Acts 6:2–4) while deacons are over the physical and social matters (1 Tim. 5:9). Deacons, compared to elders, could be younger in the faith, not as apt to teach or refute others (1 Tim. 3:2, 6; 1:10). All Apostles by gift were elders by office. But not all elders (office) were Apostles that had the gift (2 John 1:1; 1 Peter 5:1). This is because the role of an Apostle was temporary and they had final authority in the Church. Being an elder is an office, not a spiritual gift, as is a pastor (Eph. 4:8, 11) for example.

The congregation screened its own membership. Unbelievers are not prescribed as part of the church but are described as having "crept in" (Jude 4). The congregation is responsible for choosing their leaders (Acts 6:2–6), exercising church discipline (1 Cor. 5:1–5), making final decisions in cases of offense (Matt. 18:15–17), commissioning missionaries (Acts 13:2), and involved in doctrinal decisions (Acts 2:42; Eph. 2:20; 2 Thess. 3:6; Acts 15:2–6).

As set out in the New Testament, each local church has autonomy. They judge their own members (1 Cor. 5:13) and if needed, the local church performs excommunication. They elect or choose their own officers (Acts 6:1–6), they have authority to guard and observe the ordinances (1 Cor. 11:23). They settle their own internal difficulties (1 Cor. 6:1–5). They have authority in their relations of different local churches (Acts 15:1–2). They have final authority for its own affairs (Matt. 18:17). They have the "say so" in the voluntary cooperation and fellowship with other churches which is possible and desirable (Rom. 15:26; Gal. 2:10); as well as prayer for other churches (1 Thess. 5:25; 2 Thess. 3:1).

Women are equal to men by nature (Gen. 1:27), by redemption (Gal. 3:28), and spiritual gifts (1 Cor. 12:4ff.). Women are functionally superior to men in that they bear children (1 Tim. 2:15). Women should not usurp authority over men in the church (1 Cor. 11:3; 1 Tim. 2:11). Women should not function as elders (or bishops) and none were a part of the Twelve Apostle (who were elders by office and apostles by gift). Elders are to be the "husband of one wife" (1 Tim. 3:2) and Elder is a position of authority, which they are not to exercise over a man in the church (1 Tim. 2:12–14). The reason for this is not cultural, but the order of creation and the fall. Were there women deaconesses? The term "deaconesses" was used of Phoebe (Rom. 16:1) and deacon wives are described (1 Tim. 3:11). However, there is no mention of them being part of a group of deacons, and cannot be reconciled with the qualifications of being a "husband of one wife" (1 Tim. 3:2).

God in His omnisapience knew His local churches would consist of finite, fallible and depraved people. Hence, human depravity calls for the existence of independent, self–governing churches. Such churches are better able to operate and control things when they go wrong (3 John 9), such as false teaching or immorality. Self–rule with spiritual overseer and congregational check tends to create better checks and balances.

ORDINANCES OF THE VISIBLE CHURCHES

The term *sacrament* is used to express a *cause* of grace, as Roman Catholic and Greek Orthodox hold. Others understand sacrament to be a *means* of grace, as Anglicans and Lutherans believe. The term *ordinance* is used to express a *symbol* of grace as in Baptist and other congregational churches.

The sacraments of the Roman Catholic and Eastern Orthodox Churches are seven: Baptism, Confirmation, Eucharist, Penance, Extreme unction, Holy Order, and Matrimony. Despite claims found in Roman Catholicism of condemnation on all who deny them, there is no basis for all seven sacraments in the Bible, the early church Fathers, or even the early church councils. As for a means of grace, reading the word of God serves well (Ps. 119:9, 11; Rom. 10:17; Rev. 1:3).

The ordinances of Protestantism are two: Baptism, Matthew 28:18–20 says,

> All authority has been given to Me in heaven and on earth. Go therefore and make disciples of all the nations, baptizing them in the name of the Father and the Son and the Holy Spirit, teaching them to observe all that I commanded you; and lo, I am with you always, even to the end of the age.

And the Lord's Supper or Communion, Luke 22:19–20 says,

> And when He had taken *some* bread *and* given thanks, He broke it and gave it to them, saying, "This is My body which is given for you; do this in remembrance of Me." And in the same way *He took* the cup after they had eaten, saying, "This cup which is poured out for you is the new covenant in My blood.

BAPTISM

There are no difference among Christians on the command to be baptized (Matt. 28:18–20), but there are differences over the *candidate*: believers or infants, over the *mode*: effusion (sprinkling or pouring) or immersion, and over *efficacy*: this concerns regeneration as found in Eastern Orthodox, Lutheran and Anglicans, or a symbol of identification as is found with Presbyterian, Methodist and Baptist.

Who should be baptized? The difference is over candidate for baptism: Pedobaptists, which means child–baptizers argue for infant baptism, and Anabaptists or rebaptizers argue for believer's baptism. Pedobaptists argue that New Testament water baptism replaces circumcision. Colossians 2:11–12 says,

> In Him you were also circumcised with a circumcision made without hands, in the removal of the body of the flesh by the circumcision of Christ; having been buried with Him in baptism, in which you were also raised up with Him through faith in the working of God, who raised Him from the dead.

They also point to whole households that were baptized (Acts 16:15, 38; 18:8; 1 Cor. 1:16). In response to the Pedobaptist (child–baptizers) position, the text (Col. 2:11–12) says nothing about baptizing infants. Since only males were circumcised in the Old Testament this is a weak analogy and an inconsistent comparison to baptism. Even this texts mentions "faith" as the means of being saved and infants cannot have faith.

There are four times (Acts 16:15, 38; 18:8; 1 Cor. 1:16) households are mentioned as being converted, but there is no evidence in these texts that any infants were baptized. In fact, whole households "believed." In 1 Corinthians 1:16 the household of Stephanas it says they were old enough to serve (1 Cor. 16:15). In Acts 16:31they said, "Believe in the Lord Jesus, and you will be saved, you and your household." In Romans 6:4 it says, "Therefore we have been buried with Him through baptism into death, so that as Christ was raised from the dead through the glory of the Father, so we too might walk in newness of life." It should be noted that there are no prohibitions of infant baptism, but also there is no Scriptural support that this is who or how Christ ordered believers to be baptized.

Anabaptists (rebaptizers) and modern Baptists argue only adults or children old enough to believe independently should be baptized. Every instance of New Testament baptism is someone old enough to believe (Matt. 3; John 3; Acts 2, 8, 10, 19). Belief is a condition for baptism and infants cannot believe (Rom. 6:23; 14:12). Acts 16:31 says "Believe in the Lord Jesus, and you will be saved, you and your household." Baptism is an outward symbol of the inner reality. Romans 6:4 says, "Therefore we have been buried with Him through baptism into death, so that as Christ was raised from the dead through the glory of the Father, so we too might walk in newness of life." Hence, it follows that only those who *can* believe should receive baptism.

What is the mode of baptism? The difference of mode of baptism concerns effusion or immersion. While pouring and sprinkling are symbols, they are never used for water baptism in the New Testament (Acts 2:4, 17; Heb. 12:24). Death and resurrection are the heart of the gospel, and are best symbolized by immersion. Jesus was baptized by immersion (Matt. 3:16). John baptized where there was "much water" (John 3:23) and the Eunuch was baptized by immersion. Acts 8:36–39, says

> "Look! Water! What prevents me from being baptized?" And Philip said, "If you believe with all your heart, you may." And he answered and said, "I believe that Jesus Christ is the Son of God." And he ordered the chariot to stop; and they both went down *into the water*, Philip as well as the eunuch, and he baptized him. When they came *up out of the water* . . . (emphasis added)

Paul taught that baptism is depicted as burial (Rom. 6:3–5). The earliest roots of Christendom do show that tanks were used for baptism. Immersionists or Baptists do allow for other modes when health or other reasons prevent immersion. But exceptions should not become the regular practice.

THE LORD'S SUPPER

Four views have developed over Jesus saying "This is my body . . . my blood" (Luke 22:19–20). The Roman Catholic view is called Transubstantiation or physically and says the bread and wine are transformed into the literal body and blood of Jesus Christ under the administration of a Roman Catholic priest. Hence, for them this is a cause of grace and an unbloody re–enactment of the sacrifice of Christ on the cross or Mass. The Eastern Orthodox view agrees at consecration it actually or "really" becomes the body and blood of Christ, yet they never explain "how."

The Lutheran view is called Consubstantiation (although Luther did not use this term). This says at consummation the actual body of Christ is "in, with, and under" the elements. Such as fire penetrating metal. This view rejects the Roman Catholic Mass as a sacrifice, but believes Christ is present in the sense that He penetrates and permeates the bread and wine.

The Reformed view is called Spiritually Presence. John Calvin taught that the bread and wine contain the body and blood of Christ spiritually.

The Swiss Protestant reformer Zwingli (1484–1531) and the Baptist view is Memorial or symbolically presence. That is, the communion is primarily a commemoration of Christ's death on the cross.

Since Christ was there bodily at the last supper, this view reasons it is absurd to take the elements He held in His hands as His actual physical body. Hence, Christ must have been speaking, as He often did, in metaphors.

In response to the Transubstantiation and Really view, since Jesus was there bodily, it is absurd to take the elements He held in His hands as His physical body. Since Jesus often used and taught with metaphors, such as when He said, "I am the door." Therefore it is not necessary to take the phrase literally or physically. And if one does, then Christ was holding His own body in His own hands which is contradictory. Also, it is idolatrous since Catholics worship the host which, if any non–literal/physical view is correct, is not God. Furthermore, this view undermines the reliability of the senses, since we are told not to trust them at communion, but trust them when seeing Jesus' resurrected body. It is also contradictory in another sense, since His bodily (corporeal) form must be in two different places at the same time, holding body and blood.

In response to the spiritual view it also is unnecessary since in Jesus' divine nature He is already everywhere spiritually (omnipresence), and in His human nature He is in heaven until He comes (1 Cor. 11:26). Given that Paul's account in 1 Corinthians 11 says nothing about Christ's presence in the elements, it is best to emphasize a remembrance and proclamation of the Lord's death.

Hence, the event is essentially memorial and proclamation and not a means of grace. As Paul says in 1 Corinthians 11:24–26:

> He broke it and said, "This is My body, which is for you; do this in remembrance of Me." In the same way He took the cup also after supper, saying, "This cup is the new covenant in My blood; do this, as often as you drink it, in remembrance of Me." For as often as you eat this bread and drink the cup, you proclaim the Lord's death until He comes.

Finally, nothing is automatic about the ordinance's effect; instead the results are dependent upon the condition of the participants. As Paul continues (v. 27–30),

> Therefore whoever eats the bread or drinks the cup of the Lord in an unworthy manner, shall be guilty of the body and the blood of the Lord. But a man must examine himself, and in so doing he is to eat of the bread and drink of the cup. For he who eats and drinks, eats and drinks judgment to himself if he does not judge the body rightly. For this reason many among you are weak and sick, and a number sleep.

SUMMARY

Our study of the church (Ecclesiology) shows it was a mystery in the Old Testament, but revealed in the New Testament as the means in which the gospel would be taken to the Gentiles. Christ predicted the Church, and the Apostles were its foundation, made up of all believers since Pentecost. Universally it is invisible, consisting of only saved, living and dead believers constituting the body of Christ. It is manifested locally in churches. The New Testament shows that the churches are autonomously consisting of the Congregation, Elders and Deacons with different requirements and responsibilities. The two ordinances of the Church issued by Christ himself are baptism and the Lord's Supper.

QUESTIONS TO ANSWER

1. What is the difference between the universal and visible (local) churches?
2. What are five purposes of the church stated in Scripture?
3. How do the three main forms of church government differ?
4. What are the different views of baptism?
5. What are the different views of the Lord's Supper or communion?

6. Did you read?

14

Last Things ~ Part 1

The LORD Jesus will be revealed from heaven with His mighty angels in flaming fire, dealing out retribution to those who do not know God and to those who do not obey the gospel of our LORD Jesus.
These will pay the penalty of eternal destruction, away from the presence of the LORD and from the glory of His power, when He comes to be glorified in His saints on that day, and to be marveled at among all who have believed.
2 Thessalonians 1:6–10

OUR study finally turns to the Last Things (Eschatology). In Part 1, we cover the final state of the saved (heaven) and the final state of the lost (hell). In Part 2 (Chapter 15) we cover the Second Coming and Millennium as well as the Tribulation and Rapture.

FINAL STATE OF THE SAVED (HEAVEN)

The term *heaven* is used in three ways in Scripture: It is used of earth's atmosphere (Matt. 6:26), the stars or space (Matt. 24:29) and the abode of God, the "third heaven" or "paradise" (2 Cor. 12:2, 4). Biblically *heaven* is used in the present to describe the intermediate blissful state of departed sprits that have yet to be resurrected or re-united with their glorified bodies (2 Cor. 5:7; 1 Thess. 4:16–17). The term *heaven* is also used for the future eternal state, that is, the New Heaven and New Earth (Rev. 21:1).

HEAVEN: INTERMEDIATE STATE

What is the nature of death? Death is the moment the soul leaves the body (Gen. 35:18; James 2:26). The soul survives death in a disembodied state (Gen. 25:8). The body returns to dust, but the soul is gathered to other spirits in heaven. This is described as a place of peace. Jesus called "Abraham's bosom" (Luke 16:22) which is a place of conscious bliss. The phrase consistently used in the Old Testament is "gathered to" implies a get–together of spirits. "When Jacob had finished giving instructions to his sons, he drew his feet up into the bed, breathed his last and was gathered to his people" (Gen. 49:33). Job 19:25–26 says, "As for me, I know that my Redeemer lives, and at the last He will take His stand on the earth. Even after my skin is destroyed, yet from my flesh I shall see God."

For departed spirits, the Bible never shows any hint of nonexistence or unconsciousness between death and resurrection.

Jesus teaches in Luke 16:22–24,

> Now the poor man died and was carried away by the angels to Abraham's bosom; and the rich man also died and was buried. In Hades he lifted up his eyes, being in torment, and saw Abraham far away and Lazarus in his bosom. And he cried out and said, 'Father Abraham, have mercy on me, and send Lazarus so that he may dip the tip of his finger in water and cool off my tongue, for I am in agony in this flame.'

In Luke 23:43 Jesus said to the thief on the cross next to him, "Truly I say to you, today you shall be with Me in Paradise."

Stephen during his stoning said in Acts 7:56, 59, "Behold, I see the heavens opened up and the Son of Man standing at the right hand of God. . . . They went on stoning Stephen as he called on the Lord and said, 'Lord Jesus, receive my spirit!'"

Paul asserts in 1 Corinthians 5:5, "I have decided to deliver such a one to Satan for the destruction of his flesh, so that his spirit may be saved in the day of the Lord Jesus." And in Philippians 1:21, 23–24 "For to me, to live is Christ and to die is gain. But I am hard–pressed from both directions, having the desire to depart and be with Christ, for that is very much better; yet to remain on in the flesh is more necessary for your sake."

The author of Hebrews (12:22–23) says, "But you have come to Mount Zion and to the city of the living God, the heavenly Jerusalem, and to myriads of angels, to the general assembly and church of the firstborn who are enrolled in heaven, and to God, the Judge of all, and to the spirits of the righteous made perfect."

Some say *sheol*, which is the Old Testament word sometimes used to describe the place of departed spirits, had a compartment where Old Testament saints went before Christ died on the cross. And after His resurrection Christ took them to heaven at His ascension. In response, the New Testament shows no basis for such a view. Jesus' teaching in Luke 16 has a gulf between heaven and hell, not two sections of *sheol*. Ephesians 4:8–6 cited in support of this view, is not about taking Old Testament saints to heaven, but about taking evil forces captive by His death/resurrection (Ps. 68). Christ's announcement in 1 Peter 3:19 is about His victory to the fallen spirit world or angels, not Old Testament saints. Paul teaches that Jesus Christ is the first to go to heaven with His glorified body (1 Cor. 15:22) and it is in His glorified presence that saints during the Old and New Testament times together await the resurrection of their bodies (Heb. 12:23; 1 Thess. 4:13–17).

A spirit in the intermediate state is still an incomplete human being. Paul uses the term "naked" (2 Cor. 5:1–4) to describe it. The human person to be completed must be reunited with a glorified resurrected body. This follows since the image of God includes the body and matter is "good" (Gen. 1:3), (Chapter 9). Both the Old and New Testament teach that there will be two resurrections one of the saved (the just) and of the unsaved (the unjust).

Daniel 12:2 says, "Many of those who sleep in the dust of the ground will awake, [1] these to everlasting life, but the [2] others to disgrace and everlasting contempt" (emphasis added).

Jesus' teaching in John 5:28–29: "Do not marvel at this; for an hour is coming, in which all who are in the tombs will hear His voice, and will come forth; [1] those who did the good deeds to a resurrection of life, [2] those who committed the evil deeds to a resurrection of judgment" (emphasis added) (see also Paul in 1 Cor. 15:21–26).

Revelation 20:4–6 says,

> Then I saw thrones, and they sat on them, and judgment was given to them. And I *saw* the souls of those who had been beheaded because of their testimony of Jesus and because of the word of God, and those who had not worshiped the beast or his image, and had not received the mark on their forehead and on their hand; *and they came to life and reigned with Christ for a thousand years. The rest of the dead did not come to life until the thousand years were completed. This is the first resurrection.* Blessed and holy is the one who has a part in the first resurrection; over these the second death has no power, but *they will be priests of God and of Christ and will reign with Him for a thousand years.* (Emphasis added)

Scripture teaches that the nature of the resurrected body will be like that of Jesus Christ (1 John 3:2). It will be numerical identical to the pre-resurrected body. This is seen in that it has the same scars (John 20:27), is flesh and bones (Luke 24:39), can eat food (Luke 24:42), and is tangible (Matt. 28:9). It will be material since it is "out from the dead" (Luke 24:45), "sown" (1 Cor. 15:42), and the term *body* always means a physical body; that is, transforms into our bodies (Phil. 3:21; 1 John 3:2-3). The resurrected body will have glory (Phil. 3:21, cf. Matt. 17), mobility (Acts 1:10-11), agility (John 20:19), and be supernaturally dominated in power (1 Cor. 15:44). The timing of the Resurrections for believers is at the Rapture (1 Thess. 4:16-17) which is, a we shall see, separated by the Tribulation and Millennium (Chapter 15), and the end of this is the resurrection of unbelievers (Rev. 20:14-15). Unbelievers also have a resurrected body that is immortal. This is so they can remain in their chosen destiny (1 Cor. 15:26).

God's nature (omnipotent and omnibenevolent) shows that He can cause the human soul to survive death since He can do anything not impossible. It is not impossible for the Creator of souls to sustain their existence after death since He is the originating cause and sustaining cause. God will, because He is all good, cause the soul to survive death (Col. 1:17; Lam. 3:22). Since we are in the image of God (Gen. 1:27), God annihilating His image would be an act of God against God. So it is a reasonable inference that God will preserve His creation that is in His image. Since God is omnipotent He can resurrect our bodies, since God is omnibenevolent He will resurrect us and make us complete because of His Mercy. In God's omnisapience Christ's resurrection manifests the victory over death and the Devil: they did crucify Him, and God, in His infinite wisdom, allowed it in order to defeat sin and restore His creation (Rev. 21-22).

HEAVEN: ETERNAL STATE

The constituents of heaven are the Triune God (Rev. 4:2, 8), good angels (Rev. 4:4-6) and redeemed humans (Rev. 7:9; Heb. 12:22-23; Rev. 5:13). The duration of heaven is everlasting, since God is eternal. This constitutes the fulfillment of His promises (Titus 1:2; Matt. 25:46; Rev. 5:13).

Heaven is described as better than earth (Phil. 1:23; 2 Cor. 6:8), a place of no sorrow (Rev. 21:4; 2 Cor. 1:4-5), no curse (Gen. 3:17-19; Rev. 22:3 cf. Rom. 8:18-21), no darkness (Rev. 21:23, 25), no sickness or pain (Rev. 21:4), no death (Rev. 21:4 cf. 1 Cor. 15). A place of perfect bodies (1 Cor. 15:51-53), with many dwelling places (John 14:1-3), perpetual worship (Rev. 4:8, 10 cf. 5:13-14), everlasting service (Rev. 22:3), a grand reunion (1 Thess. 4:13-18), a great heavenly wedding (Rev. 21:2–3). It is a heavenly city (Heb. 12:22–23), a place of perfect knowledge (1 Cor. 13:9–20), moral perfection (1 Cor. 13:10; Rev. 21:17) and indescribable beauty and glory (2 Cor. 12:2–4; Rev. 21:18–21).

It is also the place of the Beatific Vision: when we see God face to face. Mortal man cannot see God (John 1:18; Ex. 33:18–23), but immortal man will see God (Rev. 22:4). This is the fulfillment of all divine aspirations. It brings direct and perfect knowledge of God (1 John 3:2; 1 Cor. 13:9–12). It is the experience that brings the perfect Love of God (Matt. 22:37–38). The beatific vision makes sin impossible thereafter and fulfills our freedom. True freedom is the freedom to do only good. It is evil that keeps us in bondage. Beholding absolute Good overpowers any attraction or desire for the unholy. This Beatific Vision is only for believers (Heb. 11:6) and brings a permanent and dynamic state of perfection.

God is immutable but not immobile; likewise, in heaven we will be immutable (though finitely) perfect without being immobile (static). God is the Unmoved Mover, but He is not an Unmoving Mover. In fact, as Pure Actuality, He is the most active being in the universe. He is Pure Actuality, having no potentiality (Chapter 1). Likewise, when we reach the most godlike state of absolute perfection possible (via the Beatific Vision), we do not become less active but more active. We will not be God's frozen chosen—we will be His mobile millions, actively worshiping and serving Him. Our action will not be that of striving but enjoying, not of seeking but of treasuring what was found. Our minds will be active, not in searching for truth but in rejoicing over the infinite truth discovered.

Questions about Heaven

Will there be babies in heaven? Probably not, since heaven is a place of maturity and perfection. Those who die in infancy will be granted maturity in heaven.

Is heaven a place or a state of mind? The right state of mind and heart can lead to salvation. But heaven is much more than a state of mind: it is a real place (John 14:2–4), the New Heaven and New Earth.

Where is heaven located? Heaven is the abode of righteous human souls and angelic spirits in God's presence (2 Cor. 5:8; Heb. 12:23). For the intermediate state this may be in the space–time world (Acts 1:10; Zech. 14:4), just hidden from us. Or it may be in another dimension (Luke 24:31; John 20:26). For the eternal state it is on the New Earth (2 Peter 3:12–13; Rev. 21:1–2).

Where is heaven located? On Earth! 2 Peter 3:12–13 says, "Looking for and hastening the coming of the day of God, because of which the heavens will be destroyed by burning, and the elements will melt with intense heat! But according to His promise we are looking for new heavens and a new earth, in which righteousness dwells." Revelation 21:1–2 says, "Then I saw a new heaven and a new earth; for the first heaven and the first earth passed away, and there is no longer any sea. And I saw the holy city, New Jerusalem, coming down out of heaven from God, made ready as a bride adorned for her husband."

Will everyone be equally blessed or rewarded in heaven? Everyone will be fully blessed, but not equally. Everyone's cup will be full and running over, but not everyone's cup will be the same size. Our temporal obedience determines our reward in eternity (2 Cor. 5:10; 1 Cor. 3:11–15).

Will we experience "time" in heaven? Some say yes, seeing the phrase "day and night" forever (Rev. 4:8; 7:15) as descriptive of duration. However, others say no, since we will be changeless perfection. Actually, the finite changeless state is aeviternal and there is no way to change perfection. How do you make what is perfect better?

Will we learn and morally improve in heaven? Some say yes (Eph. 3:10–11; 1 Peter 1:12), but others say no, since heaven is a place of perfection, not progress (1 Cor. 13:2). Heaven is a place of receiving, not working (1 Cor. 3:11; Rev. 22:12) and heaven completes and finalizes what is done here and now (Matt. 16:19). The Beatific Vision results in perfection which is the ultimate vision of God's infinite nature (Phil. 3:12–13).

Moral Perfection on Earth	Moral Perfection in Heaven
Changing	Unchanging
Growing	Matured
Striving for	Resting in
Seeking	Enjoying
Desiring of	Delighting in
Our goal	Our reward
Our aim	Our attainment

Table 14.1 Perfection on Earth Compared to Heaven

In heaven we will know everything our finite capacity will allow us to know directly through the infinite mind of God. As He knows the entire universe in and through Himself, so will we know the universe by virtue of knowing everything directly in and through His Mind (essence). Hence, with effortless ease, we will be able to explore the entire universe, insofar as it is finitely possible. Such exploration will not be that of ceaseless discovering, but of endless delight in that we have already discovered in God.

FINAL STATE OF THE LOST (HELL)

There are several terms used for hell. The Hebrew *sheol,* as we have seen, is used for the "the unseen world" of departed spirits, the grave and is also used for the world of the "wicked" unseen spirits (Ps. 9:17). The New Testament uses *hades* for the "departed wicked spirits." There are two words usually translated "hell" one is taken from the Valley of Gehenna which was a putrid dump that burned perpetually (Matt. 5:22, 29–30). The other is used of eternal damnation of fallen angels (2 Peter 2:4). Finally the phrase "Lake of Fire" is used for the eternal state of the lost where "death and hades" are cast (Rev. 20:14–15).

BASIS FOR HELL

The Old Testament teaches the existence of hell (Ps. 9:17, 16:10–11, Isa. 66:22–24). Daniel 12:2 says, "Many of those who sleep in the dust of the ground will awake, these to everlasting life, but the others to disgrace and everlasting contempt." Jesus in the New Testament taught and warned people of hell more than anyone else (Matt. 5:29–30, 10:28, 11:23, 13:40–41, 13:49–50, 22:13, 23:15–33, 25:41; Mark 9:43–48; Luke 12:5, 16:19–31). Jesus said, "Do not fear those who kill the body but are unable to kill the soul; but rather fear Him who is able to destroy both soul and body in hell" (Matt. 10:28). Other places in the New Testament also teach on hell (2 Thess. 1:7–9; Heb. 9:27; 2 Peter 2:4, 9; Jude 6, 12–13; Rev. 2:11, 14:10–11, 19:20, 20:10, 20:11–15, 21:8). Paul taught, "These will pay the penalty of eternal destruction, away from the presence of the Lord and from the glory of His power" (2 Thess. 1:7–9). Revelation says, "He who has an ear, let him hear what the Spirit says to the churches. He who overcomes will not be hurt by the second death" (Rev. 2:11).

Biblically several things require the reality of hell. God's sovereignty demands a hell. Evil frustrates good. If there were no hell, there would be no final victory over evil (1 Cor. 15:24–28; Rev. 20–22). God's justice demands a hell. God is just (Rom. 2). God will do what is right (Gen. 18:25). Not all evil is punished in this life (Ps. 73:3). Therefore, it is necessary to punish the wicked after this life to maintain God's justice. God's love demands a hell. God is love (1 John 4:16). Love is persuasive, but cannot force people to love Him (1 John 4:19; 2 Cor. 9:7). Those who do not wish to love God, must be released, and separated from Him. Human depravity demands a hell. The just punishment for sin against the eternal God is eternal punishment (Isa. 59:7–8; Rom. 3:19, 22–23). Unrepentant, depraved rebellion against the flawless, unblemished holiness is deserving of God's wrath. Human dignity demands a hell. God created humans free and cannot force people into heaven against this freedom (Matt. 23:37). As C. S. Lewis aptly said: "There are only two kinds of people in the end: those who say to God, 'Thy will be done,' and those to whom God says, in the end, '*Thy* will be done'" (*The Great Divorce*, 69). Finally, the cross of Christ implies a hell. Why the cross and all His suffering unless there is a hell? If there is no hell to shun, then the cross was in vain. Christ's work is robbed of its eternal significance unless there is an eternal hell that sinful souls need to be delivered from. We can tell ourselves that it would be wonderful if there were no hell or no final day of judgment at which we will be held accountable for all our deeds, but we shouldn't fail to note that all of this is exactly what we naturally want to be true.

Nature, Location and Duration of Hell

What is hell like? Hell is a horrifying reality. It is like being left outside in darkness; a wandering star, waterless cloud, a perpetually burning dump, a bottomless pit, an everlasting prison, place of anguish and regret (Matt. 8:12; Jude 13; Mark 9:44–48; Rev. 20:1, 3; 1 Peter 3:19; Luke 16:28). It is a Great Divorce since "a great gulf" is fixed between heaven and hell (Luke 16:26).

Hell is depicted as eternal fire. Fire is real, but not necessarily physical since even the lost will have imperishable physical bodies (John 5:28–29). Revelation 20:13–15 says, "And *death and Hades* gave up the dead which were in them; and they were judged, every one of them according to their deeds. Then *death and Hades* were thrown into the lake of fire. This is the second death, the lake of fire" (emphasis added). Figures of speech are used to describe hell. This we know because they are contradictory if taken literally. For example, hell has flames, yet is outer darkness. Hell is a dump, yet it is bottomless pit.

Hell is not torture, that is, pain inflicted from without against one's will. Instead hell is torment or self-inflicted by one's own will. The door to hell is locked from the inside. Torment is living with the consequences of one's own bad choices. Torment is the anguish that results from realizing they used their freedom for evil and chose wrongly. Everyone in hell will know the pain is self-induced (Matt. 22:13).

Where is hell located? Relational terms are used, but they do not need to be taken as spatial. Hell is "under the earth" (Phil. 2:10) or "outside" the heavenly city (Rev. 22:15). Hell is "away from the presence of the Lord" (2 Thess. 1:7–9). Hell is the other direction from God. God must hold hell and those in it in existence, but He has no positive relation with them.

What is the duration of hell? Since God is eternal, hell will be everlasting; it has a beginning but no end. Jesus says, "If your hand or your foot causes you to stumble, cut it off and throw it from you; it is better for you to enter life crippled or lame, than to have two hands or two feet and be cast into the *eternal* fire" (Matt. 18:18, emphasis added). The same word "eternal" is used for both heaven and hell and does not entail an ending but everlasting (Matt. 18:18, cf 19:16; Heb. 9:14). There is no means of escape after arriving (Luke 16:26; Heb. 9:27). Some say those in hell will be annihilated (Annihilationism). However this is contrary to an all–loving God. It is inconsistent with an all loving God to snuff out the souls of those who do not do what He wishes. It is also contrary to the nature of humans in the image of God. Suffering does not justify annihilation any more than one is justified in killing a child because they are in pain.

Questions about Hell

Why punish people in hell, why not reform them for Heaven? God does try to reform people; it is called *life* (2 Peter 3:9). After this life is the time of reckoning (Heb. 9:27). Hell is not for the reformable, it is for the unreformable and unrepentant (1 Tim. 2:4). This question assumes someone would want to leave hell and be saved without Christ. But God cannot force free creatures to be reformed. C. S. Lewis said, "To be 'cured' against one's will . . . is to be put on a level with those who have not yet reached the age of reason or those who never will; to be classed with infants, imbeciles, and domestic animals" (*God in the Dock*, 292).

Isn't eternal damnation for temporal sins overkill? Only everlasting punishment will suffice for sins against the eternal God. Sins committed in time are perpetrated against the eternal God. Forcing people into heaven would be "hell" for them since they would be where everyone is loving and praising the One they want to avoid. Annihilating them would be an attack on God's own image. There is no comparison to be made between non–existence and existence. Without an eternal separation of good from evil (in hell), there could be no heaven, an eternal preservation of good.

Is it right or just to send people to hell when they can't help being sinners? Sin sends people to hell for two reasons: 1) they are bent to sin because of their fallen nature, and 2) they choose to sin because of their will. As Augustine said, "We are born with the propensity to sin and the necessity to die." Their sin nature does not force them to sin; they still choose to sin. Everyone is held responsible for their decision to accept or reject God's offer of salvation from sin and its penalty. Sin against an infinite God is infinitely evil and worthy of infinite punishment.

How can we be happy in heaven knowing a loved one is in hell? This question assumes that we are more merciful than God. God is happy in heaven, yet He knows not everyone will be there. We can be happy the same way God is because of the Beatific Vision. We can be happy eating even knowing that others are starving—if we have offered them food but they have refused to eat. Otherwise, those who reject heaven's bliss could inflict woe on those who chose it. But hell cannot veto heaven!

Why did God create people He knows would go to hell? Nonbeing or nonexistence cannot be compared to being or existence. Jesus' statement about it being better if Judas had never been born (Mark 14:21) is a strong expression about the severity of his sin. The fact that not all people will "win" in the game of life, does not mean it should not be played. It is better to have loved all the people of the world (John 3:16) and have lost some than not to have loved them at all.

Why not annihilate sinners instead of consciously tormenting them? It is because we are not animals, that we are not treated like animals. A good parent does not kill his son just because he does not do what he wants him to do. It is more merciful for God to allow us to choose our own way—even against His will—than to force His will on us.

Some say hell has no redeeming value. But such awesome punishment befits the nature of an awesome God. All the saved in heaven magnify God's mercy and the lost magnify his justice. An eternal and final separation of good from evil triumphs good over evil so that evil no longer contaminates good.

Some say hell is contrary to the mercy of God. God's mercy and pain and suffering are not incompatible in this world or hell. Mercy in God is not a passion or emotion that overcomes His justice. Since God's attributes are not inconsistent with each other; it follows that God is not unmerciful to allow hell (Chapter 3). In heaven we will be conformed to God's eternal vantage point: Love what He loves and hate what He hates. In the end, God will have done everything possible to save people. God cannot make their decision for them, or force a free decision.

SUMMARY

This part of the study of Last Things (Eschatology) shows that the final state of the saved is heaven. Their intermediate state is a state of blissfulness with the Lord awaiting their resurrected bodies. In their eternal state they will see God face to face, and dwell in the New Heaven and Earth for ever more. Hell is the final state of the lost; it is the horrifying reality of realizing the result of their choice to be eternally separated from their loving Creator.

QUESTIONS TO ANSWER

1. What is the nature of heaven in the intermediate state?
2. What will the Beatific Vision be like?
3. What will heaven be like?
4. What is the nature of hell in the intermediate state?
5. What will hell be like?
6. Why can't God annihilate those who go to hell?
7. Did you read?

15

Last Things ~ Part 2

*In that day His feet will stand on the Mount of Olives, which is
in front of Jerusalem on the east; and the Mount of Olives will
be split in its middle from east to west by a very large
valley, . . . And the LORD will be king over all the earth; in that
day the LORD will be the only one, and His name the only one.*
Zechariah 14:4, 9

THE previous chapter (14) in our study of Last Things (Eschatology)
covered the final state of the saved and lost. Here we study the
Second Coming and Millennium followed by the Tribulation and
Rapture. Those not as familiar with the sequence of the Pretribulation
Premillennial view may want to view the summary at the end of this
chapter.

INTERPRETATION OF PROPHECY

Debate over the interpretation of prophecy has resulted in two main
schools of thought: *literal* and *allegorical*. As applied to prophecy, as
well as the rest of Scripture, the literal (*sensus literalis*) seeks the normal or plain sense of the text as understood in its historical and grammatical setting. The allegorical approach to prophecy gives a nonlit-
eral or spiritual meaning to the prophetic text. Both schools claim
the historical grammatical method. However, there is good reason
to reject the allegorical method: 1) it cannot be used consistently
on other parts of Scripture, such as doctrine, narrative or history. 2)
There are no controls or limits on the meaning which must be sin-
gular and objective (Chapter 1). As such it can lead to subjectivism

and mysticism. And 3) it is self-defeating since it relies on the literal hermeneutic to affirm itself as a method of interpretation.

SECOND COMING AND MILLENNIUM

Dispensationalism which means "stewardship" seeks to identify distinguishable economies between God and man in Scripture. All see at least three and some as many as seven: 1) Innocence (Gen. 1:28–3:6), 2) Conscience (Gen. 4:1–8:14), 3) Government (Gen. 8:15–11:9), 4) Promise (Gen. 11:10–Ex 18:27), 5) Mosaic law (Ex, 19:1–Acts 1:26), 6) Grace (Acts 2:1–Rev. 19:21), and 7) Millennium (Rev. 20:4–6). Covenant Theology seeks to identify covenants or differing agreements that God makes, they usually have two or three: 1) Covenant of Works: God & Adam (Gen. 1:27–3:26), 2) Covenant of Grace: God & Man, (Gen, 3:7–Rev. 20:15) and the Reformers add 3) Covenant of Redemption: Father and Son.

However, neither approach is explicitly in Scripture. To fully appreciate the nature of the Second Coming and the Millennium a study of the covenants in Scripture is required. Hence our approach is to study the biblical covenants themselves. There are seven covenants found in Scripture.

COVENANTS

The term *covenant* means "agreement" or "arrangement" between God and particular human beings. There were three before God began dealing with Israel.

1) The Edenic Covenants (Gen. 1–2)
2) The Adamic Covenant (Gen. 3)
3) The Noahic Covenant (Gen. 9)

Four deal with Israel:

4) The Abrahamic Covenant (Gen. 12)
5) The Mosaic Covenant (Ex. 19)
6) The David Covenant (2 Sam. 7)
7) The New Covenant (Jer. 31)

The first of Israel's covenants, the Abrahamic Covenant is an unconditional agreement God made with Abraham and his descendants. Genesis 12:1–3 says,

> Go forth from your country, And from your relatives And from your father's house, To the land which I will show you; And I will make you a great nation, And I will bless you, And make your name great; And so you shall be a blessing; And I will bless those who bless you, And the one who curses you

I will curse. And in you all the families of the earth will be blessed.

There are at least five important things to note in this covenant:
1) It is unconditional "I will bless you"
2) It is national "I will make you into a great nation"
3) It is geographical "Promised Land"
4) It is perpetual "to you and your offspring"
5) It is international in scope "all peoples on earth will be blessed through you"

The unconditional gift of the land (Gen. 15:18) is from the Mediterranean Sea (west) to Northern Jordan and Northern Iraq (east), from Egypt (south) to Lebanon and Syria (north).

This covenant is repeated throughout the Old Testament (Gen. 13:14–17. 15:7–18, 17:1–8, 22:17–18, 26:3–5, 35:10–12, 46:10–1, Deut. 28:8–12; Joshua 1:2–6; 1 Chron. 16:15–18; Isa. 49:6; Jer. 25:9–12; Ezek. 37:21–25; Dan. 9:22, 46:3–4; Amos 9:14–15).

This promise has never been fulfilled at any time in history, either prior to or after the Advent. Even after Jesus' time on earth, the kingdom of Israel, which included its unconditional land–promises (forever), had not yet been fulfilled. Jesus implied that it was coming but did not say when (Acts 1:6–7, 3:19–21, 15:14–17; Rom. 11:1–32; Heb. 11:8–10, 12–16; Rev. 7:4).

Because Israel rejected their Messiah–King who is to rule in Jerusalem (Matt. 19:28) over the whole land God gave Abraham, and since this reign is to be forever, the event is yet future; it will not be fulfilled until Christ returns (24:30; 25:31–34). At this time Abraham, Isaac, Jacob, David, and all other Old Testament saints will be raised and literally will reign over the whole earth in physical, resurrected bodies (Matt. 19:28; Rev. 20:4–6).

The Mosaic covenant was conditional and its blessings dependent on Israel's legal obedience. The Mosaic covenant involved the conditions for being blessed in the land. The Mosaic covenant was bilateral. God required Israel to obey His word as a condition for being "a kingdom of priests and a holy nation" (Ex. 19:4–6; cf. Deut. 28:1–45; Jer. 31:31–33; Heb. 8:7, 13; Rom. 7:1–4; Gal. 3:17–25; 4:1–7, 4:21–31; 2 Cor. 3:7–11; Rom. 10:3–4; Col. 2:14, 17; Heb. 7:12).

The covenant was not permanent. The Abrahamic covenant takes precedence over the Mosaic covenant. The Mosaic covenant

	Abrahamic Covenant	Mosaic Covenant
Nature	Unconditional	Conditional
Agreement	Unilateral	Bilateral
Parties	God Alone	God and Israel
Condition	None	Obedience to God
Duration	Everlasting	Temporal
Beginning	Genesis 12	Exodus 19
End	No End	At the Cross

Table 15.1 Abrahamic and Mosaic Covenants

was instituted because of human sinfulness, while the Abrahamic covenant was given because of God's graciousness (Table 15.1).

While the Abrahamic covenant centers around the land, the Mosaic covenant centers around conditioned obedience, and the Davidic covenant centers around the throne. While the former covenants provide the land and the nation; the latter provides a king to rule over the kingdom (2 Sam. 7:11–16; Isa. 55:1–3; Ps. 89:20–37). Despite countless acts of disloyalty on Israel's part, God has been and will be absolutely faithful. The Davidic covenant promised to Israel a political, religious, moral, visible, earthly kingdom, and God personally guaranteed that it would endure forever, and that all nations would be blessed through it, as with the Abrahamic covenant.

In addition to these covenants, the Old Testament sets forth a future New Covenant (Table 15.2).

	The Old Covenant	The New Covenant
Duration	Temporal	Everlasting
Replaced	Yes	Never
Written	In Stone	On hearts
Initiated	By the blood of animals	By the blood of Christ
Number of sacrifices	Many sacrifices	One Sacrifice forever
Mediator	Moses	Jesus
Forgiveness	Anticipatory	Realized by the Cross
Holy Spirit	No permanent indwelling	Permanent indwelling
Approach to God	Through Aaron the high priest	Through Christ our High Priest
Celebrated	By sacrifices (looking forward to the Cross)	By Communion (looking backward to the Cross)

Table 15.2 Old and New Covenant

Jesus and writers of the New Testament saw this New Covenant as applicable to the Church in its fulfillment (Jer. 31; Matt. 26:26–28; cf. 1 Cor. 11:23ff.). There will be an ultimate fulfillment of the New Covenant after Israel has been resurrected and returned to the Holy Land (Ezek. 37). This shows that the promise is not entirely fulfilled before that. That this covenant was *made* with Israel does not mean spiritual benefits cannot be *applied* to Gentiles (Heb. 8:7–9) such as the forgiveness of sins applied to Jewish and Gentile believers alike. Jesus' inaugurated a spiritual kingdom in Matthew 13. This, however, does not annul a future messianic kingdom to come.

The overall testimony of the covenants reveals seven features.

1) The Promised Land Forever (Gen. 13:14–15)
2) A Nation Forever (Gen. 12:1–2)
3) A King Forever (Isa. 9:6)
4) Restoration of Israel Forever (Dan. 2:44)
5) Presentation of the Messianic King (Matt. 3:1–2)
6) Rejection of the Messianic King (Matt. 21:43)
7) Restoration of the Messianic Kingdom (Rom. 11)

The New Testament distinguishes Israel from the Church (1 Cor. 10:32) and after the Church age God will restore Israel as a nation (Rom. 11). So Israel and the Church have a great deal in common. They are both part of the people of God (Rev. 4–5). They are part of God's spiritual kingdom (John 3:3). They are designed to glorify God (Rev. 4:10–11). They both participate in the spiritual blessings of the Abrahamic Covenant (Gen. 12:3; Rom. 4:16). They both participate in the spiritual blessings of the New Covenant (Jer. 31:31–33; Heb. 8:7, 13). And both will endure forever (2 Tim. 2:10; Rev. 21:2–3). There are also several significant differences to note, see Table. 15.3.

	The Nation of Israel	The Church
Headship	Moses	Christ
Origin	Abraham	Pentecost
Nature	Earthly (a political body)	Heavenly (a spiritual body)
Governing Principle	Law of Moses	Grace of Christ
Holy Land	Divine inheritance	No inheritance
Davidic Covenant	Promised to Israel	Not promised to Church
Constituents	Jews only	Jews and Gentiles
Membership	By physical birth	By spiritual birth
Function	Channel of blessing to the world	To provoke Israel to repent

Table 15.3 The Nation of Israel and the Church

THE MILLENNIUM

There are three views on the Millennium (Rev. 20:1–6). Premillennialism, Amillennialism, and Postmillenialism. Premillennialism is the view that Jesus Christ will physically (bodily) return to reign on earth setting up a worldwide kingdom that will last for one thousand years. Amillennialism denies a literal or physical earthly reign of Christ following the Second Coming deciding to interpret Rev. 20 spiritually or allegorically. Postmillenialism sees the Church, not the Second Coming, as inaugurating the Millennium by Christianizing the world and then Christ will return. These views are compared in contrasted below (Table 15.4).

	Pre-millennialism	Amillennialism	Postmillennialism
Literal Millennium	Yes	No	No
Resurrection before Millennium	One	None	None
"Thousand years" of Revelation 20	Future	Present	Present
Resurrection(s)	Two	One	One
Consistent literal understanding of prophecy	Yes	No	No
Unconditional Old Testament Covenants	Yes	No	No
Distinctions between Israel and the Church	Many	None	None
Messianic kingdom	Future	Present	Present
Rapture/Second Coming	Separate events	Same event	Same event
Binding of Satan	In the future (during Millennium)	In the Past	In the Present
Moral progress	Not inevitable	Not inevitable	Inevitable
Final judgment	Two events	One event	One event

Table 15.4 Views on the Millennium

The Premillennial view sees the Millennium as a future literal reign of Christ for one thousand years (Matt. 24:30; Zech. 14:4) that teaches two resurrections one before, for the saved (1 Thess. 4:15–17), and one after, for the lost (Rev. 20:11–15). Biblically this view is grounded in the land promise to Israel (Rom. 11:29), the eternal Davidic Throne (2 Sam. 7:11–16; Ps. 89), the promises yet to be fulfilled and Israel's expectation of the Messianic Kingdom (Isa. 9:6–7; Mal. 3:1).

Further biblical support is found in John the Baptist and Jesus offering Israel the Messianic Kingdom (Matt. 3:1–2; 4:17). Jesus promised to restore the Messianic Kingdom to Israel. Jesus said in Matthew 19:28: "Truly I say to you, that you who have followed Me, in the regeneration when the Son of Man will sit on His glorious throne, you also shall sit upon twelve thrones, judging the twelve tribes of Israel." Jesus implied it was still future at His Ascension (Acts 1:6–7). Paul affirming the irrevocability of God's promised Kingdom to Israel (Rom. 9:3–4). Peter promised Israel the Messianic Kingdom in Acts 3:19–21: "Therefore repent and return, so that your sins may be wiped away, in order that times of refreshing may come from the presence of the Lord; and that He may send Jesus, the Christ appointed for you, whom heaven must receive until the period of restoration of all things about which God spoke by the mouth of His holy prophets from ancient time." Paul specified in 1 Corinthians 15:22–28 that Christ's future reign would end:

> But each in his own order: Christ the first fruits, after that those who are Christ's at His coming, then comes the end, when He hands over the kingdom to the God and Father, when He has abolished all rule and all authority and power. For He must reign until He has put all His enemies under His feet. The last enemy that will be abolished is death. For He has put all things in subjection under His feet. But when He says, "All things are put in subjection," it is evident that He is excepted who put all things in subjection to Him. When all things are subjected to Him, then the Son Himself also will be subjected to the One who subjected all things to Him, so that God may be all in all.

This fits with John's affirming two resurrections, one at the beginning of the thousand years that is the saved and one at the end of the thousand years that is the lost, and specifying that the Kingdom would be for a thousand years (Rev. 20:1–6).

The period is repeatedly called "a thousand years" (Rev. 20:2–6). It is also known as Isaiah's "Little Apocalypse" (Isa. 24:21–23). During the Millennium Christ will reign (Matt. 19:28) and judge the nations by separating the sheep which are the saved from the goats which are the lost (Zech. 14:2–4; Matt. 25:31–41). Resurrected humans will take part (Rev. 20:6), and one faith will exist over the earth (Isa. 66:23; Zech. 14:16–18). Peace and prosperity will be restored (Mic. 4:3; Zech. 3:10; Isa. 65:21) and creation will be delivered from bondage (Rom. 8:18–23). Animals will not be carnivorous (Isa. 11:6–8; 65:25 cf. Gen. 2:9:3:2), human longevity is restored (Isa. 65:20–22), and death will only exist for rebellion and punishment (Isa. 11:4).

The Millennium is not heaven—it will not be absolutely perfect, but it will be as perfect as it can be on earth with unsaved people still in the mix (Matt. 13:29–30). The Millennium is not the first chapter of heaven but the last chapter of earth—not the completed victory, but the last chapter in the ultimate victory: He must reign until He has put all his enemies under his feet (1 Cor. 15:25; cf. 13:20–12), (Table 15.5).

	Millennium	New Heaven and New Earth
Terminus	At end of Christ's reign	No end
Evil	Present	Not present
Death	Death occurs	No death occurs
Location	On earth	In heaven and on earth
Final Judgment	Not yet occurred	Completed
Constituents	Saved and unsaved	Saved only
Satan	No yet finally judged	Finally judged.

Table 15.5 Millennium Compared to New Heaven and Earth

Premillennialism alone has a comprehensive hermeneutic that accounts for these two different aspects of God's future kingdom. It is also a consistent hermeneutic that shows what was lost in the garden on earth (Gen. 2) is restored on earth (Rev. 21). History has a linear consummation that results in victory over sin, evil and death (1 Cor. 15:24–25). This surely adds urgency to evangelism since it holds to the immanency of Christ's return (Luke 19:13; John 9:40).

The all wise eternal God, who knows all things by His omniscient knowledge, makes unconditional promises based on His immutable character, plans all things by His unchangeable will, and achieves them with His omnipotent power. God foretold and will accomplish the future messianic Millennial Kingdom in which Christ the Messiah, chosen by the Father to this end, will reign.

Premillennialism shows the complete victory of God. Human history started in a literal Paradise (Gen. 2), with a literal geographical location with no evil or suffering with Adam and Eve in a perfect environment. This Paradise was lost by sin that brought suffering and death on the whole human race which expelled the first humans from the Garden (Paradise). If the Paradise lost is not a Paradise regained, then God will have lost the war; if physical death is not reversed by physical resurrection, then Satan obtains ultimate victory; if literal perfection is not restored, then God will have lost what He created. He will reverse the curse and gain victory over the Satan–damaged creation. This He will do by a literal resurrection and by a literal earthly reign of Christ. He will reign until death is actually defeated (1 Cor. 15:24–27; Rev. 20:4–6), at the end of the Millennium and the beginning of the new heaven and earth (Rev. 21:4).

Premillennialism has a historical consummation through the linear view of history, that is, history moving forward toward a goal. Such a view is a result of Judeo–Christian revelation. Without a literal Millennium, there is no real end to history. The Millennium is not the first chapter of eternity, but the last chapter of time—when sin, suffering, and death are finally overcome by Christ's reign on earth (1 Cor. 15:24–25). It also employs a consistent hermeneutic. Other views inconsistently take parts of the Bible non–literally or allegorically. For example, some take the predictions and fulfillments of Christ's death and resurrection literally, but not his predictions and fulfillments of His return and reign (Matt. 19:28; 24–25). They also inconsistently apply literalism and allegory to the same sentence (Isa. 61:1–2; Luke 4:18–21). For example, they take the second resurrection literally and the first spiritually (Rev. 20:5–6; John 5:25–29).

Premillennialism adds urgency to evangelism and is an incentive for holiness. Premillennialism upholds the immanency of Christ's return. We must live with a sense of expectation (Luke 19:13; John 9:4). Only Premillennialism can preserve immanency: we do not know when He will return, since it could be at any moment. Human souls are in the balance, as 2 Peter 3:10–12 says, "Since all these things are to be destroyed in this way, what sort of people ought you to be in holy conduct and godliness, looking for and hastening the coming of the day of God, because of which the heavens will be destroyed by burning, and the elements will melt with intense heat!"

ANSWERING OBJECTIONS TO PREMILLENNIALISM

Some object to Premillennialism saying it is rarely mentioned in Scripture. However, a scriptural truth is not dependent upon its frequency of mention and a truth can be taught without its name being used. John 3:3, 7 is the only mention of being 'born again' yet evangelicals correctly emphasize the high importance of this.

Some say all the covenants are conditional. But as shown above, some promises in the Old Testament (e.g., Jonah) and covenants (e.g., Mosaic) are conditional, but not all. The Abrahamic and Davidic covenants are unilateral, being unconditional (Heb. 6:13–14, 17–18, Ps. 89:30–37).

Some say the land promises were already fulfilled in Joshua's day (Josh. 21:43–45) or Solomon's day (1 Kings 4:20). But Joshua 21 refers to the conditional Mosaic covenant (Num. 34) not the

Abrahamic (Gen. 15:18–21), and the continual giving of the prophecy after Joshua and Solomon, whose reign was short (Amos 9:14–15), indicates they were not fulfilled. Also, the geographic land was never possessed (Jude 1:27–34) and the New Testament sees it as unfulfilled (Luke 19:11; Acts 1:6–7; Rom. 11:25).

Some say the promises are fulfilled spiritually in the Church. But this confuses application of the New Covenant (Heb. 8:7–13) to Israel and the Church by negating its literal fulfillment. This is something Scripture never does.

Some say that Jesus said His kingdom was not of this world (John 18:36). However, this was to indicate its rejection and spiritual nature now and not a rejection of its literal establishment later (Acts 1:6–8).

Some say animal sacrifices (Ezek. 40–48) in the Millennium contradict Hebrews 8–10 that says they are abolished. But this fails to distinguish between the atoning sense which is abolished and the memorial sense (as in the Lord's Supper–1 Cor. 11:26) in which some believe it will be celebrated in the millennium. Celebration of the Eucharist will end at the Second Coming (1 Cor. 11:26). After this, Israel will be restored (Rom. 11:25–27), along with her Sabbaths and sacrifices, which will be with her during the Millennium.

Premillennialism is rooted in a consistent literal hermeneutic; based in God's unconditional covenants with Abraham and David, points to a literal, political, earthly messianic kingdom. A denial of this position forsakes consistent application of the historical–grammatical hermeneutic, and if the allegorical method were applied to other Scripture it would undermine the whole of evangelical Christianity.

TRIBULATION AND RAPTURE

That there will be a time of tribulation before Christ's return to earth is foretold and taught throughout Scripture. Moses foretold of an end–time tribulation for Israel in Deuteronomy (4:23–32), it says, "When you are in distress and all these things have come upon you, in the latter days you will return to the Lord your God and listen to His voice. For the Lord your God is a compassionate God; He will not fail you nor destroy you nor forget the covenant with your fathers which He swore to them." It is the Seventieth "Week" of Daniel 9:24–27, says, "And its end will come with a flood; even to the end there will be war; desolations are determined. And he will make a firm covenant with the many for one week, but in the middle of the week he will put a stop to sacrifice and grain offering; and on the wing of abominations will come one who makes desolate, even until a complete destruction, one that is decreed, is poured out on the one who makes desolate." Daniel goes on to elaborate on the Antichrist (Dan. 11:31–39). It is the Time of Jacob's Trouble (Jer. 30:3–14). It was taught by Jesus in the Mount Olivet Discourse (Matt. 24) and is the Tribulation mentioned in the Book of Revelation (Rev. 6–18).

The term *rapture* is used for being "caught up" to heaven (2 Cor. 12:2–4; Acts 8:39; Rev. 12:5) it is used by Paul in 1 Thessalonians 4:16–18: "For the Lord Himself will descend from heaven with a shout, with the voice of the archangel and with the trumpet of God, and the dead in Christ will rise first. Then we who are alive and remain will be caught up together with them in the clouds to meet the Lord in the air, and so we shall always be with the Lord. Therefore comfort one another with these words" (cf. 1 Cor. 15:50–58). John also mentions it in (14:1–3): "Do not let your heart be troubled; believe in God, believe also in Me. In My Father's house are many dwelling places; if it were not so, I would have told you; for I go to prepare a place for you. If I go and prepare a place for you, I will come again and receive you to Myself, that where I am, there you may be also."

The Rapture involves Jesus Christ returning and appearing to believers (1 Thess. 4:16), first resurrecting dead believers (v. 16), calling up living believers (v. 17) and a reunion with departed loved ones (v. 17). This event should be used to bring reassurance or comfort by our looking forward to this event (v. 18).

There are many indicators that the Rapture will take place prior to the Tribulation which is called Pretribulationism. The Church is never mentioned on earth during the Tribulation (Rev. 6–18). The Church (bride) is mentioned as being in heaven during the Tribulation, it is only the apostate "church" that is on earth (Rev. 18:2; cf. 3:12; 19:7). This is supported by the references to heaven dwellers (Rev. 13:6), Saints, Apostles, and Prophets (Rev. 18:20; 19:14). These come with Christ. If so, they must have previously been taken up or raptured. Further they are mentioned as being in heaven as Twenty–Four Elders since they are sitting on thrones that are promised to believers (Rev. 3:21), they are clothed in white robes also promised (3:3; 18) and they are given crowns (2:10; 3:11).

The reference to earthly believers in Revelation is not about the Church. The term *believers* is mentioned twice during the Tribulation and this is a reference to Jewish converts from the twelve tribes of Israel. The "saints" are either the 144,000 saved Jews or those converted during the Tribulation. Furthermore, the Church is delivered from the Hour of Testing. Revelation 3:10 says, "Because you have kept the word of My perseverance, I also will keep you from the hour of testing, that hour which is about to come upon the whole world, to test those who dwell on the earth." This is not a promise to keep them *through* it or merely from trials, but *from* the whole "hour." The only way to be kept from the hour is to be kept from any part of it.

The Church is saved from God's wrath according to 1 Thessalonians 1:10: "and to wait for His Son from heaven, whom He raised from the dead, that is Jesus, who rescues us from the wrath to come." And 1 Thessalonians 5:9 says, "For God has not destined us for wrath, but for obtaining salvation through our Lord Jesus Christ."

Daniel considered the whole "seventieth week" (of seven years) as part of the Day of the Lord, a day of wrath (Dan. 12:1, 7). Salvation from God's wrath means deliverance from the whole Tribulation period. Only the Church's Rapture explains the sudden apostasy. Since the Restrainer of all sin–which is the Holy Spirit of God (John 16:7–8) Who indwells the Church–is removed. Once the Church is removed, this also explains the ultimate lawlessness of the Antichrist.

The imminence (at any moment) of Christ coming for His saints clearly implies a pretribulation rapture. Paul says in 1 Corinthians 15:51–52: "Behold, I tell you a mystery; we will not all sleep, but we will all be changed, in a moment, in the twinkling of an eye, at the last trumpet; for the trumpet will sound, and the dead will be raised imperishable, and we will be changed." This is a sign–less, imminent event. Quickly does not necessarily mean 'soon' but swiftly.

The Church is not destined to "the time of Jacob's trouble." This is for His people Israel (Jer. 30:7; 9:24). It is not for the Church, just as God took Enoch to heaven and allowed Noah to endure the Flood. So God will take the Church, and allow Israel the time of trouble and purification to prepare for her Messiah (Rom. 11:25).

Our blessed hope implies a pretribulation Rapture (1 John 3:2–3; Titus 2:12–13). Believer's rewards imply a pretribulation Rapture (2 Cor. 5:10; 1 Cor. 3:11–15; Rev. 22:12). Christ is coming for and then with His saints also implies a pretribulational Rapture (1 Thess. 4:16–17; John 14:3; Matt. 24: 29–31). The sheep nations going into the Millennium also supports the pretribulation Rapture. Matthew 25:31–34:

> But when the Son of Man comes in His glory, and all the angels with Him, then He will sit on His glorious throne. All the nations will be gathered before Him; and He will separate them from one another, as the shepherd separates the sheep from the goats; and He will put the sheep on His right, and the goats on the left. Then the King will say to those on His right, 'Come, you who are blessed of My Father inherit the kingdom prepared for you from the foundation of the world.'

The sheep of Matthew 25 are the 144,000 Jews saved and the multitude they win (Rev. 7:4, 9). Other views such as Posttribulationism

Rapture	Second Coming
Meeting them in the air (1 Thess. 4:17)	Taking them to the earth (Zech. 14:4; Acts 1:11)
Taking believers to heaven (John 14:3)	Bringing believers back to Earth (Rev. 19:14)
Coming for His saints (2 Thess. 2:1)	Coming with His saints (Jude 14)
Only believers see Him (1 Thess. 4:17)	All people see Him (Rev. 1:7)
No signs precede it (1 Thess. 5:1–3)	Many signs precede it (Matt. 24:3–30)
The Tribulation begins (2 Thess. 1:6–9)	The Millennium begins (Rev. 20:1–7)

Table 15.6 Rapture Compared to Second Coming

have no one to populate the millennium in unresurrected bodies. Also, the Rapture is a mystery which supports pretribulation 1 Cor. 15:51–53). The Rapture is not part of the "Day of the Lord." This is often used of end time events, but it is never used of the Rapture. Paul in 2 Thessalonians 2:2 uses "that Day" which he did not have to explain, but he did need to explain the Rapture. Finally it is Christ, not His angels (Matt. 24:31), Who will come back to gather the elect, to take them to His Father's house, and not keep them on earth (John 14:1–3).

Hence a distinction is made between the Rapture and the Second Coming (Table 15.6).

OBJECTIONS AND ALTERNATIVE VIEWS

Some object to Pretribulationism saying it is a late doctrine. In response this is the fallacy of chronological snobbery that argues that truth can be determined by time. It is also a genetic fallacy, saying a view is wrong because of its origin. Some early doctrines are false such as Docetism – a denial of Christ's humanity and baptismal regeneration. Doctrinal development can be very progressive. But it also is not true, since many believe that imminence and Pretribulationism were taught in the early church. Ephraem of Syria (c. 306–373) may have taught it. And it is a derivative of Premillennialism which was taught by many early Fathers. However, the question is not was it taught by the *early* church, but by the *earliest* church in the New Testament?

Some object saying Preterism is true. This is the view that says past claims of apocalyptic biblical prophecy (Matt. 24–25 and Rev. 6–18) have already been fulfilled in the first century. In response, the

Tribulation (Rev. 6–18) is spoken in connection with the Second Coming, final resurrection, and kingdom (Rev. 19–22). However, these teachings of the book of Revelation are an inseparable unit, and all orthodox Christians hold the resurrection as future (2 Tim. 2:18). Further, no literal fulfillment (in A.D. 70) of many events (Matt. 24) can be found. For example, the stars did not fall from heaven (24:29); Certainly Jesus did not return (v. 30); the abomination of desolation (v. 15) has not occurred; Christ did not set up His kingdom, and separate sheep and goats (Matt. 25:34–41). Furthermore, there is no literal fulfillment of the Abrahamic promises to possess the Holy Land and Davidic promise that Messiah would sit on His throne and reign forever. Also, the events of the Tribulation are not local to Jerusalem (Rev. 1:7; 9:18; 16:3; 16:14) but global.

An alternative view Midtribulationism says the Rapture occurs halfway through the Tribulation after the "beginning of sorrows" (Matt. 24:8) but before the "great tribulation" (v. 21). In response, this loses any sense of imminence, since it has signs that come before it occurs. And the signs in 2 Thess. 2:3–4 are not prior to the Rapture, but during the Tribulation. There is just no reference to the Church being raptured in the middle of the Tribulation.

Another version places the Rapture before the wrath of God. This Pre–Wrath view says the Rapture occurs between the sixth and seventh seals in the book of Revelation (Rev. 6:12–8:1). In response, the wrath and tribulation are not different periods. The seven seals are all part of the same sequence; the only difference is in intensity. God often uses humans to execute His wrath (Ex. 9:16). The forth seal is clearly God's wrath because it inflicts death that alone comes from God (Rev. 6:8; cf. Deut. 32:39). Even the unsaved recognize the judgment as the "wrath of the Lamb" (Rev. 6:15–16).

Another alternative view Posttribulationism sees the Rapture and Second Coming as one event at the end of the Tribulation. In response, Matthew 24 (and 13:24) refers to Christ's return at the end of the Tribulation to set up the Millennial Kingdom, not the Rapture. Revelation 20:4–6 speaks of believers who died during the Tribulation, not those resurrected at the Rapture (1 Thess. 4:1–17). Revelation 3:10 means "out of" the time of trial, not through it. Hence, you cannot be saved from the hour by being part of it.

The final alternative is the Partial–Rapture View. It says faithful saints are raptured before the Tribulation while unfaithful Saints are left to endure. In response, the Rapture is never connected with being worked for; it is part of salvation which is not by works (Titus 3:5–7). The Rapture, which is the resurrection for believers, is never connected with being lost. Rewards are lost, not the Rapture or res-

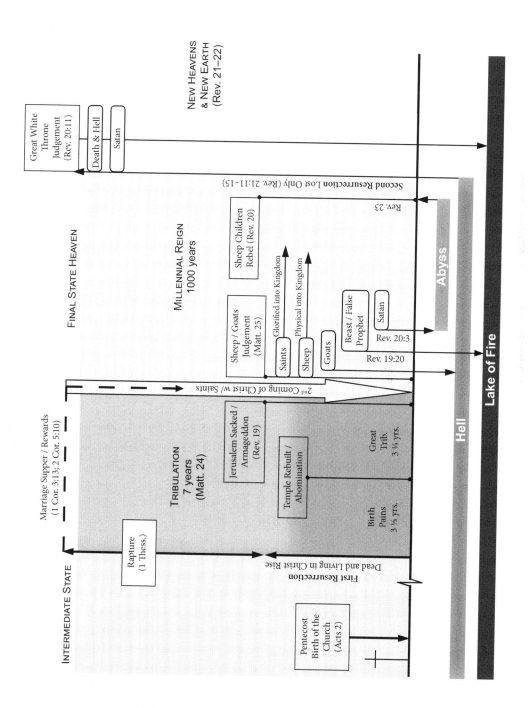

Figure 15.1 Pretribulation Premillenial View

urrection (1 Cor. 3:13–15). First Corinthians 15:51–52 clearly states "all" will be changed, not just the "faithful."

Although it is not one of the fundamentals of the Faith, the Pretribulation view does seem to be a best explanation of the many possibilities. By this it is meant the view which, given all the biblical data, offers the most plausible explanation.

Summary

This part of the study of Last Things (Eschatology) shows the events according to the Pretribulation Premillenial view. They can be summarized as follows (Figure 15.1).

Church: After the birth of the church, the next event is the Rapture of the Church. No one on earth knows when that will occur. After the Church is raptured, the Tribulation can take place, but nothing necessitates that the start is immediately after the Rapture. The Tribulation is described in Rev. 6–18. Events unfolding are taken either simultaneously or sequentially.

Tribulation: A global political leader called the Antichrist makes a seven year treaty with the Jewish nation, and allows them to offer sacrifices and rebuild the temple (Dan. 9:27). Birth pains (beginning of sorrows) are wars that involve mass deaths, famines and natural disasters. Many come to faith, or believe after the Rapture, as a result of the testimony and witness of the 144,000 Jews (Rev. 7:4, 9). Many of them are also martyred (Matt. 24:5–11; Rev. 6:1–11).

Mid Tribulation: The Antichrist puts a stop to the sacrifices/offerings of the Jews. He demands worship claiming to be God (Rev. 13:14), preforms many counterfeit signs and sets up a false religion under the false prophet. The last half of the Tribulation is the culminating judgment "the day of the Lord" (2 Thess. 2:2). Those that do not take the mark of the beast are forbidden to buy or sell (Rev. 13:16–18). Many are martyred for their faith (v. 14).

Many will flee into the wilderness and be protected by God (Rev. 12:6). These will be the ones that enter the millennium in mortal or unresurrected bodies. These are the sheep of Matthew 25:32–33. At the end of the Tribulation 200 million soldiers from the east will come across the Euphrates River, likely a collection from all nations, to invade Israel (Rev. 9 & 16). They will surround Jerusalem (Zech. 12 & 14).

End of Tribulation: God will miraculously intervene, save Israel and restore the house of David by Christ returning and setting foot on the Mount of Olives to deliver His people. National Israel will recognize Christ as their Messiah. Israel will be re-grafted into the redemptive line and the "time of the gentiles" will end.

The Millennium: The Abrahamic Covenant, guaranteeing the Promised Land will be fulfilled, the Davidic Covenant that promised a King in the line of David perpetually will be fulfilled, and the New Covenant (Jer. 31) will end.

- The Millennium is described in Isaiah 4, 24, 32, 56, 60, 65; Zechariah 14, Revelation 20.
- It begins with the Second Coming: Matthew 24:29-30.
- Satan is bound 1000 years: Revelation 20.
- The Antichrist and false prophet are thrown into the Lake of Fire.
- Christ will judge the nations and separate the sheep (saved) from the goats (lost) (Zech. 14:2-4; Matt. 25:31-41).
- Christ will reign on a throne in Jerusalem (Matt. 19:28).
- Christ's followers will be positionally rewarded in His reign (2 Cor. 5:10; 1 Cor. 3:11-15).
- Resurrected humans will take part (Rev. 20:6; 21:2).
- One Faith will be established over all the earth (Isa. 66:23; Zech. 14:16-18).
- Peace will be restored to the earth (Micah 4:3).
- Prosperity will be restored to the earth (Zech. 3:10; Isa. 65:21).
- Creation will be delivered from bondage (Rom. 8:18-23).
- Animals will not be carnivorous (Isa. 65:25 cf. Gen. 2:9:3:2).
- Longevity will be restored (Isa. 65:20, 22).
- Death will result from rebellion and punishment (Isa. 11:4).
- Evil and death in the Millennium implies an end (Rev. 12:5; Isa. 65:20; Rev. 20:7-10).
- Some children born during the Millennium will not believe in Jesus.
- End of the Millennium: Revelation 20.

Satan is released from the Abyss to deceive the nations that includes children born during the Millennium who do not believe and/or follow Jesus.

- They will be gathered for war and surround Jerusalem.
- God will devour them with fire from heaven.
- Satan is thrown into the lake of fire (Rev. 20:7-10).
- The Great white thrown Judgment takes place (Rev. 20:11-15).
- First heaven and earth pass away (Rev. 21; 2 Peter 3:10-12)
- Eternal State: Revelation 21-22.

- After the Millennium, the New Heavens and New Earth will be created (Rev. 21).

Revelation 21:23–27:

> Its city has no need of the sun or of the moon to shine on it, for the glory of God has illumined it, and its lamp is the Lamb. The nations will walk by its light, and the kings of the earth will bring their glory into it. In the daytime (for there will be no night there) its gates will never be closed; and they will bring the glory and the honor of the nations into it; and nothing unclean, and no one who practices abomination and lying, shall ever come into it, but only those whose names are written in the Lamb's book of life.

Revelation 22:3–5:

> There will no longer be any curse; and the throne of God and of the Lamb will be in it, and His bond–servants will serve Him; they will see His face, and His name will be on their foreheads. And there will no longer be any night; and they will not have need of the light of a lamp nor the light of the sun, because the Lord God will illumine them; and they will reign forever and ever.

Questions to Answer

1. What are the Covenants mentioned in Scripture?
2. What are the different views on the Millennium?
3. What is the scriptural support for the Premillennial view?
4. What is the scriptural support for the Pretribulation view of the Rapture?
5. What is the sequence of events for the Petribulational Premillennial view of last things?

Bibliography

Adler, Mortimer J. *Truth in Religion.* New York: MacMillan, 1990.

Allis, Oswald T. *Prophecy and the Church.* Nutley, NJ: Presbyterian and Reformed, 1974.

Aquinas, Thomas. *Compendium of Theology.* St. Louis: B. Herder Book, 1948.

_____. *Summa Theologica.* Translated by Fathers of the English Dominican Province. Vol. 1–5. Allen, TX: Christian Classics, 1948.

Arminius, Jacob. *The Writings of James Arminius.* 3 vols. Trans. From the Latin by James Nichols and W. R. Bagnall. Grand Rapids, Baker, 1956.

Babylonian Talmud, Tosephta Sotah. Peabody, MS: Hendrickson, 2005.

Beckwith, Roger. *The Old Testament Canon of the New Testament Church and Its Background in Early Judaism,* Grand Rapids: Eerdmans, 1986.

Brown, Harold O. J. *Heresies.* Peabody: Hendrickson, 1988.

Calvin, John. *Institutes of the Christian Religion.* 2 vols. Ed. John T. McNeill. Translated by Ford Lewis Battles. In Library of Christian Classics. Vols. 20–21. Eds. John Baillie, John T. McNeill, and Henry P. Van Dusen. Philadelphia: Westminster, 1960.

Chafer, Lewis Sperry. *Systematic Theology.* Vol. 1–2. Abridged Edition. Edited by John F. Walvoord. Wheaton: Victor Books, 1988.

Charnock, Stephen. *The Existence and Attributes of God.* Grand Rapids: Baker, 1996.

Culver, Robert D. *Systematic Theology: Biblical & Historical.* Bercker, Germany: Mentor, 2005.

Darwin, Charles. *On The Origin of Species* (1859). New York: New American Library, 1958.

Denzinger, Henry. *The Sources of Catholic Dogma.* Translated by Roy J. Deferrari. London: B Herder, 1957.

Dickason, Fred C. *Angels: Elect and Evil.* Chicago: Moody Press, 1975.

Edwards, W. D., et al. "On The Physical Death of Jesus Christ" *Journal of the American Medical Association,* 255:11, March 21, 1986, 1463.

Elwell, Walter A., ed. *Topical Analysis of the Bible.* Grand Rapids: Baker, 1991.

Enns, Paul. *The Moody Handbook of Theology.* Rev. ed. Chicago: Moody Press, 2008.

Erickson, Millard. *Christian Theology.* Grand Rapids: Baker, 1991.

Eusebius. *Ecclesiastical History.* Grand Rapids: Baker, 1990.

Geisler, Norman L. & J. Kerby Anderson. *Origin Science: A Proposal for the Creation–Evolution Controversy*. Grand Rapids: Baker, 1987.

Geisler, Norman L. & William C. Roach. *Defending Inerrancy*. Grand Rapids: Baker, 2011.

Geisler, Norman L. & William E. Nix. *From God to Us*. Rev. & Exp. Chicago: Moody Press, 2012.

Geisler, Norman L. & William E. Nix. *General Introduction to the Bible*. Rev. ed. Chicago: Moody Press, 1986.

Geisler, Norman L. & Ron Rhodes. *Conviction without Compromise*, 2008.

Geisler, Norman L. & William Watkins. *Worlds Apart*. Grand Rapids: Baker, 1989.

Geisler, Norman L. *Chosen but Free: A Balanced View of Divine Election*. 3rd ed. Minneapolis: Bethany, 2010.

_____. *Creating God in the Image of Man?* Minneapolis: Bethany House, 1997.

_____. *Knowing the Truth About Creation*. Ann Arbor: Servant Books, 1989.

_____. *Miracles and the Modern Mind*. Grand Rapids: Baker, 1992.

_____. *Systematic Theology*. Minneapolis: Bethany, 2011.

_____. *The Battle for the Resurrection*. Nashville: Thomas Nelson, 1989.

_____. *Thomas Aquinas: An Evangelical Appraisal*. Grand Rapids: Baker, 1991.

_____., ed. *Inerrancy*. Grand Rapids: Zondervan, 1980.

Gromacki, Robert. *The Virgin Birth: Doctrine of Deity*. Baker, 1981.

Hagopian, David G., ed. *The Genesis Debate: Three Views on the Days of Creation*. Mission Viejo: Crux Press, 2001.

Hodge, Zane. *Absolutely Free*. Dallas: Redencion Viva, 1989.

Irenaeus. *Against Heresies*. in *The Ante–Nicene Fathers*. Eerdmans, 1885.

Josephus, *The New Complete Works of Josephus*, translated by William Whiston. Grand Rapids: Kregel, 1966.

Ladd, George. *The Pattern of New Testament Truth*. Grand Rapids: Eerdmans, 1977.

Lewis, C. S. *Christian Reflection*. Edited by Walter Hooper. Grand Rapids: Eerdmans, 1967.

_____. *God in the Dock, Essays in Theology and Ethics*. Edited by Walter Hooper. Grand Rapids: Eerdmans, 1970.

_____. *Mere Christianity*. New York: Macmillan, 1943.

_____. *Miracles*. New York: Macmillan, 1947.

_____. *The Abolition of Man*. New York: Macmillan, 1947.

_____. *The Great Divorce* New York: Macmillan, 1946.

_____. *The Problem of Pain*, New York: Macmillan, 1940.

_____. *The Weight of Glory*, New York: Macmillan, 1949.

Lightner, Robert P. *Sin the Savior and Salvation*. Grand Rapids: Kregel, 1991.

_____. *The Death Christ Died: A Biblical Case for Unlimited Atonement*. Kregel, 1998.

_____. *The Last Days Handbook*. Nashville: Thomas Nelson, 1990.

MacArthur, John F. Jr. *Charismatic Chaos*. Grand Rapids: Zondervan, n.d.

_____. *The Gospel According to Jesus*. Panorama City: Word of Grace, 1988.

O'Hair, J. C. *The Unsearchable Riches of Christ*, Grand Rapids: Grace, 1976.

Pentecost, J. Dwight. *Things to Come*. Grand Rapids: Academie Books/Zondervan, 1964.

Radmacher, Earl. *The Nature of the Church*. Portland: Western Baptist Press, 1972.

Ramm, Bernard. *The Christian View of Science and Scripture*. Grand Rapids: Eerdmans, 1981.

Rhodes, Ron. *Angels Among Us: Separating Truth From Fiction*. Eugene, OR: Harvest House, 1994.

_____. *Christ Before the Manger: The Life and Times of the Preincarnate Christ*. Grand Rapids: Baker, 1992.

Ryrie, Charles C. *A Survey of Bible Doctrine*. Chicago: Moody Press, 1972.

_____. *Basic Theology: A Popular Systematic Guide to Understanding Biblical Truth*. Chicago: Moody Press, 1999.

_____. *The Holy Spirit*. Chicago: Moody Press, 1997.

_____. *Dispensationalism*. Rev. ed. Chicago: Moody Press, 1995.

_____. *So Great Salvation*. Chicago: Moody Press, 1997.

_____. *The Premillennial Return of our Lord*. Neptune, NJ: Loizeaux Brothers, 1953.

Saucy, Robert L. *The Church in God's Program*. Chicago: Moody, 1972.

Sauer, Erich. *From Eternity to Eternity: An Outline of Divine Purposes*. Grand Rapids: Eerdmans, 1978.

Schaff, Philip. *A Select Library of the Nicene and Post-Nicene Fathers of the Christian Church*. Grand Rapids: Eerdmans, 1988–1991.

Seiss, J. A. *The Apocalypse*. Grand Rapids: Zondervan, 1970.

Shedd, W. G. T. *The Doctrine of Endless Punishment*. Carlisle, PN: The Banner of Truth Trust, 1990.

Showers, Renald. *Maranatha: Our Lord Come! A Definitive Study of the Rapture of the Church*. 5th ed. Bellmawr, NJ: The Friends of Israel Gospel Ministry, 2002.

Thiessen, Henry Clarence. *Lectures in Systematic Theology*. Rev. ed. Grand Rapids: Eerdmans: 1979.

Unger, Merrill F. *Biblical Demonology*. Wheaton: Van Kampen Press, 1952.

Walvoord, John F. *Jesus Christ Our Lord*. Chicago: Moody Press, 1969.

_____. *The Holy Spirit*. Grand Rapids: Academie Books/Zondervan, 1958.

_____. *The Millennium Kingdom*. Grand Rapids: Zondervan, 1959.

_____. *The Blessed Hope and the Tribulation: A Biblical and Historical Look at Posttribulationism*. Grand Rapids: Zondervan, 1976.

Walvoord, John, & Roy Zuck, eds. *The Bible Knowledge Commentary*. Vols. 1–2. Wheaton: Victor, 1987.

Warfield, B. B. *Counterfeit Miracles*. The Banner of Truth Trust, 1983.

Wenham, John. *Christ and the Bible*. InterVarsity, 1972.

Wesley, John. *The Works of John Wesley*. 14 vols. in 7. Grand Rapids: Baker, 1996.

Woodbridge, John. *Biblical Authority: A Critique of the Rogers/McKim Proposal*. Grand Rapids: Zondervan, 1982.

NORM GEISLER INTERNATIONAL MINISTRIES

Norm Geisler International Ministries is dedicated to carrying on the life's work of its co-founder, Norman L. Geisler. Described as a cross between Billy Graham and Thomas Aquinas, Norm Geisler, PhD, is a prolific author, professor, apologist, philosopher, and theologian. He has authored or co-authored over 96 books and co-founded 2 seminaries.

NGIM is focused on equipping others to proclaim and defend the Christian Faith by providing evangelism and apologetic training.

More Information

Website: http://NormGeisler.com

Training: http://NGIM.org (Norm Geisler International Ministries)

e–Books: http://BastionBooks.com

Email: Dr.NormanGeisler@outlook.com

Facebook: http://facebook.com/normgeisler

Twitter: https://www.twitter.com/normgeisler

Videos: http://www.youtube.com/user/DrNormanLGeisler/videos

Biblical Inerrancy: http://DefendingInerrancy.com

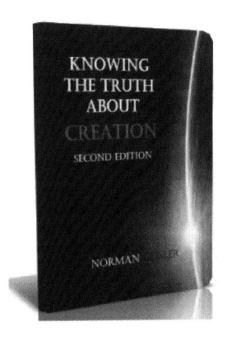

THE truth about creation is not limited to the arena of science. There are also biblical, philosophical, moral, and spiritual dimensions to the topic. The aim of this book is not to defend a particular doctrinal point of view but to emphasize what orthodox Christians hold in common. Part One covers the biblical view of God and creation, both spiritual and material. Part Two explores the philosophical and scientific aspects of creation. Part Three discusses the moral and spiritual implications of creation